Communications
in Computer and Information Science   1764

Rationale

The CCIS series is devoted to the publication of proceedings of computer science conferences. Its aim is to efficiently disseminate original research results in informatics in printed and electronic form. While the focus is on publication of peer-reviewed full papers presenting mature work, inclusion of reviewed short papers reporting on work in progress is welcome, too. Besides globally relevant meetings with internationally representative program committees guaranteeing a strict peer-reviewing and paper selection process, conferences run by societies or of high regional or national relevance are also considered for publication.

Topics

The topical scope of CCIS spans the entire spectrum of informatics ranging from foundational topics in the theory of computing to information and communications science and technology and a broad variety of interdisciplinary application fields.

Information for Volume Editors and Authors

Publication in CCIS is free of charge. No royalties are paid, however, we offer registered conference participants temporary free access to the online version of the conference proceedings on SpringerLink (http://link.springer.com) by means of an http referrer from the conference website and/or a number of complimentary printed copies, as specified in the official acceptance email of the event.

CCIS proceedings can be published in time for distribution at conferences or as post-proceedings, and delivered in the form of printed books and/or electronically as USBs and/or e-content licenses for accessing proceedings at SpringerLink. Furthermore, CCIS proceedings are included in the CCIS electronic book series hosted in the SpringerLink digital library at http://link.springer.com/bookseries/7899. Conferences publishing in CCIS are allowed to use Online Conference Service (OCS) for managing the whole proceedings lifecycle (from submission and reviewing to preparing for publication) free of charge.

Publication process

The language of publication is exclusively English. Authors publishing in CCIS have to sign the Springer CCIS copyright transfer form, however, they are free to use their material published in CCIS for substantially changed, more elaborate subsequent publications elsewhere. For the preparation of the camera-ready papers/files, authors have to strictly adhere to the Springer CCIS Authors' Instructions and are strongly encouraged to use the CCIS LaTeX style files or templates.

Abstracting/Indexing

CCIS is abstracted/indexed in DBLP, Google Scholar, EI-Compendex, Mathematical Reviews, SCImago, Scopus. CCIS volumes are also submitted for the inclusion in ISI Proceedings.

How to start

To start the evaluation of your proposal for inclusion in the CCIS series, please send an e-mail to ccis@springer.com.

Abbas M. Al-Bakry · Safaa O. Al-Mamory ·
Mouayad A. Sahib · Loay E. George ·
Jaafar A. Aldhaibani · Haitham S. Hasan ·
George S. Oreku
Editors

New Trends in Information and Communications Technology Applications

6th International Conference, NTICT 2022
Baghdad, Iraq, November 16–17, 2022
Proceedings

Springer

Editors
Abbas M. Al-Bakry
University of Information Technology
and Communications
Baghdad, Iraq

Safaa O. Al-Mamory ⓘ
University of Information Technology
and Communications
Baghdad, Iraq

Mouayad A. Sahib
University of Information Technology
and Communications
Baghdad, Iraq

Loay E. George
University of Information Technology
and Communications
Baghdad, Iraq

Jaafar A. Aldhaibani
University of Information Technology
and Communications
Baghdad, Iraq

Haitham S. Hasan
University of Information Technology
and Communications
Baghdad, Iraq

George S. Oreku
Open University of Tanzania
Dar es Salaam, Tanzania

ISSN 1865-0929   ISSN 1865-0937 (electronic)
Communications in Computer and Information Science
ISBN 978-3-031-35441-0   ISBN 978-3-031-35442-7 (eBook)
https://doi.org/10.1007/978-3-031-35442-7

This Springer imprint is published by the registered company Springer Nature Switzerland AG
The registered company address is: Gewerbestrasse 11, 6330 Cham, Switzerland

Preface

The 6th International Conference on New Trends in Information and Communications Technology Applications (NTICT 2022) was hosted and organized by the University of Information Technology and Communications, Baghdad, Iraq. It was held in Baghdad on November 16–17, 2022. NTICT 2022 was a specialized international conference that aimed to present the latest research related to information and communications technology applications. NTICT was the first conference in Iraq to have its proceedings published in Communications in Computer and Information Science (CCIS) by Springer. NTICT 2022 aimed to provide a meeting for an advanced discussion of evolving applications in machine learning and computer networks. The conference brought both young researchers and senior experts together to share novel findings and practical experiences in their fields. The call for papers resulted in a total of 67 submissions from which only 53 articles passed the prescreening stage. In the second stage, each submission was assigned to at least three international reviewers for double-blind reviews. After receiving the review comments, the Program Committee decided to accept only 14 papers based on a highly selective review process with an acceptance rate of 26%. The accepted papers are categorized to 4 fields; 7 papers in computer methodologies, 2 papers in information systems, one paper in network systems, and 4 papers in security and privacy. The conference organizing committee would like to thank all who contributed to the success of this conference, in particular the members of the Program Committee and the respected international reviewers for their scientific efforts in carefully reviewing the contributions and selecting high-quality papers. The reviewers' efforts to submit the review reports within the specified period were greatly appreciated. Their comments were very helpful in the selection process. Furthermore, we would like to convey our gratitude to the keynote speakers for their excellent presentations. A word of thanks is extended to all authors who submitted their papers and for letting us evaluate their work. The submitted papers were managed using Springer Nature's EquinOCS conference management system; thanks to the Springer team for publishing these proceedings. We hope that all participants enjoyed a successful conference, made a lot of new contacts, engaged in fruitful discussions, and had a pleasant stay in Baghdad.

November 2022

Abbas M. Al-Bakry
Safaa O. Al-mamory
Mouayad A. Sahib
Jaafar A. Aldhaibani
Haitham S. Hasan
Loay E. George
George S. Oreku

Organization

General Chair

Abbas M. Al-Bakry   President of UOITC, Iraq

Co-chair

Hassan Shaker Magdy   Al-Mustaqbal University College, Iraq

Program Chairs

Abbas M. Al-Bakry	UOITC, Iraq
Safaa O. Al-mamory	UOITC, Iraq
Mouayad A. Sahib	UOITC, Iraq
Loay E. George	UOITC, Iraq
George S. Oreku	Open University of Tanzania, Tanzania
Haitham S. Hasan	UOITC, Iraq
Jaafar A. Aldhaibani	UOITC, Iraq

Steering Committee

Loay Edwar George	UOITC, Iraq
Jane J. Stephan	UOITC, Iraq
Mahdi N. Jasim	UOITC, Iraq
Ahmed A. Hasim	UOITC, Iraq
Inaam Rikan Hassan	UOITC, Iraq
Ahmed Sabah Ahmed	UOITC, Iraq
Ali Hassan Tarish	UOITC, Iraq
Nagham Hamid Abdul-Mahdi	UOITC, Iraq

International Scientific Committee

Abbas Al-Bakry	UOITC, Iraq
Abdel-Badeeh Salem	Ain Shams University, Egypt

Abdelghani Aissaoui	University Tahri Mohamed of Bechar, Algeria
Abdelnaser Omran	Bright Star University, Libya
Abdulamir Karim	University of Technology, Iraq
Abdulrahman Jasim	Al-Iraqia University, Iraq
Yahya Abid	BUIST, Botswana
Adolfo Guzmán-Arenas	Instituto Politécnico Nacional, Mexico
Ahmad Bader	Middle Technical University, Iraq
Ahmad Mohammad	Mustansiriyah University, Iraq
Ahmed Hashim	UOITC, Iraq
Ahmed Shamil Mustafa	Al-Maarif University College, Iraq
Aini Syuhada Md Zain	Universiti Malaysia Perlis, Malaysia
Alaa Al-Waisy	Imam Ja'Afar Al-Sadiq University, Iraq
Alaa Abdulateef	Universiti Utara Malaysia, Malaysia
Alaa Al-Hamami	British University of Bahrain, Bahrain
Alaa Taqa	University of Mosul, Iraq
Alejandro Zunino	ISISTAN, National Scientific and Technical Research Council, Argentina
Ali Abbas	Imam Ja'Afar Al-Sadiq University, Iraq
Ali Al-Ataby	University of Liverpool, UK
Ali Alnooh	UOITC, Iraq
Ali Al-Shuwaili	UOITC, Iraq
Ali Al-Timemey	University of Baghdad, Iraq
Ali Idrees	University of Babylon, Iraq
Amera Melhum	University of Duhok, Iraq
Athraa Jani	Al-Mustansiriyah University, Iraq
Attakrai Punpukdee	Naresuan University, Thailand
Aws Yonis	Ninevah University, Iraq
Ayad Abbas	University of Technology, Iraq
Azhar Al-Zubidi	Al-Nahrain University, Iraq
Basim Mahmood	University of Mosul, Iraq
Belal Al-Khateeb	University of Anbar, Iraq
Buthainah Abed	UOITC, Iraq
Cik Feresa Mohd Foozy	Universiti Tun Hussein Onn Malaysia, Malaysia
Dena Muhsen	University of Technology, Iraq
Dennis Lupiana	Institute of Finance Management, Tanzania
Kumar	JNTU Anantapur, India
Wafaa Abedi	City University College of Ajman, UAE
Duraid Mohammed	Al-Iraqia University, Iraq
Ehsan Al-Doori	Al-Nahrain University, Iraq
Emad Mohammed	Orther Technical University, Iraq
Essa I. Essa	University of Kirkuk, Iraq
Fadhil Mukhlif	University of Technology Malaysia, Malaysia

Farah Jasem	University of Anbar, Iraq
Fawzi Al-Naima	Al-Ma'Moon University College, Iraq
George S. Oreku	Open University of Tanzania, Tanzania
Ghani Hashim	Lorraine University, France
Haider Hoomod	Mustansiriyah University, Iraq
Haitham S. Hasan	UOITC, Iraq
Hamidah Ibrahim	Universiti Putra Malaysia, Malaysia
Hanaa Mahmood	University of Mosul, Iraq
Harith Al-Badrani	Ninevah University, Iraq
Hasan Al-Khaffaf	University of Duhok, Iraq
Haydar Al-Tamimi	University of Technology, Iraq
Hemashree Bordoloi	Assam Don Bosco University, India
Hiba Aleqabie	University of Karbala, Iraq
Hussam Mohammed	University of Anbar, Iraq
Ibtisam Aljazaery	University of Babylon, Iraq
Idress Husien	University of Kirkuk, Iraq
Intisar Al-Mejibli	UOITC, Iraq
Jaafar Aldhaibani	UOITC, Iraq
Jane Stephan	UOITC, Iraq
Junita Mohd Nordin	Universiti Malaysia Perlis, Malaysia
Jyoti Prakash Singh	National Institute of Technology Patna, India
Kiran Sree Pokkuluri	Shri Vishnu Engineering College for Women, India
Kuldeep Kumar	National Institute of Technology Jalandhar, India
Kunal Das	West Bengal State University, India
Layla H. Abood	University of Technology, Iraq
Litan Daniela	Hyperion University, Romania
Loay Edwar George	UOITC, Iraq
Mafaz Alanezi	University of Mosul, Iraq
Mahdi Abed Salman	University of Babylon, Iraq
Mahdi Jasim	UOITC, Iraq
Malik Alsaedi	Al-Iraqia University, Iraq
Marinela Mircea	Bucharest University of Economic Studies, Romania
Miguel Carriegos	Universidad de León, Spain
Moceheb Shuwandy	Tikrit University, Iraq
Modafar Ati	Abu Dhabi University, UAE
Mohammad Al-Mashhadani	Al-Maarif University College, Iraq
Mohammad Sarfraz	Aligarh Muslim University, India
Mohammed Alkhabet	University Putra Malaysia, Malaysia
Mohammed Aal-Nouman	Al-Nahrain University, Iraq
Mohammed Al-Khafajiy	University of Reading, UK

Mohammed Al-Neama	Mosul University, Iraq
Mouayad Sahib	UOITC, Iraq
Muhammad Raheel Mohyuddin	Al Ain, Pakistan
Muhammad Zakarya	Abdul Wali Khan University, Pakistan
Muhsen Hammoud	Federal University of ABC, Brazil
Muthana Mahdi	Mustansiriyah University, Iraq
Nada M. Ali	University of Baghdad, Iraq
Nadhir Ibrahim Abdulkhaleq	UOITC, Iraq
Nadia Al-Bakri	Al-Narain University, Iraq
Noor Maizura Mohamad Noor	Universiti Malaysia Terengganu, Malaysia
Nor Binti Jamaludin	National Defence University of Malaysia, Malaysia
Nur Iksan	Universitas Riau Kepulauan, Indonesia
Omar Abdulrahman	University of Anbar, Iraq
Omar Saleh	Ministry of Higher Education and Scientific Research, Iraq
Omar Salman	Al Iraqia University, Iraq
Paula Bajdor	Czestochowa University of Technology, Poland
Qais Qassim	University of Technology and Applied Sciences, Oman
Qaysar Mahdy	Tishk International University, Iraq
Raja Azura	Universiti Pendidikan Sultan Idris, Malaysia
Razwan Najimaldeen	Cihan University-Duhok, Iraq
Robert Laramee	University of Nottingham, UK
Ruslan Al-Nuaimi	Al-Nahrain University, Iraq
S. Nagakishore Bhavanam	Acharya Nagarjuna University, India
Saad Dheyab	UOITC, Iraq
Safaa Al-mamory	UOITC, Iraq
Santhosh Balan	JNTU Hyderabad, India
Sarmad Ibrahim	Mustansiriyah University, Iraq
Sarmad Hadi	Al-Nahrain University, Iraq
Shaheen Abdulkareem	University of Duhok, Iraq
Shaimaa Al-Abaidy	University of Baghdad, Iraq
Shumoos Al-Fahdawi	Al-Maarif University College, Iraq
Siddeeq Ameen	Technical College of Informatics, Iraq
Sk Sarif Hassan	Vidyasagar University, India
Thaker Nayl	UOITC, Iraq
Venkatesh R.	Anna University, India
Walead Sleaman	Tikrit University, Iraq
Yafia Radouane	Ibn Tofail University, Morocco
Yaseen Yaseen	University of Anbar, Iraq
Yousif Hamad	Siberian Federal University, Russia

Yousif Sulaiman	Al-Maarif University College, Iraq
Yusra Al-Irhayim	University of Mosul, Iraq
Zailan Siri	Universiti Malaya, Malaysia
Zainab Ahmed	University of Baghdad, Iraq
Zeyad Karam	Al-Nahrain University, Iraq
Zeyad Younus	University of Mosul, Iraq
Ziad Al-Abbasi	Middle Technical University, Iraq

Secretary Committee

Jwan Knaan Alwan	UOITC, Iraq
Alya Jemma	UOITC, Iraq
Ali Abed Al-Kareem	UOITC, Iraq
Ammar AbdRaba Sakran	UOITC, Iraq
Suhaib S. Al-Shammari	UOITC, Iraq
Ali Jassim Mohammed	UOITC, Iraq

Contents

Computing Methodologies

Estimating Blur Parameters to Reconstruct the Motion Blurred Images 3
  *Nidhal K. El Abbadi, Ali Hussein Abdulkhaleq,
  and Safaa Alwan Al Hassani*

Enhancing Service Classification for Network Slicing in 5G Using
Machine Learning Algorithms 25
  *Noor Abdalkarem Mohammedali, Triantafyllos Kanakis,
  Ali Al-Sherbaz, Michael Opoku Agyeman, and Saad Talib Hasson*

MesoNet3: A Deepfakes Facial Video Detection Network Based on Object
Behavior Analysis 38
  Qasim Jaleel and Israa H. Ali

Computer Vision Techniques for Hand Gesture Recognition: Survey 50
  Noor Fadel and Emad I. Abdul Kareem

A Comprehensive Review in Using the Advances of Deep Learning
in the 3D Race Classification 77
  Noor H. Reda and Hawraa Abbas

Multi-agents as Data Mining Classifiers and Crawlers to Get Intelligent
E-Advertisements 107
  Hanan Q. Jaleel, Jane J. Stephan, and Sinan A. Naji

Automated Multi-style Iraqi Cars License Recognition Based
on Convolutional Neural Network Technology 125
  Shaimaa K. Ahmed, Zobeda H. Naji, and Maather Alshaibi

Information Systems

Food Recommendation System Based on Data Clustering Techniques
and User Nutrition Records 139
  Hayder Hussein Al-Chalabi and Mahdi Nsaif Jasim

EEG Data Compression Using Tap9/7 Wavelet Transform and Double
Shift-Coding 162
  Hend A. Hadi and Loay E. George

Network

Implementation of Network Slicing for Multi-controller Environment
Based on FlowVisor 173
   Suadad S. Mahdi and Alharith A. Abdullah

Security and Privacy

A Novel Ensemble Method for Network-Based Anomaly Intrusion
Detection System 191
   Ali H. Al-Shakarchi, Nabeel H. Al-A'araji, and Safaa O. Al-mamory

New Security Mechanism of Health Data Based on Blockchain–NFV 230
   Hayder A. Jawdhari and Alharith A. Abdullah

Use Multichannel EEG-Based Biometrics Authentication Signal in Real
Time Using Neural Network 248
   Nadhim Azeez Sayel, Salah Albermany, and Bayan Mahdi Sabbar

Machine Learning-Based DDoS Attack Detection in Software-Defined
Networking 264
   Mohammed Ibrahim Kareem and Mahdi Nsaif Jasim

Author Index 283

Computing Methodologies

Estimating Blur Parameters to Reconstruct the Motion Blurred Images

Nidhal K. El Abbadi[1]([✉]) [iD], Ali Hussein Abdulkhaleq[2] [iD],
and Safaa Alwan Al Hassani[3] [iD]

[1] Computer Techniques Engineering Department, College of Engineering & Technology,
Al-Mustaqbal University, Babylon, Iraq
nidhal.abass@fulbrightmail.org
[2] Department of Information Technology, Technical College of Management, Al-Furat
Al-Awsat Technical University, Najaf, Iraq
[3] Computer Science Department, Faculty of Computer Science and Mathematics, University of
Kufa, Najaf, Iraq

Abstract. One of the important topics of image restoration is the restoration of a motion-blurred image. The restored blurred images are based on estimating the two parameters of a point spread function (PSF) angle and length of the blur kernel. In this article, we suggested checking the quality of the input images before going further in processing when the image is not blurred, estimating the PSF parameters, and reconstructing the image based on the periodicity of motion-blurred in the frequency domain. Fourier transform is used to detect the blur in the input images, and the Hough transform is used to estimate the blurred image angle. Also, the cepstrum domain is used for blur length estimation by finding the lowest peak. After blur parameters are estimated, we determine a point spread function (PSF) to deblur the image using a wiener filter of non-blind deconvolution. The visual, as well as the peak signal-to-noise ratio (PSNR) of restored images, are compared with competent recent schemes. The experimental results of the suggested algorithm show good accuracy, robustness, and time efficiency for blur detection, estimation of the PSF parameters, and reconstruction of the image when compared with other works and methods.

Keywords: blur angle · blur length · blur image · image processing · point spread function

1 Introduction

Modern image processing sciences, including photography, astronomical images, medical images, and microscopy images, have evolved well over recent years and many advanced techniques have emerged. These advances have allowed images to be acquired at higher speeds and higher resolution. High-resolution techniques can lead to degraded acquired image quality, which is an example of a blur. The effect of image de-blurring is effectively a clear image when eliminating distortion and blur [1].

© The Author(s), under exclusive license to Springer Nature Switzerland AG 2023
A. M. Al-Bakry et al. (Eds.): NTICT 2022, CCIS 1764, pp. 3–24, 2023.
https://doi.org/10.1007/978-3-031-35442-7_1

Image blur is the primary cause of image loss, and the de-blurring image is a common research concern in the field of image processing [2]. Different factors can cause image degradation, such as out of focus, camera movement or object movement, and atmospheric turbulence. Any motion at the time of image capturing for the camera or objects can cause a motion blur, this is because the sensors can observe the same point on the scene [3]. Mathematically, the motion-blurred image can be modeled as a convolution of the latent image with the point spread function (PSF), also called the blur kernel [4]. Blur image restoring, is a process in which latent sharp images are restored from the observed image using part or no information about the blurring process. There are two main methods to restore the images from degraded images, non-blind and blind images. In most cases a PSF is assumed to be known before recovering the true image, this is called the non-blind restoration or classical restoration. While the second method is based on the estimation of PSF without any prior information about the blurring process [2]. Generally, the restoration of motion-blurred images aims to eliminate the effect of PSF. There are two parameters used to determine PSF: the motion length and direction, unfortunately, their values are often unknown because there is no information about motion when the image is captured [3, 4].

De-blurring is a technique to remove artifacts from images that blur. Image de-blurring can broadly divide into two classes, specifically blind and non-blind deconvolution. Some of the well-known non-blind de-blurring methods are the Lucy Richardson algorithm, Wiener filter, and Regularized filter. The accuracy of restoration depends on the estimation of blur length and blur angle that constructs the PSF itself. For instance, after the PSF reconstruction from these two parameters, a Wiener filter can restore a degraded image in the current method.

The main contribution of this paper is the ability to check the images whether it is blurred or not before any deblurring process. Also, the high accuracy of estimating the motion blur angle and length is considered a contribution that enhances the deblurring process.

The rest of the paper includes related works in Sect. 2, where there are several previous and related papers discussed. A brief idea about the motion blur, Hough transform, and cepstrum domain analysis is presented in Sects. 3, 4 and 5 respectively. The methodology of the proposed method is introduced in detail in Sect. 6, while the results of the proposed method are displayed in Sect. 7. Finally, introduce the conclusions in Sect. 8.

2   Related Works

This section is focused on the reviews of previous methods that have worked in this field of study, emphasizing the studies with the most relevance to the method suggested in this work.

(Li et al. 2021) Introduced a method to recover the motion blurred image captured by mobile device. They suggested using a generative adversarial network based on the mobile net network. The backbone of the network is already trained (where only the generator is trained), so the entire network is trained by the authors [5].

(Zhang and Zheng, 2020) incorporated the Fourier image spectrum with the identification of edges dependent on phase consistency. The blurring angle is defined by measuring the direction of the central bright stripe's edge. Bilinear interpolation is then used for producing the sub-pixel image of the spectrum, measuring the distance between the dark bands, and estimating the blurring length [6].

(**Y. Elmi et al., 2020**) presented an approach for estimating parametric PSF. This approach can be used to estimate the linear motion blur vector parameters. This method is used to determine the angle and length of the motion blur vector in a single image to produce PSF for de-blurring. This blind approach takes small vectors in all trends and deburrs with the PSF of those candidate vectors. A no-reference quality measurement metric assesses the goodness of the deblurred image. The no-reference image quality metric assesses measuring the edge degradation in the sharpness, and the quantity of artifact produced from saturated pixels in the deblurred image. In the next iteration, the unacceptable blurring caused by motion vectors is eliminated. The approximation has been enhanced by extending the length of the rest vectors, and the same procedure is continued recursively. The method continues until only one vector remains as the estimate for movement vector blur. In this method there is no additional hardware is needed, fully automatic, and doesn't require operator intervention, use the blurred image for estimating PSF only, improved movement accuracy blurred vector parameters, and less computational time [7].

(**Murthy et al., 2018**) introduced a technique used to estimate motion blur parameters by formulating the trigonometric relationship between the movement of blurred spectral lines of the image and the blurred parameters. The length of motion blur is calculated by rotating the Fourier spectrum to the estimated motion angle. This allows forehand angle estimation to be performed. By exploring the trigonometric relation between spectral lines, the suggested approach estimates both length and angle simultaneously, thus eliminating spectrum rotation for length estimation [8].

(**Albluwi et al., 2018**) proposed a method based on a convolution neural network (CNN) for deblurring images and increasing image resolution of blurred low-resolution images. The super-resolution CNN architecture is composed of four layers, two for input and output and two hidden layers, the first hidden layer focus on extracting the overlapping patch. Each patch represents a high-dimensional vector. While the second hidden layer maps the high dimension vector to another high-dimensional vector to represent a high-resolution patch [9].

(**Kumar, 2017**) suggested an efficient method of estimating parameters of the point spread function (PSF) based on the Histogram of Oriented Gradients (HoG) and the statistical characteristics of an image. In specific, HoG and statistical characteristics help to estimate the motion-based PSF angle and velocity parameters. Once all the parameters have been estimated, the blurred image reconstruction is carried out using a newly introduced non-blind process in the moment domain. The benefit of using the moment domain is quick convergence, and the variations in the PSF parameters are robust [10].

3   Motion Blur Model

The 2D linear shift-invariant model that case the blur and the degraded image is represented by Eq. 1.

$$g(x, y) = f(x, y) * h(x, y) + \eta(x, y) \tag{1}$$

where:

    $f(x, y)$: is the original image.

    $g(x, y)$: is the blurred image.

    h: is PSF.

    $\eta(x, y)$: is Gaussian noise.

The angle and length of linear blur motion are related directly to the camera properties during the time of the image captured. After estimating the two parameters of the blur kernel's length and angle, PSF could be reconstructed, and a blurred image restoration could be done [4].

4 Hough Transform

The Hough transform is a technique used to find shapes in a digital image. The classical Hough transform is most commonly used to detect regular curves such as lines, circles, ellipses, etc. In this paper, we use a polar mathematical model (Eq. 2) to detect lines:

$$\rho = x * \cos(\theta) + y * \sin(\theta) \tag{2}$$

where ρ (rho) is the distance of the perpendicular vector from the origin to the line, θ (theta) is the angle between the x-axis and the ρ vector. The values ρ and θ are limited to $\theta \in [0, 180]$ in degrees, and $\rho \in [-D, D]$ where D is the maximum distance between opposite corners in an image. A line in image space can be represented as a single point in the parameter space (also called Hough space) with the parameters θ and ρ. Each point in the image space can produce a sinusoid curve in the Hough space. A line in image space consists of many pixels or points, these points can define curves in the Hough space, and all the lines (belonging to points of a single line in image space) in the Hough space pass through a single point. When the Hough transform is applied to the image for the entire pixels, then it is easy to detect the lines that have the high vote. The result of the Hough transform is stored in a matrix that is often called an accumulator table. Where one dimension of this matrix is the theta values (angles), and the other dimension is the rho values (distances) [11].

5 Cepstrum Domain Analysis

Cepstrum transform is used to separate the blur components from the image components. Without the additive noise, image $g(x, y)$ is defined in the Cepstrum transform as follows:

$$Cp = F^{-1}log|F\{G(x, \}|) \tag{3}$$

$$= F^{-1}\{log[H(u, v)].log[F(u, v)]\}$$

$$= F^{-1}\{log[H(u, v)] + log[F(u, v)]\}$$

$$= C_h(p, q) + C_f(p, q)$$

where F {.} denotes Fourier transform, G (u, v), H (u, v), and F (u, v) are Fourier transforms of the blurred image, PSF, and the original image respectively. As a blurred image, it is better to separate motion blur from the cepstrum domain than the Frequency domain. In the frequency domain, it is possible to represent *sinc* function. So, uniform motion blur has periodic patterns by zero-crossing of *sinc* function, this is displayed in the cepstrum domain as negative peaks as shown in Fig. 1, where the original image blurred with uniform motion blur by an angle equal to 45° and length equal 15. The *sinc* function in the frequency domain is shown in Fig. 1 (c), and the negative peaks of the blurred image's cepstrum are shown in Fig. 1 (d) [12].

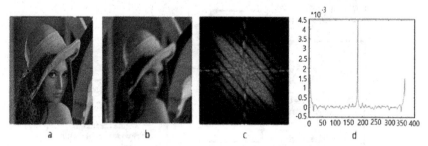

Fig. 1. (a) Original image (b) Blurred image (c) Fourier transform (d) Negative peaks.

6 Methodology

Blurring the image with a linear motion makes the edges in the image expand in the direction specified by the PSF. This research aims to determine the length and direction of the edge extension which represents the PSF parameters. The proposed system consists of four main stages: blur detection, blur angle estimation, blur length estimation, and construction of the PSF algorithm. The construct of the PSF algorithm depends on the blur angle algorithm and the blur length algorithm. Figure 2 shows a flowchart of the proposed system.

6.1 Check the Image Quality

The first step in the proposed algorithm is to check the quality of the input image, when the input image is blurred then continue with other steps; otherwise, when the image has no blur (clear) then no need to remove the blur. Algorithm 1 summarized the main steps for checking the image quality.

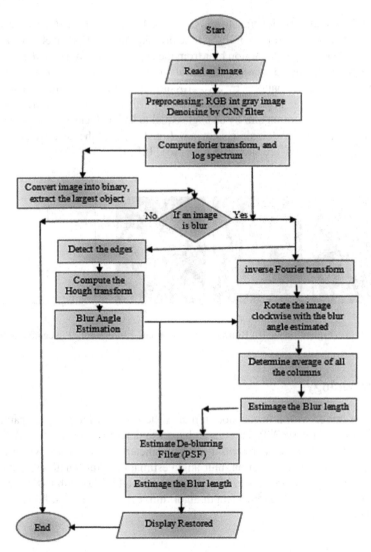

Fig. 2. General flowchart of the proposed system

Algorithm 1: Checking Image Quality

Input: Image
Output: Decision "Blur or Clear image"

Begin
Step 1: Input color image.
Step 2: Convert RGB image to grayscale image.
Step 3: Compute the Fourier transform F (u, v).
Step 4: Compute the log spectrum of F (u, v).
Step 5: Convert the image to a binary image.
Step 6: Extract the largest object (connected component)
Step 7: Plot an ellipse around the selected object.
Step 8: Determine whether the input image is blurry or not by calculating
The length of the long diagonal of the ellipse and comparing it with
the threshold values.

End.

If the input image is colored, then it is converted into a grayscale image. The suggested algorithm works efficiently with the grayscale images. The gray image will be transformed by using discrete Fourier transformation. In this step, horizontal lines of the spectrum (in dark, light, and white strips) are obtained in case of a blurry image, but these lines are not clear. So, a logarithmic transformation is applied to the spectrum to increase the contrast of the lines, and the lines become more clear. Detection of these horizontal stripes in the spectrums of an image can help determine the quality of the image; so, the resulting image is converted to a binary image. From the binary image, the largest object (connected component) is selected. Ellipse will be plotted around the selected object. The length of the long diagonal of the ellipse is selected. When the length of the long diameter of the ellipse is larger than the threshold value (these values are determined by the experiment to be the threshold value that separates between clear and blurs images as shown in Table 1) then the image is blurred, otherwise, the image is clear. Figure 3 illustrates the steps of determining the image quality.

Table 1. The threshold value between clear and blurred images is according to image size.

Image size	Limit value
256 × 256	47.5
500 × 500	135
600 × 600	160
700 × 700	173.4

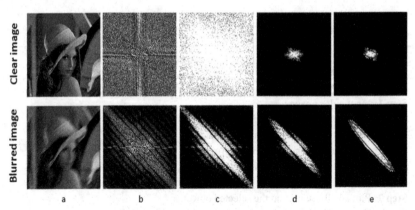

Fig. 3. (a) Authentic Image (b) frequency spectrum of an image (c) logarithmic transformation (d) Binary image (e) Extract the largest object and draw an ellipse.

6.2 Motion Blur Angle Estimation

One of the important parameters that are used in deblurring is motion blur angle. Steps for estimating motion blur angle are summarized in Algorithm 2.

Algorithm 2: Motion Blur Angle Estimation

Input: Blurred image (gray image)
Output: Blur angle

Begin
Step 1: Compute the Fourier transform F (u, v).
Step 2: Compute the log spectrum of F (u, v).
Step 3: Detect the edges of the image by using Sobel edge detection.
Step 4: Compute the Hough transform.
Step 5: Blur angle is the angle corresponding to the median of the largest five
votes resulting from Hough peaks.
End.

The input image into Algorithm 2 is grayscale, the suggested method works efficiently with the grayscale images. The gray image will be transformed by using discrete Fourier transformation, in this step, we get spectrum horizontal lines (in dark, light, and white strips) which are perpendicular to the blur direction as shown in Fig. 4(c), but these lines are not clear, so, the logarithmic transformation is applied to the spectrum to increase the contrast of the lines, and the lines become more clear as shown in Fig. 4(d). Detection of these horizontal stripes in the spectrums of blurred images (created due to uniform linear motion) can help to estimate the blur angle.

The fourth step is the edge detection in the image resulting from step three by using the Sobel filter, the result is shown in Fig. 4(e), in this case, the image will be displayed as parallel lines (mostly discontinuous lines) around the sides of the spectrum center which called the top and bottom edges for the spectrum. So, to get continuous lines, the Hough transform will be applied on these edges to discover the direction of the line and determine the blur angle as shown in Fig. 4(f). The median of the five-largest votes will be selected from Hough peaks and the corresponding theta is the angle of blur direction.

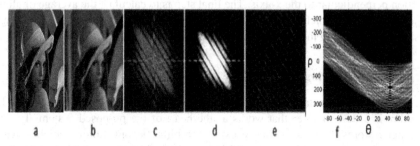

a   b   c   d   e   f   θ

Fig. 4. (a) Authentic Image (b) Blurred image with angle 45 and length 15 (c) frequency spectrum of blurred image (d) logarithmic transformation (e) Sobel edge detection (f) Hough Transform

6.3 Motion Blur Length Estimation

The second essential parameter that is used in deblurring is motion blur length. The blur length estimation is based on the value of the blur angle estimated in Algorithm 2. The steps of estimating the blur length are summarized in Algorithm 3.

Algorithm 3: Motion Blur Length Estimation

Input: Blurred image (gray image), and motion blur angle.
Output: Blur length

Begin:
Step 1: Transform the blurred RGB image to a grayscale image.
Step 2: De-noising image based on the CCN denoising method.
Step 3: Compute the Fourier transform F (u, v).
Step 4: Compute the log spectrum of F (u, v).
Step 5: Performing inverse Fourier transform to get the image in the cepstrum domain.
Step 6: Rotate the image clockwise with the blur angle estimated from algorithm 2.
Step 7: Determine the average of all the columns of the image in step 6.
Step 8: Blur length is estimated by finding the lowest peak value.
End.

The input gray image will be denoised by using the convolution neural network (CNN) denoising method which works efficiently to remove unwanted particles. Then, the image is transformed into the cepstrum domain, because the cepstrum can be used to estimate the zero patterns in the frequency response from which one can estimate motion length. To transform an image into the cepstrum domain, first, transfer the image by Fourier transform and calculate logarithmic transformation for it. After that, the inverse Fourier transform was taken, which transform the image into the cepstrum domain. Next, rotate the image clockwise by the angle estimated in Algorithm 2 to make the blur direction perpendicular to the x-axis. The final step is to calculate the average of all the perpendicular lines which convert 2D images to one dimension vector. The blur length is estimated by finding the smallest peak values of the vector.

6.4   Create De-blurring Filter (PSF)

One of the most important de-blurring algorithms is generated in this section. This algorithm is a de-blur filter that works as the heart of the proposed system. The de-blur filter restores the original image using non-blind deconvolution, which is based on previously estimated blur angle and length. Steps for creating a de-blur filter are summarized in Algorithm 4.

Algorithm 4: Generate De-Blur Filter

Input: Length (*len*), and Angle (*theta*)

Output: De-Blur Filter

Begin

Step 1: Rotate half of the length estimated around the center, where

$$half = (len-1)/2$$

Step 2: Convert the estimated angle from degree to radian.

Step 3: Compute *sin* and *cos* of the estimated angle.

Step 4: Compute the size of the half matrix according to *sin* and *cos*, where

$$sx = half*\cos(theta) + 1 - len*eps$$
$$sy = half*\sin(theta) + 1 - len*eps$$

Step 5: Construct two matrices according to *sx* and *sy*.

Step 6: Construct a new matrix based on step 5 by finding the shortest distance between each pixel location (i, j) and the rotating line, where the distance is perpendicular to the line, as shown below:

$$dist = y*\cos(theta) - x*\sin(theta)$$

Step 7: Find points beyond the endpoint of the line but within the width of the line, where

$$pix = (rad >= half) \& (abs(dist) \le 1)$$
$$rad = \sqrt{x^2 + y^2}$$

Step 8: Compute the distance between points outside the endpoint of the line and the endpoint of the line, where

$$xpix = half - abs((x(pix) + dist(pix)*sinphi)/cosphi)$$
$$dist(pix) = \sqrt{dist(pix).^2 + xpix.^2}$$
$$dist = 1 + eps - abs(dist)$$

Step 9: Convert the negative *dist* value into zero as follows:

$$ist(dist < 0) = 0$$

Step 10: Rotate the matrix counter at a 180-degree angle clockwise.

Step 11: Convert the half-matrix to full size, where

$$H(end + (1:end) - 1, \ end + (1:end) - 1) = dist$$

Step 12: Normalization of the filter.

Step 13: Flip the upper rows with lower rows if the cosine of theta is greater than zero.

Step 14: De-Blur Filter has been created.

End.

The image can be divided into two halves. As a result, the line will cut the image into symmetric parts, whether horizontal, vertical, or diagonal. Therefore, the work will be based on the half-length of the line. The first step is to determine the size of the half-matrix based on the half-length, *cosine*, and *sine* of the blur angle. The size of the half-matrix will depend on the estimated angle and length in the previous algorithms. Two matrices are constructed depending on the size of the half-matrix calculated in the previous step. One of the matrices represents the horizontal line, and the other represents the vertical line. The orthogonal line is constructed based on these two matrices by finding the shortest distance between each pixel location and the rotating line, where the distance between these points and the line is perpendicular. To get an ideal line, first, find points far beyond the line's endpoint. The distance between these points and the line's endpoint is calculated. Finally, the values of these points are modified, and the matrix's values are updated according to the algorithms of the last two equations in step eight. After that, check whether the matrix values are less than zero, and update them to zero. Next, the matrix is rotated counterclockwise at 180° and modified to become a full-size matrix. The full-size matrix's values are normalized. Finally, the upper rows of the full-size matrix are flipped with the lower rows if the cosine of an angle is greater than zero. The line direction of the De-blur filter (Full-Size Matrix) is the same as the image's blur motion direction.

6.5 Deblured Image

Finally, non-blind Deconvolution techniques such as Wiener and Lucy-Richardson Filters were used to recover the sharp image using the PSF function created in the previous algorithm.

The following equation can be used to restore the original image using the Wiener filter:

$$\hat{F}(u, v) = W(u, v)G(u, v) \tag{4}$$

$\hat{F}(u, v)$ is the restored image, $W(u, v)$ is the Wiener filter, and $G(u, v)$ is the blurred image all in the frequency domain? The Wiener filter $W(u, v)$ can be described as the equation below:

$$W(u, v) = \frac{H^*(u, v)}{|H(u, v)|^{\wedge 2} + \frac{S\_U(u,v)}{S\_X(u,v)}} \tag{5}$$

where $H(u, v)$ is the point spread function in the frequency domain, S_X is the signal power spectrum and S_U is the noise power spectrum. After the image was restored, it converted from the frequency domain to the spatial domain.

Also, the iterative Lucy-Richardson algorithm can be used to recover the original image by using the equation below:

$$\hat{f}_{k+1} = \hat{f}_k \left(h * \frac{g}{h \otimes \hat{f}_k} \right) \tag{6}$$

where $\hat{f}_{k+1}$ is the estimate of a restored image after k iterations, $*$ is the correlation operator, and h refers to the point spread function. The image $h \otimes \hat{f}_k$ is a blurred image.

7   Experimental Results and Discussion

In this proposal, the standard images such as Lena, Cameraman, Peppers, Baboon, Girl, Corridor, and Characters with different sizes of 256×256, 500×500, 600×600, 688×688, and 700×700 are selected to use in the evaluation the proposal efficiency under control environments. Images are blurred with different lengths and angles ranging from 10 to 85 pixels and 10 to 180°.

The first test was to detect if an image has blurred or not, a test implemented with different image sizes 256×256, 500×500, 600×600, and 700×700. The test was performed by using 1000 clear images from the VOC 2012 dataset. Also, blurred images were created by artificially blurring the images (fourteen standard and natural images were blurred with various lengths ranging "from 10 to 90 pixels", and various angles ranging "from 10 to 180°") to produce 8092 blurred images, in addition to fifty blurred images from (VOC 2012 dataset), that produces 8142 blurred images.

Figures 5, 6 and 7 illustrate the process of detecting a blur and the elapsed time required to determine whether an image has blurred or not for various image sizes. When images were blurry or clear, the proposed method produces good results for all image sizes.

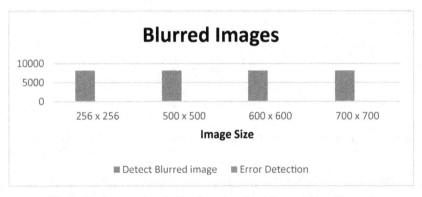

Fig. 5. Implementation of blur detection algorithm on blurred images.

Mean absolute error (MAE) was calculated for blur detection in the blurry image; the value of MAE was very small, specifically for image sizes 256×256 and 700×700. In addition, when the image was clear, the MAE for the 500×500 and 600×600 image sizes has very small MAE, as shown in Table 2.

It is concluded that the detection of blur can be achieved very efficiently for different image sizes.

The second test was to measure the best image size that can be used to determine the blur angle. Blurred images with sizes 256×256, 500×500, and 600×600, and different blur lengths and angles are used in this test. The estimation of the angles for each image size is shown in Figs. 8, 9 and 10. Angles estimated when image size 256×256 gives good estimation when the blur length is from 10 to 60 but shows some error, specifically when the blur length is equal to (70, 80, and 85) which is eliminated when the image size is bigger.

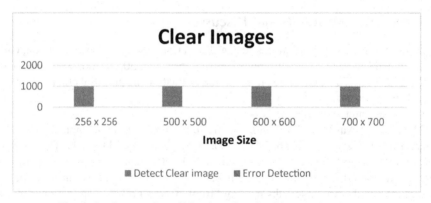

Fig. 6. Implementation of blur detection algorithm on clear images.

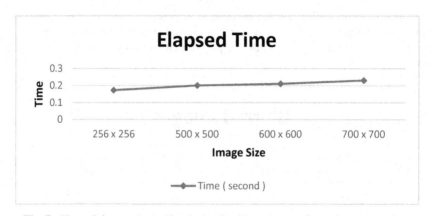

Fig. 7. Elapsed time to detect if an image has blurred or not for various image sizes

Table 2. Illustrate the MAE of the proposed method for different image sizes.

Image size	Number of clear images	Number of blurred images	MAE of Clear image	MAE of a blurred image
256 × 256	1000	8142	0.005	0.0001
500 × 500	1000	8142	0.003	0.001
600 × 600	1000	8142	0.003	0.001
700 × 700	1000	8142	0.009	0.0002

It is concluded from the testing results that the increasing image size will enhance the angle estimation specifically for blur lengths ranging from 15 to 85.

The errors that result when estimating blur angles for different length is shown in Fig. 11. The error is very small, one degree or less for just blur length equal to 10 and maybe a very small value with blur length equal to 15 and 25, while the others have no error.

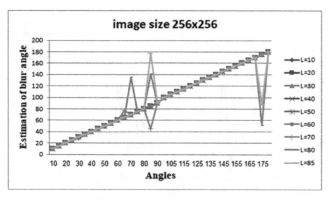

Fig. 8. Angle estimation for image size 256 × 256.

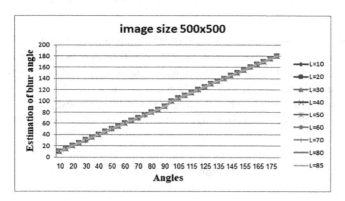

Fig. 9. Angle estimation for image size 500 × 500.

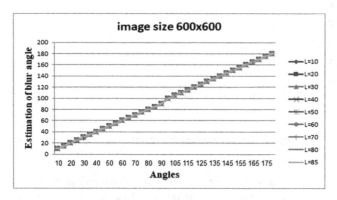

Fig. 10. Angle estimation for image size 600 × 600

Estimation of blur length for various blur angles to find the best image size that can give a more accurate estimation is the second test. The results from Fig. 12 approved

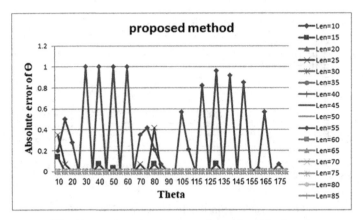

Fig. 11. Angle estimation errors for various blur length

that the small image size is not a good choice for estimating the length and direction of the blur. At the same time images with size 600 × 600 (Fig. 14) give some errors in the estimation of blur length for some images such as the cameraman image which gives a length of 11 instead of the real length of 15 when the angle was 40°. Also, the corridor image gives an outlier length when the angle equals 80. The best accuracy for length estimation was achieved when the image size is 500 × 500 as shown in Fig. 13.

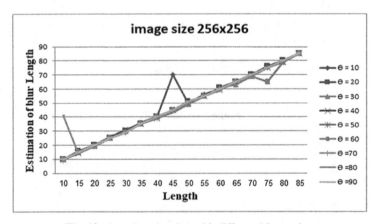

Fig. 12. Length estimation with different blur angles.

The errors that result when estimating blur length for different angles are shown in Fig. 15. The error is very small, less than one pixel mostly when the angles are 30 and 40.

We argue that the best accuracy can be achieved when the image size for this proposal is 500 × 500. At this size, there is a very good angle estimation and a very good length estimation.

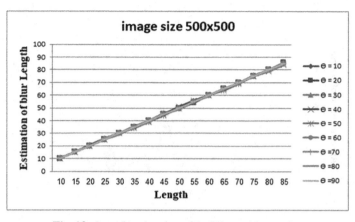

Fig. 13. Length estimation with different blur angles.

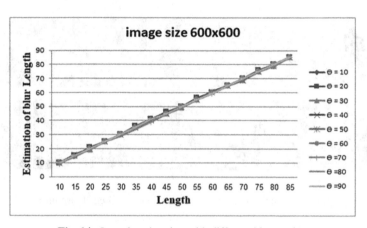

Fig. 14. Length estimation with different blur angles.

The other test is to measure the image quality after de-blurring. Different images with different lengths and angles were used in this test as shown in Fig. 16, the image size was 500 × 500, and the first row of images in Fig. 16 shows the blurred image, while the second row of images shows the de-blurred image after restoration by the proposed algorithm. The information about these images is summarized in Table 3. Table 3 shows the details about the PSF parameters used to blur images, while the last row shows the value of PSNR after image de-blurring.

Deblured images visually seem like pleasant images, where the values of PSNR encourage values.

Another test was to calculate image quality after blur was removed using Richardson-Lucy Filter. The test used eighty images from the VOC 2012 dataset entered into the system that was originally blurred at different lengths and angles, and the image size was 500 × 500, as shown in Fig. 17. Figure 17 shows the blurred image in the first row and

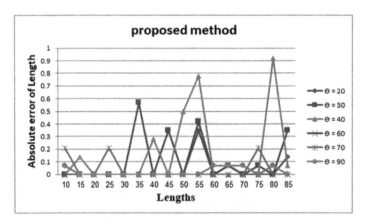

Fig. 15. Length estimation error for different angles.

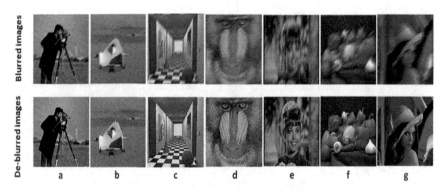

Fig. 16. Deblur images according to the proposed algorithm

Table 3. Information about the images in Fig. 16.

Images	A	b	c	d	e	F	g
Blur angle	45	30	70	10	80	40	20
Blur length	15	20	25	30	35	40	50
PSNR after de-blurring	111	112	103	101	113	114	109

the de-blurred image in the second row. After eliminating the blur, the Brisque values decreased, indicating that the image quality improved significantly.

The suggested blur angles estimated values, and run times are compared with other previous approaches such as Dash [13], Kumar [10], Wang [4], and Iraei methods [3], for different images with different sizes as shown in Table 4. From Table 4 it is concluded

Fig. 17. Deblur images according to the proposed algorithm using Richardson–Lucy Filter

that the result of the proposed method is more accurate than other estimation methods and the time is also the best.

Another comparison is listed in Table 5, which compared the suggested motion length estimation and the run time with the same methods used in comparing angle estimation. Different lengths for different image sizes are used in this comparison. The proposed method results achieve very good estimation, although some of the other previous methods produce comparatively good accuracy for length estimation than the proposed method.

Also, the absolute error of blur angles estimated shown in Fig. 11 are compared with other previous approaches such as Dash [13], Kumar [10], Wang [4], and Iraei methods [3].

The Dash method has a pretty good result to estimate angles smaller than $\theta = 45°$ for all blur lengths, in opposite for angles larger than $\theta = 45°$, where the absolute error rate is greatly increased. Kumar's method has estimated various angles as uniformly as possible rather than the two previously mentioned methods. This method still has a very high absolute error for $L = 10$, $L = 20$, and $L = 30$, and functionally is not suitable for these lengths. In the Wang method, there is a reasonably good approximation for all

Table 4. Results comparison of blur angle estimation using different methods.

Image	Original	Dash		Kumar		Wang		Iraei		Proposed Method	
	θ	θ	Time	θ	Time	θ	Time	θ	Time	θ	Time
	(˚)	(˚)	(s)	(˚)	(s)	(˚)	(s)	(˚)	(s)	(˚)	(s)
Lena 256x256	40	38.92	0.76	39.31	0.31	40.45	0.41	40.22	0.38	40	0.12
Cameraman 256x256	70	68.99	0.71	69.57	0.31	69.69	0.45	69.83	0.38	70	0.14
Pepper 256x256	10	9.11	0.79	10.65	0.31	10.4	0.42	9.76	0.39	10	0.126
Corridor 256x256	30	30.82	0.78	30.36	0.3	30.31	0.41	30.13	0.38	30	0.127
Building 600x600	35	33.61	1.91	33.94	1.09	35.41	1.37	35.39	1.4	35	0.129
Characters 688x688	60	61.62	2.32	60.76	1.34	59.61	1.86	59.62	1.82	60	0.135

Table 5. Results comparison of blur length estimation using different methods.

Image	Original	Dash		Kumar		Wang		Iraei		Proposed Method	
	L	L	Time	L	Time	L	Time	L	Time	L	Time
	(Pixel)	Pixel	(s)	Pixel	(s)	Pixel	(s)	Pixel	(s)	Pixel	(s)
Lena 256x256	30	28.88	0.62	30.37	0.34	29.69	0.44	30.16	0.64	30	2.37
Cameraman 256x256	20	21	0.6	20.41	0.34	19.71	0.43	20.26	0.63	20	2.40
Pepper 256x256	40	41	0.6	39.52	0.31	40.39	0.44	39.88	0.61	40	2.47
Corridor 256x256	50	49.55	0.61	49.61	0.32	49.64	0.41	50.17	0.62	50	2.31
Building 600x600	40	41.87	1.41	41.22	1.05	39.89	1.15	40.37	1.44	40	6.02
Characters 688x688	50	50.59	1.54	51.05	1.21	49.34	1.24	49.76	1.57	50	7.34

blur lengths at all angles, and the absolute error rate is reduced. Iraei method show high absolute error rate at $L = 10, L = 20$, and $L = 30$, but the error rate for some angles drops to less than 0.1 and has zero error when $L = 50, L = 70$, and $L = 90$. Also, the amount of this error will be reduced by increasing the blur angle. As it is clear in Fig. 11, the suggested method that used Hough transform for edges detect, exhibit a great decrease of the absolute error rate for all angles and all blur length down to zero when the length of motion $L = 20$, $L = 30$, $L = 40$, $L = 50$, $L = 60$, $L = 70$, $L = 80$ and $L = 85$ for all angles.

Figure 15 shows the absolute error rate of the proposed method when blurred with blur lengths from 10–85 (with step 5 pixels) for six different blur angles. Figure 15 also shows that the proposed method has a maximum absolute error of 0.9 in the worst case. Most lengths have an absolute error of less than 0.3, which means restoring the blurry image is more accurate than other methods.

Another test is implemented on noisy blurred images to prove the robustness of the de-blurring method to noise. Gaussian noise was added to eight different images with different sizes of signal-to-noise ratio (SNR = 25 dB). The five methods (Dash's, Kumar, Wang, Iraei, and the proposed methods) are used to estimate the PSF parameters, and then reconstruct the original images. The results showed in Table 6. As Table 6 shows, the maximum absolute error for the estimated blur angle by the proposed method is reached zero, and it is a very good result compared with other methods, although the results of other methods were very good in general. Same thing for the blur length the results were very good except for a small deviation of estimation lengths for some images.

Table 6. Results comparison of blur parameters estimation in noisy states (SNR = 25 dB)

Image	Original		Dash			Kumar			Wang			Iraei			Proposed Method		
	θ	L	θ	L	PSNR	θ	L	PSNR	θ	L	PSNR	θ	L	PSNR	θ	L	PSNR
Lena 256x256	40	30	38.71	28.7	25.29	40.48	29.2	31.22	39.59	29.57	37.16	40.27	29.84	44.03	40	30	99.14
Camerama n 256x256	70	20	68.91	21	25.46	70.46	19.2	30.12	69.62	19.69	36.8	69.71	20.31	43.36	70	20	100.95
Pepper 256x256	10	40	9.03	39.04	25.07	9.33	40.5	30.09	10.41	40.42	36.27	9.73	39.79	42.88	10	40	93.63
Corridor 256x256	30	50	28.94	49.15	26.39	29.29	49.5	31.54	29.57	49.59	36.73	29.8	50.22	43.46	30	50	94.59
Baboon 256x256	40	60	39.09	61	27.1	39.24	60.8	31.87	39.6	59.57	37.86	40.23	60.17	44.68	40	60	91.04
Girl2 256x256	20	85	21.06	85.45	27.24	19.64	84.6	31.98	20.28	85.39	37.35	19.79	85.29	44.19	20	85	90.78
Building 600x600	35	40	32.84	42.03	24.74	34.06	41.1	30.56	35.04	39.72	36.07	35.56	40.34	42.45	35	40	99.77
Characters 688x688	60	50	61.73	51.6	25.51	60.88	51	30.64	39.63	49.4	35.47	59.78	49.75	41.97	60	50	101

Moreover, the PSNR of de-blurred noise was good in general, and it reflects the good robustness of the noise.

8   Conclusion

In this work, the deblur image restoration is constructed by determining the PSF. The estimation of angle and length by the proposed method gives more accurate results than the other methods. The main contribution of this work is the ability to check the blurred image before the de-blurring process. The range of estimation angles and length is wider than the previous methods. In this work, we prove that size of the image will have significant effects on the accuracy of estimation of the PSF, and then restore the de-blurring image. Generally, the absolute errors are reduced. This method is robust and works very well even with noisy images. The suggested method produces a pleasant deblur image and it is reliable.

References

1. Dawood, A.A.M., Saleh, M.F.: Image deblurring techniques: a review. J. Sci. Eng. Res. **6**(3), 94–98 (2019)
2. Gowthami, S., Harikumar, R.: Conventional neural network for blind image blur correction using latent semantics. Soft. Comput. **24**(20), 15223–15237 (2020). https://doi.org/10.1007/s00500-020-04859-y
3. Iraei, I., Sharifi, M., Baleghi, Y.: A new approach to enhancing the estimation of blur parameters in blurred images. Optik **224**, 165298 (2020). https://doi.org/10.1016/j.ijleo.2020.165298
4. Wang, Z., Yao, Z., Wang, Q.: Improved scheme of estimating motion blur parameters for image restoration. Digit. Signal Process. A Rev. J. **65**, 11–18 (2017). https://doi.org/10.1016/j.dsp.2017.02.010
5. Li, N., Chen, S., Tang, M., Kan, J.: Deblurring method for motion blurred images based on GAN. Int. J. Circ. Syst. Signal Process. **15**, 106–113 (2021). https://doi.org/10.46300/9106.2021.15.12
6. Zhang, G., Zheng, T.: Estimation method of blurred parameters in moving blurred image. J. Phys. Conf. Ser. **1616**(1) (2020). https://doi.org/10.1088/1742-6596/1616/1/012096
7. Elmi, Y., Zargari, F., Rahmani, A.M.: Iterative approach for parametric PSF estimation. Multimedia Tools Appl. **79**(39–40), 29433–29450 (2020). https://doi.org/10.1007/s11042-020-09511-3
8. Murthy, K.V.V., Gajjar, R., Zaveri, T., Banerjee, A.: Trigonometry-based motion blur parameter estimation algorithm. Int. J. Image Min. **3**(1), 67 (2018). https://doi.org/10.1504/ijim.2018.10014060
9. Albluwi, F., Krylov, V.A., Dahyot, R.: Image deblurring and super-resolution using deep convolutional neural networks, pp. 1–6 (2018). https://doi.org/10.1109/MLSP.2018.8516983
10. Kumar, A.: Deblurring of motion-blurred images using histogram of oriented gradients and geometric moments. Signal Process. Image Commun. **55**, 55–65 (2017). https://doi.org/10.1016/j.image.2017.03.016
11. Win, Z.M., Aye, N.: Detecting image spam based on file properties, histogram, and hough transform. J. Adv. Comput. Netw. **2**(4), 287–292 (2014). https://doi.org/10.7763/jacn.2014.v2.127
12. Park, J., Kim, M., Chang, S., Lee, K.H.: Estimation of motion blur parameters using cepstrum analysis. In: Proceedings of International Symposium on Consumer Electronics, ISCE, pp. 406–409 (2011). https://doi.org/10.1109/ISCE.2011.5973859
13. Dash, R., Majhi, B.: Motion blur parameters estimation for image restoration. Optik (Stuttg). **125**(5), 1634–1640 (2014). https://doi.org/10.1016/j.ijleo.2013.09.026

Enhancing Service Classification for Network Slicing in 5G Using Machine Learning Algorithms

Noor Abdalkarem Mohammedali[1]([✉]), Triantafyllos Kanakis[1], Ali Al-Sherbaz[2], Michael Opoku Agyeman[1], and Saad Talib Hasson[3]

[1] Centre for Smart and Advanced Technologies (CAST), University of Northampton, Northampton, UK
noor.mohammedali@northampton.ac.uk
[2] School of Computing and Engineering, University of Gloucestershire, Gloucestershire, UK
[3] College of Information Technology, University of Babylon, Babylon, Iraq

Abstract. In a virtualization aspect, Network Function Virtualization (NFV) has a role in implementing network slicing. Using NFV to slice the network, make the network more flexible, but very complicated in term of management. A slice is a set of services that the network needs based on the user requirements. Moreover, each slice has a set of services called sub-slice, or one type of service. This research aims to improve the availability and scalability of the services in network slicing by managing the performance of the inter/intra slice in real-time. Also, this research will enhance the Quality of Service (QoS) for the network resources and services and the Quality of Experience (QoE) for the users within the slice when we applied machine learning algorithms to classify and predicate accurate service to the user.

With this research, we implemented the slices based on the principles of NFV to deliver flexibility in the 5G network by creating multiple slices on top of the physical network. When the implementation of the prototype is completed, traffic generated tool was used to send traffic over the slices. After data collection, we classified different services using machine learning algorithms. The optimizable tree model had almost high accuracy among other algorithms which was 99.3%.

Keywords: 5G · Network Slicing · NSSF · Traffic-Classification · QoS · inter-slice · NFV · E2E · Machine Learning

1 Introduction

Next-generation networks will be configured with softwarization techniques based on a Software-Defined Network (SDN) and NFV. The implementation of the network elements will be started from the core layer to the access layer. The key benefits of using the SDN are to reduce time configuration for complex networks, reconfigure them easily and optimize the resources using a programmable interface [1]. In addition, there are different aspects that lead the future network using NFV because it is bringing a great effect on the network especially when it is optimizing the Network Functions (NFs), while the SDN optimises the fundamental system [2].

© The Author(s), under exclusive license to Springer Nature Switzerland AG 2023
A. M. Al-Bakry et al. (Eds.): NTICT 2022, CCIS 1764, pp. 25–37, 2023.
https://doi.org/10.1007/978-3-031-35442-7_2

The NF is a functional block built on top of the physical or virtual infrastructure to create a network service and define the functional behaviour of the networks. With future systems, all NFs and resources will be virtualized and reconfigured in the core network to provide scalability and flexibility to the networks [3]. The network resources such as storage, computing and radio access network will be virtualized and dynamically managed to scale up/down the resources in the network. A network slice considered a logical network contains a set of resources [4] These resources will be provided in the slice by the service provider based on the requirements that have been agreed upon in the service level agreement (SLA) between the service provider and customers (slice owner).

The 3G Partnership Project (3GPP) in their TS 28.801 explained the concept of network slicing, the network functions and the connection between them. Also, 3GPP explained and standardised the QoS and QoE for future mobile networks. In this survey [5], the 3GPP TS 23.501 and 23.502 reviewed in terms of the mobility management in 5G with inter-slice handover in a service level. In their research directions, authors mentioned that the continuity between the slices is not given in the 3GPP TS. Furthermore, the creative concept of the Network Slice Subnet Instance (NSSI) is explained within the 3GPP TR 28.801. Network Slice Management Function (NSMF) send a request to the Network Slice Subnet Management Function (NSSMF) to create the NSSI. The NSSI depends on the availability and reliability of the physical and logical resources, and it is work on the run-time operations. The 3GPP TR 23.799 discussed all that in their technical specification document.

The QoS set of policies needs to be considered in real-time traffic with a group of functions and services to guarantee the required bandwidth for each application. With the QoE, the performance of the service needs to be improved to bring an efficient service to cover the demands of the end-user. However, there are three types of verticals that will be considered in this work: eMBB (enhanced Mobile Broadband), URLLC (ultra-Reliable Low Latency Communications) and MIoT (Massive IoT) [6]. Furthermore, managing the priority of the slice and the QoS flow during the session setup of the service are still open issues. In addition, slice and mobility management at the service level in real-time is discussed in a state-of-the-art paper in [7].

In Sect. 2, we summarize the related research to implement the slice approach on 5G systems. In Sect. 3, we propose our slicing prototype and classification model using our dataset. In Sect. 4, we explain and evaluate the performance of the model. Finally, in Sect. 5, we conclude this paper.

2 Related Works

By increasing the number of user requirements, the future network was invented to be flexible as possible. Network slicing is used to provide the flexibility needed in the new radio network. The programmability of network service is realized in slice selection. Vertical slice, radio access slice and air interface slice mentioned in [1]. With vertical slicing, they could slice one network into multiple vertical networks. Each slice could have its own core network and architecture for End- to-End network slicing in the 5G network. In addition, this architecture gives flexibility, scalability and efficiency for air interface network slicing [8].

Vassilaras et al. [9] reviewed all the network slice problems. In addition, their concentration on controlling and managing the resource allocation in the virtual network using a real-time management algorithm.

Yousaf et al. in [10] proposed a network slicing with flexible mobility and QoS/QoE support for 5G networks represented an open research problem. They mention many issues that need to be considered, such as packet filter for 5G services. Zhang et al. in [11] presented a network slicing architecture, the concept and the management of the network slicing and the handover management scheme for handover between different access networks.

Many issues and challenges discussed in network slicing for the future network. The new approach to mobility management needs to be developed to support seamless handover for 5G new radio in network slicing to improve the continuity and scalability of the user experience [12].

Oladejo and Falowo demonstrated the network capacity of Mobile Virtual Network Operators (MVNOs) in a multi-Tenancy. In their work, the resource allocation is realized based on the hierarchal model by setting a priority to different slices to solve the resources allocation problem. Moreover, SLA between infrastructure providers and MVNOs was taken into consideration [13]. Zhang et al. in [14], proposed flexible rescheduling network services over multi Virtual Network Function (VNF) within different orders in run-time process. Their sharing and preemption model was developed using the Integer Linear Programming algorithm to increase the number of legal resources. Also, the result showed that this model beats the other models in terms of resource sharing acceptance in the virtual network.

Mobility management architecture based on a network slicing explained in which means each slice manages its users across heterogeneous radio access technologies. In this architecture, each slice has the slice configuration and service characteristics control different requirements such as latency and speed [15]. Mobility [16] is one of the key issues in a service level for future networks because the management in the mobility is in two levels of mode: idle mode for the user reachability and connected mode for the handover. Sattar and Matrawy in [17] mentioned two key challenges in network slicing for 5G core Networks in terms of isolation and End-to-End delay. The End-to-End slice means creating a connection between the core network and RAN. The relationship between this connection could be one-to-one or one-to-many with a real-time application. They applied Mixed-Linear Integer Programming (MILP) as a formulation for a model optimization algorithm. In the end, they simulated the 5G core network and slice request and their simulation result met the minimum requirement, but it need more enhancement.

A slice management schema proposed in [18] to reduce the interference in a wireless network by defining different policies within their routing protocol. A virtual function is used to satisfy the QoS requirement when the resources isolated between slices are done based on their priority. In this paper, traffic policy flows based on two types of priority: high and low priority. So, the highest weight gets through the shortest path to provide a better QoS and lower interference to VIP slices. Their proposed solution is based on brute-force search to find the shortest path and k-hop distance interference algorithm because it is used with different types of wireless networks. Besides, they evaluated the routing algorithm performance for the wireless network environment. In the end, a comparison between their result and the naive slice management method showed that their method defeated NSM in terms of the QoS, throughput and delay performance.

Shurman et al. in [19] designed network slicing over a mmwave bands with a frequency range between (30–300) GHz to prove that their work supports the 5G channel. Their scenario has two types of priorities based on the reserved value. Moreover, this value is set as a tag on the frame, which corresponds to a slice priority after sending the packet to the switch. The Work in [20] proposed a set of policies that work with network slicing and sub-network slicing in a dynamic way. Their ontologies managed the lifecycle for the slices dynamically based on two types of policies: inter-slice policy and intra-slice policy. In their model, the resources and the services came from remote health scenarios to support eHealth and Ultra HD video to support multimedia services. Virtual resources allocation within slice priority identified in [21] to change the traffic dynamically without affecting the QoE for the users. The inter and intra-slice priority will depend on the QoS requirement for various users and services in the future network.

A dynamic management resource approach applied a reinforcement learning algorithm to meet the end-users requirement [22]. In this approach, the authors managed the resources using a Markov Decision Process (MDP). Then, they utilized Q-learning for managing the resources dynamically. In the end, they compared their result with different algorithms using an inelastic flow to demonstrate that the number of the resources increase, the amount of profit increase and the satisfaction rate for the QoS increase in the dynamic resource allocation.

Kim et al. in [23] addressed the complexities of the 5G network, where each user within the slice has two service function chains (SFCs). The first SFC handles the traffic in the control plane and the second one is used to carry the traffic in the data plane. Both of the SFCs work on the physical and virtual layers to reduce the traffic cost according to the users' requirements in different verticals in terms of latency and bandwidth. Supervised learning algorithm is used to classify and predict slice traffic over the 5G network [24]. 5G services are allocated dynamically in real-time. Their work is done based on open-source code to program the slice decisions.

Based on the authors' knowledge, none of the above research paper deal with the 5G function to solve the open research issues, such as resource allocation, mobility and slice management. For that reason, we will build a set of slices on top of the 5G core using open-source code to send traffic, collect the slice traffic and predict the 5G services using the best machine learning model that's fit our dataset. This solution will enhance the QoS and QoE for the user when applying more services to future networks and let the users connect to multiple slices at the same time.

3   The Proposed Model

This system will be developed using softwarization approaches based on SDN and NFV. All NFs will be implemented according to the 5G functions. The 5G means a wireless network standard by a group of telecommunications companies to increase the speed of data communication, capacity and coverage in logical networks instead of the traditional networks. The compensation between SDN, NFV and 5G functions introduced real-time dynamic programming services to the network based on the use cases demand.

From the diagram below in Fig. 1, the infrastructure layer will be represented as a user plane which contains all the slices that will be implemented as virtual Tenants. The 5G core will work as the brain of the network to control the top layer of the network (application plane) and the lower layer (user plane). The Proposed slice model builds on top of Free5gc open-source code for the 5G core [25] and UERANSIM open-source code is used for the users and radio access network [26].

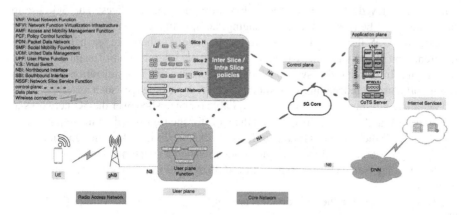

Fig. 1. System Prototype

All the slice resources and services will be reconfigured by the 5G core using the N4 interface. In addition, the application plane will contain all the functions and services. The 5G core needs to manage the slices in the data plane such as slice policy, data flow and slice management. All the future networks will need to implement the slice in the core network to control the users in the data plane. The slice implementation will use Access and Mobility Function (AMF) for controlling the user data, mobility state and authentication, Police Control Function (PCF) for policy rules and authorization and Network Slice Service Function (NSNF) to manage the policies for the network slicing. According to the 3GPP specifications, all functions will be implemented at the core layer and will run through different types of interfaces based on the function. All these functions will be connected using a specific interface named Service-Based Interface (SBI) through the SBI Message Bus. In this system, many functions will be configured, such as mobility, policy control, and priority with different functional requirements such as latency, mobility, availability, reliability and data rates to serve the specific users. Furthermore, all 5G functions will be configured in the core network and then will be run in the user plane depending on the requirement of the slice management in the future network as listed below:

Adding/scaling a set of services and resources that support the slice.

Moving the users from one slice to another and assigning the users for more than eight slices at the same time for a specific purpose based on the user demands or in emergency cases.

Isolating the slices from each other to prevent any interference between the slices.

In slice management, flexibility is one of the features required in the future network, which means that scale the slice up and down. Specifically, the network slice priority will be changed based on the network situation, such as an emergency state or disaster. Moreover, the priority of the user per service needs to be changed depending on the service regulations.

Network policies will be divided into two types: inter-slice and intra-slice policies. The inter-slice priority deal with the devices inside the slice. On the other hand, the intra-slice policy deals with devices within different types of slices. The 5G core in this system will be responsible for managing the mobility as a service, managing slice policies, the QoS flow and the life cycle for the slice. Furthermore, each Tenant has a different type of service such as Tenant 1 for emergency services and Tenant 2 for video live stream. In the end, this system needs to use management optimization techniques to support a users. Indeed, network slicing faced many challenges such as:

Guaranteeing that the SLAs will be available on each slice over the 5G networks at the same time and increase the QoS and the QoE for the user based on the requirement.

Combining the main keys for the future networks: flexibility, efficiency and lightness.

Slicing is used to combine multiple applications on a single network.

Minimising the Operating Expenditure (OPEX) and improving the revenue of the networks.

Time increases for the network services in two cases Time-to-Market (TTM) and Time-to-Customer (TTC).

4   Result and Discussion

In this section, we will explain our prototype and how we generated the traffic over the 5G networks. Free5gc is required for the 5G core on the core layer, and it is run on the Ubuntu server. For the access layer, the User Plan Function (UPF) is run on the Ubuntu server and connects to another server containing UERANSIM, which is used for the Radio Access Layer (RAN) and the user device. Inter and intra slice were configured over the 5G core, UPF and RAN. Each user can connect to more than eight slices and generate traffic over them based on the user requirements.

Traffic is generated over the slices and over the 5G core. The traffic was collected from the core and user plane using Wireshark. From the Wireshark file, we checked the performance of the network in terms of delay, throughput and window size on different streams.

TCP stream sent over slice number five with 60.64.0.1 as the IP address for the slice to show the throughput of the connection from the online server with IP address 140.110.240.80. The number of the packets plotted over time in steven's graph as is shown in Fig. 2. The number of the TCP packets increased regularly until 26 s then the TCP packets become stable until 36 s when the TCP packets start increase. The number of the TCP packets in our work is better than the result for the TCP protocol in [27].

The throughput average for six streams is shown in Fig. 3. This traffic was sent from the online server using a traffic-generated tool to slice number six that the user connected to using 60.65.0.1 as IP for slice number six. On the other hand, the throughput average for 44 streams is shown in Fig. 4. This traffic was sent from the online server using a

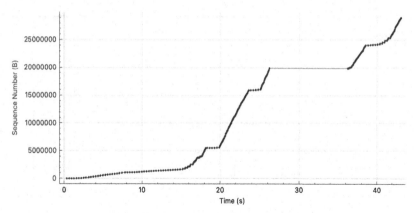

Fig. 2. Steven's graph for TCP traffic

traffic-generated tool to slice number five that the user connected to using 60.64.0.1 as IP for a slice. The connection dropped between 28 s–38 s as is shown in the graph. TCP packets length in the blue line, the throughput stream in yellow and the goodput in the green line. The average throughput for the 5G slices is important with and without the user mobility. The average packets arrival on the system is better than the result in [28].

After sending the traffic over slice number five, we calculated the duration for the packet when it is sent and received from the server to the slice using TCP protocol. In this case, Round-trip time (RTT) determines the successful delivery of the packet as is shown in Fig. 5.

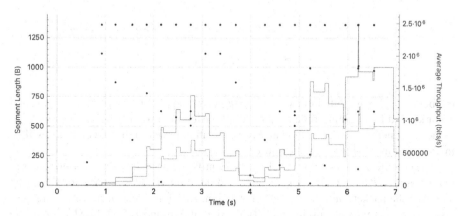

Fig. 3. Throughput for the 5G network after sending 6 streams

Window scaling for 44 streams over slice number five as is shown in Fig. 6.

After generated the traffic over the 5G network, we calculated the delay as is shown in Fig. 7.

In this research, we will classify the 5G traffic for different services using machine learning in Matlab. The idea of using different machine learning algorithms is to choose

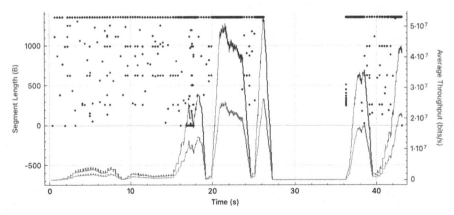

Fig. 4. Throughput for the 5G network after sending 44 streams

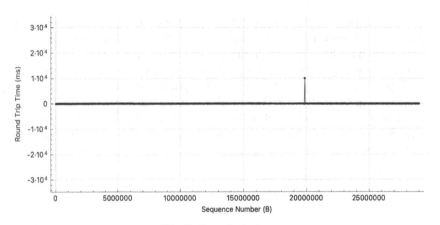

Fig. 5. Round-trip time

the best model that's fitted our purpose. We need to apply an algorithm that has good accuracy and less training time to make the decision of choosing the services faster to reduce the energy. We didn't look at the computation power in this paper, but it will be investigated more about it in our future work.

The classification model will help us to identify the best algorithms for our dataset. Our dataset contains: Traffic time, source and destination address, protocol name, the length of the packets and the packet information. Different types of protocols are generated over the 5G systems such as: TCP, UDP, ICMP and HTTP. In MATLAB, we will identify all columns as input features except the service name will be the output. Machine Learning Model Classification for the prototype is shown in Table 1. Our prediction accuracy values are enhanced in many models and get higher accuracy compared with the work in [29]. In our system, different types of traffic are classified over the End-to-End 5G slice network. The accuracy is not only our concern, but we need to predicate future services in less time. For this reason, the medium tree model has less training prediction time compared with other models.

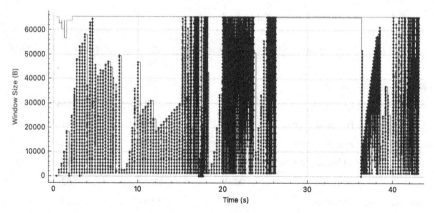

Fig. 6. Window Scaling

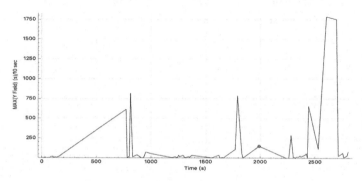

Fig. 7. Delay

After the classification model, the Confusion matrix for the best algorithm that's fitted our model is shown in Fig. 8. The optimizable tree model trained with high accuracy which is 99.3% as shown in Table 1. With our model, the maximum number of splits was 258 and the split criterion was twoing rule. The optimization result for this model is shown in Fig. 9 for the minimum classification error.

Table 1. Model Classification

Class	Classification Model	Accuracy %	Prediction Speed (obs/sec)	Train Time (sec)
Trees	Fine	**99.2**	810000	13.029
	Medium	**97.0**	900000	**11.633**
	Coarse	89.3	820000	18.956
	Optimizable	**99.3**	1300000	719.5

(*continued*)

Table 1. (*continued*)

Class	Classification Model	Accuracy %	Prediction Speed (obs/sec)	Train Time (sec)
SVM	Linear	80.1	7600	48116
	Quadratic	86.6	400	72551
	Boosted Trees	**98.8**	42000	4441.5
Ensemble	Bagged Trees	**98.8**	34000	4880.1
	RUSBoosted Trees	33.4	37000	5687.6
	Narrow	94.0	350000	5562
Neural Network	Medium	**95.2**	390000	6120.7
	Wide	**95.9**	250000	19540
	Bilayered	91.6	320000	11392
	Trilayered	89.5	310000	17325

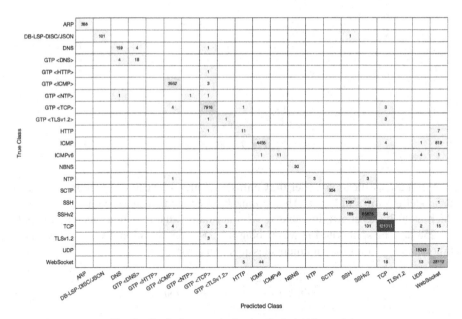

Fig. 8. Confusion matrix for the Optimizable model

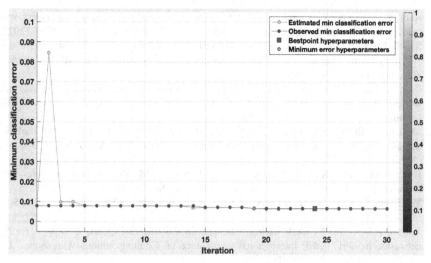

Fig. 9. Minimum classification error

5 Conclusions and Future Work

Several techniques need to be implemented to make the 5G core takes the right decision with the upcoming request to choose the slice and service within the slice. For example, when the user is on a video call, then at the same time, this user receives a phone call. So, the 5G core needs to make sure that the user will be available in both slices without any interference or cut in a call. But if the user decides to leave the video slice and move to another one, the 5G core will be able to forward the traffic based on the users' demands. Based on the authors' research resource allocation, slice and mobility management is still an open issue and under investigation by telecommunication companies and researchers especially at a service level for real-time application. In this research, we implemented the slices over the core and user plane layer and generated traffic over the slices and the core to see the performance of the traffic when we sent different types of services. After training our model with multi-machine learning algorithms. We will identify the best algorithm to fit our model to deal with real-time traffic to predict the services based on the requirements. For future work, we will implement a machine learning algorithm with an SDN controller to connect it with the 5G core to manage the mobility for inter/intra slice without effects the QoS in real-time when it is delivered to the users based on their demands and this system needs to specify the mobility types to support the 5G users.

References

1. Kheddar, H., Ouldkhaoua, S., Bouguerra, R.: All you need for horizontal slicing in 5g network. arXiv preprint arXiv:2207.11477 (2022)
2. Pérez, M., Losada, N., Sánchez, E., Gaona, G.: State of the art in software defined networking (SDN). Visión electrónica **13**(1) (2019)
3. Fitzek, F., Granelli, F., Seeling, P.: Computing in Communication Networks: From Theory to Practice. Academic Press, New York (2020)

4. Kaur, K., Mangat, V., Kumar, K.: A review on virtualized infrastructure managers with management and orchestration features in NFV architecture. Comput. Netw. 109281 (2022)

5. Sajjad, M.M., Bernardos, C.J., Jayalath, D., Tian, Y.-C.: Inter-slice mobility management in 5G: motivations, standard principles, challenges, and research directions. IEEE Commun. Stan. Mag. 6(1), 93–100 (2022)

6. Guo, S., Lu, B., Wen, M., Dang, S., Saeed, N.: Customized 5G and beyond private networks with integrated URLLC, eMBB, mMTC, and positioning for industrial verticals. IEEE Commun. Stan. Mag. 6(1), 52–57 (2022)

7. Mohammedali, N.A., Kanakis, T., Agyeman, M.O., Al-Sherbaz, A.: A survey of mobility management as a service in real-time inter/intra slice control. IEEE Access 9, 62533–62552 (2021)

8. Hurtado Sánchez, J.A., Casilimas, K., Caicedo Rendon, O.M.: Deep reinforcement learning for resource management on network slicing: a survey. Sensors 22(8), 3031 (2022)

9. Vassilaras, S., et al.: The algorithmic aspects of network slicing. IEEE Commun. Mag. 55(8), 112–119 (2017)

10. Yousaf, F.Z., et al.: Network slicing with flexible mobility and QoS/QoE support for 5G networks. In: 2017 IEEE International Conference on Communications Workshops (ICC Workshops), pp. 1195–1201. IEEE (2017)

11. Zhang, H., Liu, N., Chu, X., Long, K., Aghvami, A.-H., Leung, V.C.: Network slicing based 5G and future mobile networks: mobility, resource management, and challenges. IEEE Commun. Mag. 55(8), 138–145 (2017)

12. Gonzalez, A.J., et al.: The isolation concept in the 5G network slicing. In: 2020 European Conference on Networks and Communications (EuCNC), pp. 12–16. IEEE (2020)

13. Oladejo, S.O., Falowo, O.E.: 5G network slicing: a multi-tenancy scenario. In: 2017 Global Wireless Summit (GWS), pp. 88–92. IEEE (2017)

14. Zhang, Y., He, F., Sato, T., Oki, E.: Optimization of network service scheduling with resource sharing and preemption. In: 2019 IEEE 20th International Conference on High Performance Switching and Routing (HPSR), pp. 1–6. IEEE (2019)

15. Aljeri, N., Boukerche, A.: Smart and green mobility management for 5G-enabled vehicular networks. Trans. Emerg. Telecommun. Technol. 33(3), e4054 (2022)

16. Siddiqui, M.U.A., Qamar, F., Tayyab, M., Hindia, M., Nguyen, Q.N., Hassan, R.: Mobility management issues and solutions in 5G-and-beyond networks: a comprehensive review. Electronics 11(9), 1366 (2022)

17. Sattar, D., Matrawy, A.: Optimal slice allocation in 5G core networks. IEEE Networking Lett. 1(2), 48–51 (2019)

18. An, N., Kim, Y., Park, J., Kwon, D.-H., Lim, H.: Slice management for quality of service differentiation in wireless network slicing. Sensors 19(12), 2745 (2019)

19. Shurman, M., Taqieddin, E., Oudat, O., Al-Qurran, R., et al.: Performance enhancement in 5G cellular networks using priorities in network slicing. In: 2019 IEEE Jordan International Joint Conference on Electrical Engineering and Information Technology (JEEIT), pp. 822–826. IEEE (2019)

20. Celdrán, A.H., Pérez, M.G., Clemente, F.J.G., Ippoliti, F., Pérez, G.M.: Dynamic network slicing management of multimedia scenarios for future remote healthcare. Multimedia Tools Appl. 78(17), 24707–24737 (2019)

21. Dighriri, M., Alfoudi, A.S.D., Lee, G.M., Baker, T., Pereira, R.: Resource allocation scheme in 5g network slices. In: 2018 32nd International Conference on Advanced Information Networking and Applications Workshops (WAINA), pp. 275–280. IEEE (2018)

22. Kim, Y., Kim, S., Lim, H.: Reinforcement learning based resource management for network slicing. Appl. Sci. 9(11), 2361 (2019)

23. Addad, R.A., Bagaa, M., Taleb, T., Dutra, D.L.C., Flinck, H.: Optimization model for cross-domain network slices in 5G networks. IEEE Trans. Mob. Comput. 19(5), 1156–1169 (2019)

24. Tsourdinis, T., Chatzistefanidis, I., Makris, N., Korakis, T.: AI-driven service-aware real-time slicing for beyond 5G networks. In: IEEE INFOCOM 2022-IEEE Conference on Computer Communications Workshops (INFOCOM WKSHPS), pp. 1–6. IEEE (2022)
25. Free5GC.org. Free5GC: an open-source 5G core network (2019). https://www.free5gc.org/. Accessed 20 Apr 2022
26. Güngör, A.: UERANSIM: an open-source 5G UE and gNodeB (2021). https://github.com/ali gungr/UERANSIM. Accessed 25 Apr 2022
27. Chouman, A., Manias, D.M., Shami, A.: Towards supporting intelligence in 5G/6G core networks: NWDAF implementation and initial analysis. arXiv preprint arXiv:2205.15121 (2022)
28. Nadeem, L., Amin, Y., Loo, J., Azam, M.A., Chai, K.K.: Quality of service based resource allocation in D2D enabled 5G-CNS with network slicing. Phys. Commun. **52**, 101703 (2022)
29. Salhab, N., Rahim, R., Langar, R., Boutaba, R.: Machine learning based resource orchestration for 5G network slices. In: 2019 IEEE Global Communications Conference (GLOBECOM), pp. 1–6. IEEE (2019)

MesoNet3: A Deepfakes Facial Video Detection Network Based on Object Behavior Analysis

Qasim Jaleel[✉] and Israa H. Ali

University of Babylon- College of Information Technology, Babylon, Iraq
{qasim.jaleel1984,Israa_hadi}@itnet.uobabylon.edu.iq

Abstract. Deepfake is the process of manipulating objects with images and video. As a result of the development of deep learning techniques such as GAN, Deepfake has become closer to the truth. Many researchers are based on discovering deep fakes that were created by traditional methods. These methods produce often generate artifacts that may be subtle to humans. This paper can detect deepfakes that are perfectly created. Through the use of the new MesoNet3 algorithm to analyze behavior, facial expressions, and the appearance of an object based on a dataset. This paper consists of two stages. The first stage is to build a new MesoNet3 network that is trained on a set of data using a deepfake dataset. The second stage is to test the videos through the extraction of the face. After that, enter it into MesoNet3 and discover whether it is fake or not. The new MesoNet3 algorithm has proven its ability and accuracy in detecting fake video, compared to the old Meso-4. The accuracy of the MesoNet3 in detecting and distinguishing fake and real videos is %99.54.

Keywords: MesoNet3 · Media Forensics · DeepFake Detection · Face Detection · Meso-4

1 Introduction

FAKE videos with facial information created through digital modification, particularly using DeepFake technologies, have recently become a major public concern [1]. The phrase "DeepFake" refers to a deep learning-based technology for creating fake videos by exchanging a person's face with another person's face[2]. In addition, fake content includes fake news, hoaxes, and financial fraud [3]. As a result, the field of research, which has traditionally focused on generic media forensics, is being reenergized, with more emphasis on detecting facial modification in images and videos [4]. In general, there are types of deep fakes, among these types, full-face synthesis is the creation of a new face that does not exist [5]. Switching identity is switching one face to another. Attribute Manipulation in the treatment of some facial features, such as age, hair color, and others. Expression Swap consists of changing a person's facial expressions [6]. These methods mentioned earlier are created using deep learning. Like any other modern and rapidly

© The Author(s), under exclusive license to Springer Nature Switzerland AG 2023
A. M. Al-Bakry et al. (Eds.): NTICT 2022, CCIS 1764, pp. 38–49, 2023.
https://doi.org/10.1007/978-3-031-35442-7_3

evolving technology, Deep Learning has brought with it new obstacles. Some of these are the so-called "Deep Fakes" or "deep fakes," which are made with deep generative models that can edit video and audio recordings [4]. One of the most important deep learning techniques that can create a perfect deep fake is the generative adversarial networks (GAN) [7] as shown in Fig. 1.

Original   Deepfake

Fig. 1. Facial manipulation by GAN [8].

Videos created using GAN are more realistic and difficult to detect by traditional methods that rely on clear visual effects between video frames [9]. The diversity of the methods of GAN that create deep fakes, such as(cycle GAN, biGAN, couple GAN, etc.), as well as the great and continuous development of the tools used in the process of deep fakes [7]. This development makes it difficult to use well-known deepfake detection algorithms. Therefore, they propose a method based on analyzing the behavior of the object by comparing the behavior of the object in fake videos with the behavior of the object in real videos. One of the techniques used to detect deepfakes is Meso-4. This method is used to detect deepfakes that are created using one of the methods (Deepfake or Face2Face) [10]. The Meso-4 network is broken down into four convolution layers and a dense network with one hidden layer. It makes use of the ReLU activation functions to process non-linearities [11]. The gradient vanishing problem is likewise addressed by batch normalization in this network. Furthermore, this network employs dropout in the completely connected layer, ensuring classification endurance [12]. In Fig. 2 there are more details [13]. In this paper, the Meso-4 was modified and a new three-layer structure was created. Next, train this network using the Deepfake dataset. The reason for reducing the number of Meso-4 layers is to preserve the finer details of the object's behavior. These finer details can be used to detect abnormal behavior of the video object. Because the deep fake videos are close to the real ones. Therefore, the Meso-4 network sometimes fails to detect abnormal behavior. Whereas the Meso-3 network preserves the smallest details of the behavior of the video object. Which makes it give more accurate results than Meso-4.

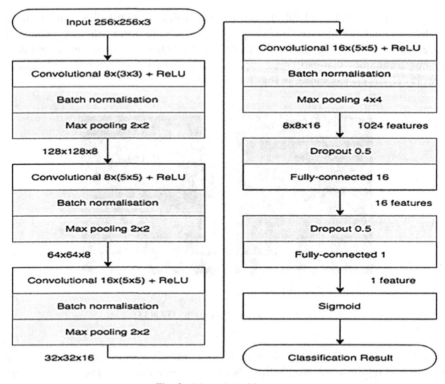

Fig. 2. Meso-4 Architecture.

2 Related Work

A lot of research has been done to discover deepfakes. We mention some of them. Robail Yasrab and et al. [14] propose a deepfake detection method using upper body language analysis. The proposal was to use LSTM in the process of training the network. The research relied on the movement of the upper part and the movement of the head in training the network. Where the network can detect deepfake videos. Shruti Agarwal and et al. [15] employed forensic technology to detect deepfakes in videos. The proposal uses the CNN network for the training and detection of deep fakes. Train network by features that represent head pose, facial landmarks, and facial expression. Hernandez-Ortega and et al. [16] applied develop a spatial-temporal representation of motion (MMSTR) for video based on heart rhythm signals. And by monitoring the heartbeat, the fake video is detected, and this depends on the network training. Chih-Chung Hsu and et al. [9] this research uses contrastive loss and deep learning to detect fake images. First, advanced GANs generate fake–real image pairs. Next, dense networks are reduced to a two-streamed network to allow pairwise input. The proposed common fake feature network is then trained to distinguish between fake and real images. A classification layer is added to the proposed common fake feature network to detect fake images. The proposed method outperformed other fake image detectors in experiments. Sawinder Kaur and et al. [17] a method that makes use of temporal sequential frames is proposed as a means of identifying deepfake videos that depict politicians. The forged video is used to extract the frames at the first level of the proposed approach, and then a deep depth-based convolutional long short-term memory model is used to identify the fake frames at the second level. The proposed model is also tested on a ground truth dataset of fake videos that we just put together. This dataset uses the source and destination video frames of well-known politicians. Zhiming Xia and et al. [10] in this paper, the authors propose a method for detecting Deepfake videos that are based on MesoNet and includes a preprocessing module. First, the preprocessing module needs to be created so that cropped face images can be preprocessed. This improves the discrimination between the different multi-color channels. After that, the images that have been preprocessed are loaded into the traditional MesoNet. Darius Afchar and et al. [13] conducted this research using the Meso-4 network and the MesoInception-4 network, based on a dataset of training. Both networks are based on the mesoscopic properties of images. This gives the ability to notice slight changes in faces in videos and detect deep fakes.

3   The Proposed Method

The proposed system consists of two stages. The first stage is the construction of the MesoNet3 network. The MesoNet3 is then trained and tested using the deepfake dataset. The second stage is the testing of videos, passing them to the MesoNet3 network, and classifying whether they are fake or real.

3.1   MesoNet3 Network

The first stage is the construction of the MesoNet3 network, which consists of three layers and can detect deepfake videos. The first and second layers consist of a convolutional layer of 8(3 * 3) and a Relu function followed by batch normalization and max pooling. The third layer consists of the convolutional layer 16(3 * 3) and the Relu function, followed by batch normalization and max pooling. In Fig. 3 there are more details.

3.2   Dataset

The used dataset is the deepfake dataset. This data consists of two groups: the training group and the evaluation group. In the following Table 1, the number of images for each group is shown. Faces were extracted from publicly available videos online. 175 videos were downloaded from various online platforms for fake images. Their duration ranges between 2 and 3 min, with a minimum resolution of 854 × 450 pixels. They were compressed using the H.264 codec but at different compression levels [13].

3.3   The Preprocessing

The preprocessing step includes resizing the image dimensions of the database images to 224 * 244 pixels, which is considered an appropriate size. However, it may not achieve the claimed accuracy in the paper. This could be due to the large size of the dataset, which may contain too many images in the test set. To counteract this, use this step to

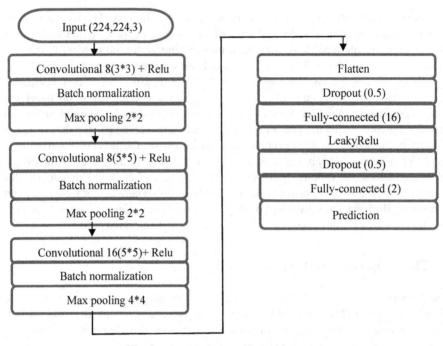

Fig. 3. MesoNet3 Network Architecture.

Table 1. Shows the number of images for the deepfake dataset.

Set	Size of the forged image class	Size of real image class
training	5111	7250
validation	2889	4259

increase the size. It takes all of the images as well as creates a new dataset by reserving only 10% of the data (randomly) for the test set (rather than 36.7 percent in the original dataset). This will be radically altered. The distribution used in the paper was as shown in Table 2.

Table 2. Shows the distribution of the number of images used in the learning and testing of the MesoNet3 network.

Set	Size of the forged image class	Size of real image class	total
training	7175	10337	17512
testing	773	1172	1945
	7948	11509	19457

3.4 Testing the Videos

In the second stage, after building and training the MesoNet3 network using the deepfake dataset. Some videos test whether they are fake or real. Fig. 4 shows the general steps for testing videos.

Input Video File. The first step is to take the videos to be tested by the system. The system receives various types of video files. But the more accurate and not bad the videos, the more accurate the result. The reason is that the MesoNet3 network depends on the behavior of the object, such as facial expressions, head movement, and others.

Face Detector (MTCNN). The Multi-task Cascaded Convolutional Networks (MTCNN) is a face identification and alignment network. It's utilized to identify faces and significant features like the eyes, nose, and mouth. As shown in Fig. 5. Through this technique, it will take the behavior of the object. This step is important in capturing the features of the object, which will be used in the later steps of deepfake detection.

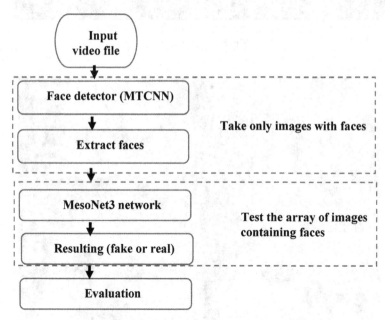

Fig. 4. General steps in testing the videos.

EXTRACT FACES. In this step, faces are combined and frames that do not contain faces are removed. It relies only on the face and its behavior of expressions and movement of the head and eyes, as shown in Fig. 6.

Mesonet3 Network. The faces are located and collected before being forwarded to the MesoNet3 network. The MesoNet3 network structure is intended to detect anomalous object behavior. Face emotions, head movement, facial position, eyes, and other features were taught to the network. This aids in spotting the object's aberrant behavior and

Fig. 5. Face detector.

Fig. 6. Extract faces.

determining if it is real or fake. Two similar videos of the same person have been sent to the MesoNet3 network, one of them is fake and the other is real. After collecting the faces, they are sent to the MesoNet3 network, where it is determined whether they are real or fake.

Evaluation. In the evaluation stage, the faces that were rated as real are evaluated correctly. Fake faces that have not been properly classified depend on confidence measures. Fig. 7 shows the result of the real classification and the percentage of confidence for each face that was recognized. Fig. 8 shows the misclassification ratio, where the confidence is very low, so it is considered a false classification. Fig. 9 shows the result of the fake classification and the percentage of confidence for each face that was recognized. Fig. 10 shows the fake misclassification ratio, where the confidence is very low, so it is considered a false classification.

Fig. 7. The real classification and the percentage of confidence.

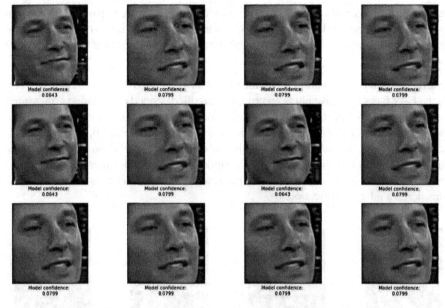

Fig. 8. The real misclassification and the percentage of confidence.

Fig. 9. The fake classification and the percentage of confidence.

Fig. 10. The fake misclassification and the percentage of confidence.

4 Experiment Results

The system consists of two stages. The first stage is to build a new network consisting of three layers. These three layers enable the detection of abnormal behavior in a person. Where the network is trained for different people based on facial expressions, eye movement, head position, and other features of the object. The second stage is the video test, where the test passes several steps. The first step is to distinguish the faces. The second step is to extract faces from videos. After that, those faces are passed to the network to discover whether these videos are fake or real, with a percentage for each of them. After training and testing the network, its accuracy is %9322. After 10 training epochs, the deepfake dataset was used in the training. The relationship between the loss of the training data and the evaluation data and the relationship between the loss and the accuracy of the model is shown in Fig. 11. The accuracy of the system in detecting and distinguishing fake and real videos is %99.54. When it was tested on the deepfake data set, it gave the accuracy of the Meso3 network as %93.22. When tested on the same deepfake data set, the Meso-4 network's accuracy was %92.94. When testing the videos, the MesoNet3 network achieved an accuracy of %99.54, while the Meso-4 network achieved an accuracy of %78.72 on the same videos, as shown in Table 3.

Table 3. Show The Accuracy of the Mesonet3 and Meso-4

Type dataset	The Accuracy of the Mesonet3	The Accuracy of the Meso-4
Deepfake dataset	%93.22	%92.94
Untitled videos	%99.54	%78.72

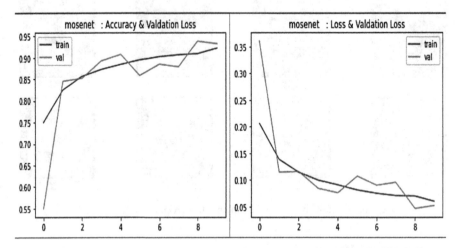

Fig. 11. The relationship between the loss, accuracy between train, and validation.

5   Conclusion

The proposed MesoNet3 network achieved good results compared to other networks such as Meso-4. The accuracy of the MesoNet3 network is due to the design of the network structure, which consists of three layers. These layers enable the detection of abnormal behavior by training the network on facial expressions and head and eye movements. This enables the network to identify fake or real videos with high accuracy. In addition, both networks depend on the accuracy of the videos; the higher the accuracy, the better the results.

References

1. Rössler, A., Cozzolino, D., Verdoliva, L., Riess, C., Thies, J., Nießner, M.: FaceForensics: a large-scale video dataset for forgery detection in human faces (2018). http://arxiv.org/abs/1803.09179
2. Huang, R., Fang, F., Nguyen, H.H., Yamagishi, J., Echizen, I.: Security of facial forensics models against adversarial attacks (2019)
3. Nguyen, T.T., et al.: Deep learning for deepfakes creation and detection: a survey (2019)
4. Yang, X., Li, Y., Lyu, S.: Exposing deep fakes using inconsistent head poses (2019)
5. Li, Y., Yang, X., Sun, P., Qi, H., Lyu, S.: Celeb-DF: a large-scale challenging dataset for DeepFake forensics (2020)

6. Kaur, S., Kumar, P., Kumaraguru, P.: DeepFakes: temporal sequential analysis to detect face-swapped video clips using convolutional long short-term memory (2020). https://doi.org/10.1117/1.JEI.29

7. Qi, H., et al.: DeepRhythm: exposing DeepFakes with attentional visual heartbeat rhythms (2020)

8. Ramachandran, S., Nadimpalli, A.V., Rattani, A.: An experimental evaluation on DeepFake detection using deep face recognition (2021)

9. Hsu, C.C., Zhuang, Y.X., Lee, C.Y.: Deep fake image detection based on pairwise learning. Appl. Sci. (Switzerland) **10** (2020). https://doi.org/10.3390/app10010370

10. Xia, Z., Qiao, T., Xu, M., Wu, X., Han, L., Chen, Y.: DeepFake video detection based on MesoNet with preprocessing module. Symmetry **14** (2022). https://doi.org/10.3390/sym14050939

11. Pashine, S., Mandiya, S., Gupta, P., Sheikh, R.: DeepFake detection: survey of facial manipulation detection solutions (2021)

12. Xia, Z., Qiao, T., Xu, M., Wu, X., Han, L., Chen, Y.: DeepFake video detection based on MesoNet with preprocessing module. Symmetry **14**, 939 (2022)

13. Afchar, D., Nozick, V., Yamagishi, J., Echizen, I.: MesoNet: a compact facial video forgery detection network (2018). https://doi.org/10.1109/WIFS.2018.8630761

14. Yasrab, R., Jiang, W., Riaz, A.: Fighting DeepFakes using body language analysis. Forecasting **3**, 303–321 (2021)

15. Agarwal, S., Farid, H., El-Gaaly, T., Lim, S.-N.: Detecting deep-fake videos from appearance and behavior (2020)

16. Hernandez-Ortega, J., Tolosana, R., Fierrez, J., Morales, A.: DeepFakesON-Phys: DeepFakes detection based on heart rate estimation (2020)

17. Kaur, S., Kumar, P., Kumaraguru, P.: DeepFakes: temporal sequential analysis to detect face-swapped video clips using convolutional long short-term memory. J. Electron. Imaging **29**, 33013 (2020)

Computer Vision Techniques for Hand Gesture Recognition: Survey

Noor Fadel[1]([⊠]) [iD] and Emad I. Abdul Kareem[2] [iD]

[1] Software Department, University of Babylon, Babylon, Iraq
noor.fadel@itnet.uobabylon.edu.iq
[2] Computer Science Department, Mustansiriyah University, Baghdad, Iraq
mmimad72@uomustansiriyah.edu.iq

Abstract. Hand gesture recognition has recently emerged as a critical component of the human-computer interaction (HCI) concept, allowing computers to capture and interpret hand gestures. In addition to their use in many medical applications, communication between the hearing impaired, device automation, and robot control, hand gestures are of particular importance as a form of nonverbal communication. So far, hand gesture recognition has taken two approaches and relied on a variety of technologies; the first on sensor technology and the second on computer vision. Given the importance of hand gesture recognition applications and technology development today, the importance of the research lies in shedding light on the latest techniques used in the recognition and interpretation of hand gestures. A survey on the techniques used from 2017–2022 has been presented in this research, with a focus on the computer vision approach. The survey was carried out as follows: the first part dealt with research based on artificial intelligence techniques for hand gesture recognition, and the second part focused on research that used artificial neural networks and deep learning for hand gesture recognition.

Keywords: AI Techniques · Deep learning · Human-computer interaction HCI · Sign language · Hand gesture recognition

1 Introduction

According to the notion of human-computer interaction (HCI) technology, humans and machines may interact naturally. Conventional human-machine contact is mostly done through devices like mice, keyboards, and displays. It goes without saying that these devices generally need to be connected to a computer. In some cases, such as virtual reality (VR), remote control (RC), and augmented reality (AR), the procedure of linking these devices is insufficient. As a result, it is critical to do research on how to create an HCI environment that is in tune with human communication behaviors [1, 2].

Gesture recognition is an important and major research topic in the field of assistive technology. The hand gesture is a convenient way to transfer the information as well as an alternative to devices such as the mouse and keyboard. Also, it helps older adults who cannot walk or talk communicate with their caregivers when they need help through hand gestures [2].

The use of hand gestures varies from one application to another, depending on the user's cultural background, application domain, and environment. Likewise, with expressive gestures [3]. One of the new paradigms today is the so-called natural user interface (NUI). The basic idea is that the user does not have to rely on additional hardware as a means of input or output and can operate the computer system in the same way that real objects would be input [3, 4].

Recognizing hand gestures has gained increasing importance in recent times for two main reasons: first, the growth of the deaf and hard of hearing population around the world, with a small percentage; and second, the development of applications based on vision and touchless control on devices such as video games, smart TV control, and virtual reality applications [4].

Hand gestures provide a non-physical link to the computer for user comfort and safety, as well as the ability to handle complicated and virtual settings in a much easier manner than the traditional ways in a significant variety of HCI applications [5]. Hand gesture applications, on the other hand, need the ability to correctly apply and comprehend various gestures [6].

1.1 Hand Gesture Methods

Gesture recognition aims to establish a system that can recognize human gestures for data transfer or command and control. It detects human hand motion and translates it into commands [6]. To collect data or information for the identification of hand gestures. This may be accomplished primarily using two techniques [7].

Sensor-Based Approaches. Collecting data consisting of finger and hand position, movement, and trajectory requires the use of sensors or devices physically attached to the user's arm or hand. The main sensor-based methods are:

1. The glove-based approach measures hand and finger position, acceleration, degrees of freedom, and flexion.
2. Electromyography (EMG) measures the electrical impulses of human muscles and decodes biological signals to detect the movement of fingers.
3. Other uses include mechanical, ultrasonic, electromagnetic, and other tactile techniques.

Vision-Based Approaches. With these approaches [8], human movements are captured by one or more cameras [9], and vision-based devices can handle many features to interpret gestures (i.e., color, texture, and shape of the hand). The sensor does not have this characteristic. Although these approaches are simple, they can pose many challenges.

Systems that require a variety of lighting, complex backgrounds, the presence of objects of hand-like skin color (clutter), and some criteria such as detection time, speed, durability, and computational efficiency [8, 9].

The term "vision-based" is most commonly used to capture images and recordings of bare hands without gloves or markers. The sensor-based approach reduces the need for preprocessing, which is the basis of traditional vision-based motion detection systems

[7, 10]. The vision-based approach also doesn't need any extra tools besides cameras, but it does need a lot of data to make a framework that can be used for scenarios that aren't visible (see Fig. 1).

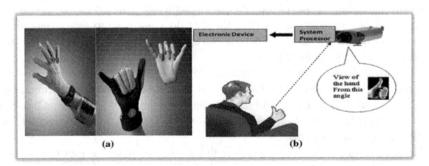

Fig. 1. Hand Gestures. (a) Glove-based attached sensor (b) computer vision–based camera [11].

There are many categories of hand gestures, conversational-gestures, manipulated (metaphoric)-gestures, fingerspelling-gestures, and communication/controlling-gestures [7].

It is very important to focus on the recent techniques that deal with the concept of recognizing gestures under the computer vision approach and to compare the recent work of researchers by highlighting the stages pursued by researchers and surveying their papers for the past five years. All phases of artificial intelligence research into hand gesture recognition were analyzed in this work, along with a summary of deep learning research into hand gesture recognition processes.

1.2 Applications of Gesture Recognition System

Gesture recognition as new interactive technology makes human-machine interactions more natural, convenient, and efficient. The gesture recognition applications are as follows:

1. Talking to the computer: instead of clicking the mouse can add citations or move images by simply flicking the hand [11].
2. Medical surgery: Gestures can be used to control the visual display and assist users with disabilities as part of rehabilitation therapy [2].
3. Gesture-based game control [13].
4. Hand gestures to control home appliances such as MP3 players and TVs, etc. [4].
5. Sign language: Sign language applications are very important in order to bridge the communication gap between deaf people and people who do not suffer from speech and hearing problems [3]. There are many sign languages, most notably American, British, Hindi, Arabic, etc.
6. The driver can be viewed from the eye to choose a radio station, and you can change the station without looking away from the road by simply flicking the hand [6].

7. When the term "immersion" is used, it is frequently associated with augmented reality [12]. Immersive media can create an environment that can be stopped and interacted with. "Immersion" is a term that has attracted much attention in technology (see Fig. 2).

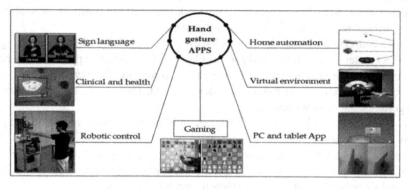

Fig. 2. Application of Hand Gesture [13].

2   Research Aims and Approach

The goal of this paper is to review current issues and advances in vision-based hand gesture recognition, as well as to identify potential future directions. The main research question is: "What are the most recent technological advances and advancements in vision-based hand gesture recognition systems?" To answer this question, all articles for hand gesture recognition systems from 2017 to 2022 have been gathered and identified the methods used. The research was a serious look at each stage of hand gesture recognition. It focused on hand gesture recognition systems based on segmentation, feature extraction, and classification.

The second section will have presented the previous research works that deal with survey research within a specific approach, as well as present a set of data sets and their specifications. The third section presents the methodology of the research sections, where a comprehensive survey will be addressed for each stage of hand gesture recognition based on artificial intelligence and deep learning (see Table 1). The last section is the conclusion view and the references used.

2.1   Related Works

Several reviews summarize a series of studies on gesture recognition. Mention a few pertinent research papers.

[14] research focuses on how to extract structural information and spatiotemporal features in a sequence of video frames by checking three groups based on the type of neural

network used in gesture recognition. Tow-dimensional convolutional networks, three-dimensional convolutional neural networks, and long-term memory (LSTM) networks. Researchers discussed the advantages and limitations of current technology.

[15] focuses on the sub-steps present in each major step associated with system design, namely: data acquisition, segmentation, tracking, feature extraction, and gesture recognition. Therefore, segmentation, tracking, feature extraction, and identification techniques were studied and analyzed. This work reviewed the comparative studies of various technologies for recognizing hand gestures.

[16] is concerned with the provision of sensory glove-based sign language recognition (SLR) systems. The trends and gaps available in this research approach have been explored to provide insights into technological environments. The review looked at the most recent research in four main areas: development, framework, recognizing other hand gestures, and reviews and surveys.

[17] focused on the latest developments in multimedia gesture recognition and presented a JMLR special topic on gesture recognition between 2011-and 2015. It also looks at the latest work on gesture recognition based on a proposed taxonomy for gesture recognition and talks about the problems researchers have had, how they solved them, and where they want to go with their research in the future.

[18] outlines the vision-based hand gesture recognition algorithms reported over the last 16 years. Methods using RGB and RGBD cameras have been validated by quantitative and qualitative comparisons of the algorithms. The algorithm uses a set of 13 metrics selected from the various attributes of the algorithm, an empirical methodology used to evaluate the algorithm, and algorithm detection accuracy to predict success in real-world applications. It will be compared quantitatively. The paper also reviewed the 26 publicly available hand gesture databases and provided web links for download.

[19] Studies centered on the applications of profound learning to RGB-D-based motion acknowledgment highlighted the strategies of encoding spatial-temporal-structural data characteristics in the video. Unlike the above literature, which provides a broad and general report on gesture recognition, this survey covers most of the new hand gesture recognition technologies based on AI and deep learning from 2017 to 2022.

2.2 A Review of Gesture Recognition Dataset

Gesture recognition is a significant focus of HCI research. The gesture can be defined as dynamic or static depending on whether it occurs during a specific time or at a specific instant. In general, dynamic gestures are more diverse and more expressive. Five datasets for gestures that have been largely adopted from publicly available datasets will be mentioned.

20 BN Jester Dataset. Dataset 20 BN-JESTER 1 is a big set of videos labeled using a laptop camera or webcam, and these videos show people making preset hand gestures (see Fig. 3). This dataset can be obtained by visiting this link: https://www.kaggle.com/datasets/toxicmender/20bn-jester/version/1.

Dvs-Gesture Dataset. This dataset was used to create the real-time gesture recognition system described in the paper [A Low-Power, Fully Event-Based Gesture Recognition System]. A DVS128 was used to record the data. The dataset contains 29 people and

Fig. 3. Examples of videos from the 20BN-jester, a randomly sampled video dataset.

11 hand gestures under 3 different lighting conditions and is released under a Creative Commons Attribution 4.0 license (see Fig. 4). This dataset can be obtained by visiting this link: https://research.ibm.com/interactive/dvsgesture/.

Fig. 4. Dvs -Gesture Dataset video frames of the gestures.

Ego-Gesture Dataset. The Ego-Gesture dataset is a large dataset for recognizing centered hand gestures. The dataset contains 2081 RGB-D videos, 24161 gesture samples, and 2953224 frames from 50 distinct clips. This dataset can be obtained by visiting this link: http://www.nlpr.ia.ac.cn/iva/yfzhang/datasets/egogesture.html. The dataset contains 83 categories of static or dynamic gestures that focus on interacting with devices (see Fig. 5).

ASL Alphabet. The dataset of images of alphabets from American Sign Language is separated into 29 volumes, representing the different categories. 87,000 images with a size of 200x200 pixels. Training data set. 26 volumes are for letters A-Z, and 3 chapters are for SPACE, DELETE, and NOTHING. These last three categories are very useful in applications and real-time classification. Only 29 images are available. The test data is on 29 images only (see Fig. 6A). This dataset can be obtained by visiting this link: https://www.kaggle.com/datasets/grassknoted/asl-alphabet.

Arabic Alphabets Sign Language Dataset (ARASL). A data set that collects Arabic language signals, and the number of images for each category varies from one category

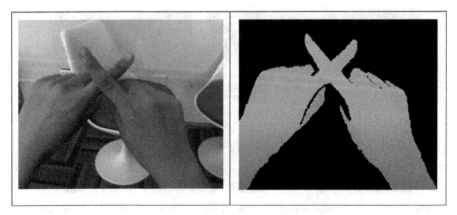

Fig. 5. Sample of Ego-Gesture.

to another. It consists of 54,049 Arabic alphabet images for more than 40 people, in addition to 32 standard Arabic signs and alphabets (see Fig. 6B). This dataset can be obtained by visiting this link: https://data.mendeley.com/datasets/y7pckrw6z2/1 .

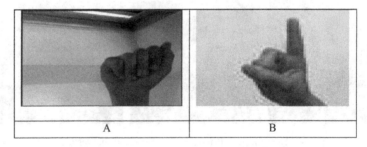

Fig. 6. A- Letter "A" from American Sign Language B- Letter "Baa" from ArASL.

3 Methodology of Research

The topic of hand gesture recognition is vast, and much research has been done in recent years. This study surveys the most recent studies on hand gesture recognition. We will also contrast the various methodologies and applications described in the examined papers. The review indicated that most articles use a single camera webcam or laptop for the data acquisition process.

In recent years, vision-based hand gesture recognition research has shifted to integrating more in-depth information sources like Microsoft Kinect and Leap Motion Controller.

The survey methodology is divided into two parts: the techniques that rely on the principle of artificial intelligence for hand gesture recognition, and the other section is based on the techniques used in artificial neural networks and deep learning for hand gesture recognition, as illustrated (see Fig. 7).

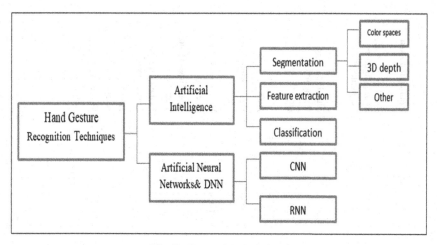

Fig. 7. Survey Methodology

3.1 Hand Gesture Recognition Based on AI Techniques

This section reviews hand gesture segmentation methods and features extracted for diverse applications as well as hand gesture classification algorithms based on AI techniques. The research deals with a serious survey of each stage of hand gesture recognition and focuses on hand gesture recognition systems based on segmentation, extraction of features, and classification, each stage separately (see Table 1).

Segmentation. Image segmentation is one of the most frequently used techniques in image processing. The appropriate method for segmenting images, in fact, depends largely on the quality of the images and the dataset, if it is static or dynamic hand motion. Many methods of segmentation have been dealt with in recognizing hand gestures, starting from discovering edges, clustering, and using threshold or contour methods [20].

Using traditional image processing approaches to recognize the person's hands, such as background reduction based on running average, skin color thresholding, upper body and face cascade classifiers, and finger recognition based on contour detection, the video frames yielded unsatisfactory results.

The research [21] examined three methods for segmenting dynamic hand gestures based on the gesture recognition system. The research suggested both segmentation methods related to skin and movement in addition to contour features. The color space has been changed to Y–Cb–Cr. Morphology operations were also applied after the contour process to obtain the hand area only and to increase the accuracy of segmentation (see Fig. 8).

To encode the color information in an image, a mathematical model can be derived from the color space, which, axiomatically, can be used. There are many different color spaces that can be used for many kinds of applications [22], including computer vision applications, image processing applications, and digital graphics applications.

Table 1. Summary of Review of Techniques for Hand Gesture Recognition.

Ref.	AI techniques			Data set	No. of Gesture	Accuracy	Application Area
	Segmentation	Feature extraction	Classification				
Hernández, I (2018)	Color space Contour& motion	Morphology operator	-	Dynamic Hand Gestures	Unlimited	98%	Sign Language Recognition
Shaik, K (2017)	YUV color	-	-	Hand Gestures	Unlimited	-	HCI
Biswas, A (2018)	fingertips	Hough transform	-	Finger Count	unlimited	-	Sign Language Recognition
Perimal M. et al. (2018)	Y–Cb–Cr	-	-	Finger Count	14	50 to 70	HCI
Huang, H (2019)	Color space	.	SVM	Hand Gestures	9		HCI
Ijawaryy, A.et al. (2017)	Y–Cb–Cr	-	-	Count Of Finger	6 Gestures	98%	Deaf. -Mute People
Prakash, J. et al. (2019)	YUV & CAMShift	-	navie Bayes	Hand Gesture	Unlimited	High	Human - Machine Interaction
Zhang, F. et al. (2020)	Landmark point	skeleton pixels	-	Finger Paint	Unlimited	-	Real Time- Hand Tracking
Karbasi, M. et al. (2017)	depth and color space	skeleton pixels	-	Hand Gesture	Unlimited	-	Malaysian Sign Language
Ma, X. et al. (2018)	local neighbor method	convex hull detection	-	Hand	6	96%	Human–Robot Interaction
Kim, M et al. (2016)	Threshold segmentation	-	-	Finger Counting & Hand Gesture	Unlimited	-	Mouse-Movement Controlling

(continued)

Table 1. (*continued*)

Ref.	AI techniques			Data set	No. of Gesture	Accuracy	Application Area
	Segmentation	Feature extraction	Classification				
Tekin, B. et al. (2019)	YCbCr, SkinMask, and HSV	-	convolutional neural network	Hand Gesture	Unlimited	95.27%96.33%, and 97.43%,	Sign Language Recognition
Wan, C. et al. (2019)	depth maps	3D hand pose	neural network	Hand Gesture	Unlimited	-	HCI
Ge, L. et al. (2019)	Single RGB image	3D hand shape & pose	-	Finger Paint Dataset	Unlimited	High	HCI
Taylor, J et al. (2017)	mask Kinect body tracker	3D hands shape	-	Hand Gesture	Unlimited	-	Interactions With Virtual And Augmented
Tsoli, A. et al. (2018)	bounding box & hand mask	-	-	Hand Gesture	Unlimited	High	Interaction With Deformable Object & Tracking
Chen, Y. et al. (2019)	feature extraction hierarchical	estimation 3D hand pose	-	Hand Gesture	-	Good	Human–Computer Interaction
Ge, L. et al. (2018)	Depth image	3D hand pose	-	Hand Gesture	-	-	Virtual/Augmented Reality
Wu, X. et al. (2018)	hand joints detection	hand pose	-	Hand Gesture	-	-	(HCI), Virtual And Mixed Reality
Cai, Y. et al. (2018)	-	hand pose	-	Hand Gesture	-	Effectiveness	(HCI), Virtual And Mixed Reality

(*continued*)

Table 1. (*continued*)

Ref.	AI techniques			Data set	No. of Gesture	Accuracy	Application Area
	Segmentation	Feature extraction	Classification				
Ahmed, K. et al (2019)	Machine learning	-	-	Hand Gesture	-	effective method	HCI
Abdul, R. et al. (2017)	Machine learning	-	-	Gesture Controlled	-	Simple and effectiveness	Control MS Windows Via Hand Gesture
Zhou, W (2017)	-	DFT	NN	Static Hand Gesture	-	-	Real-Time Implementation
Liu, Xi. et al. (2017)	Wavelet	wavelet invariant moments	SVM	Hand Gesture	-	Good	HCI
Salunke, T. et al. (2019)	-	HOG	K-NN	Hand Gesture	-	Effectiveness	HCI, Power Point Control
Saha, H. et al. (2018)	-	convex decomposition	-	Sign Finger	-	Good	American Sign Language
Molina, J. et al. (2017)	depth information	motion gesture	Motion patterns	-	26 Gesture	95%	HCI- Virtual Environments
Xi, C. et al. (2018)	YUV	skeleton points	naïve Bayes	Hand Gesture	Unlimited	High	Human And Machine System
Devin, G. et al. (2018)	hand-skeletal joints	-	CNN	-	14 28 Gesture	91.28% 84.35%	HCI

(*continued*)

Table 1. (*continued*)

Ref.	AI techniques			Data set	No. of Gesture	Accuracy	Application Area
	Segmentation	Feature extraction	Classification				
Mujahid, A. et al. (2021)	-	YOLOv3		-	gestures	97.68	HCI
Alnaim, N. et al. (2019)	-	features extraction by CNN	ADCNN	Hand Gestures	7 Hand gestures	training 100% test set 99%"	HCI People-Communicate
Chung, H. et al. (2019)	skin color detection &morphology	deep CNN	-	Hand Gestures	6 Hand gestures	training 99.9% test 95.61%	Home-Control
Bao, P. et al. (2017)	-	deep CNN	-	Hand Gestures	7 Hand gestures	simple backgrounds 97.1% complex background 85.3%	Control A Piece Of Consumer Devices
Li, G. et al. (2019)	skin color	CNN	SVM	Hand Gestures	8 hand Gesture	98.52%	HCI
Wu X,Y (2019)	Gaussian Mixture model	CNN	-	Hand Gestures	7 hand Gesture	95.96%	Hand Gesture Recognition For Human

Fig. 8. Segmentation result in [21].

Fig. 9. Skin Color Detection. (A) Use The Color Space YUV Threshold. (B) Detect and Track the Hand Using the Resulting Binary Image [22].

(See Fig. 9) is a demonstration of the YUV color space being used to identify different skin tones. [23] They used the Hough transform to extract features for the fingertips.

A new technique that describes the number of hand gestures ranging from 0 to 5 that people indicate that a computer understands has been proposed by [24]. This technique is implemented by reading a frame as an image and then extracting it only manually using the YCbCr color space filter. Then it is converted to a black and white image. The experiment was conducted using 180 random hand gesture frames taken from random people (see Fig. 10).

It was found that under-regulated lighting circumstances, high-resolution cameras, and a short distance away, gestures were examined with three criteria that directly affect the identification rate, namely noise, light levels, and hand size. The method conducts finger counting and gesture recognition based on the maximum distance between the observed fingers, with an average performance of 50 to 70% of successful detection for 14 movements based on color space-based Y–Cb–Cr segmentation. The Y–Cb–Cr color space was shown to be helpful. Lighting effects that impede detection are particularly difficult to remove.

Skin color detection using RGB channels in [25]. Because the blend of an image's color channel and intensity information has uneven features, it is not recommended for skin segmentation. Because the threshold value is an average of three-channel values, adjusted RGB color information is isolated from the brightness in a straightforward manner (r, g, and b). However, it cannot be depended on for segmentation or detection under changing illumination conditions. Converting the RGB color space to another color space in order to identify the region of interest in the hand through other hues such as red, pink, orange, and brown is an important procedure. The color may be determined. The hue of the sample may be predicted ahead of time. If it is comparable, we might

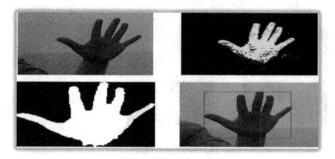

Fig. 10. Hand Gesture Detection and Foreground Segmentation Stages [24].

refer to it as the skin or the region of interest. The skin color approach has a number of obstacles, including lighting fluctuation, backdrop concerns, and other sorts of noise.

[26] found that applying the Y–Cb–Cr color scheme helps to eliminate lighting effects, but that intense light during capture affects accuracy. With the help of the CAM Shift algorithm, YUV color space was used in [27]. The background color was distinguished from skin color, and then a naive Bayes classifier was used to aid in gesture recognition.

The hand segmentation algorithm used in the research [28] was performed using a Kinect camera depth sensor, followed by a calculation of fingertip locations using 3D communication, Euclidean distance, and geodetic distance on manual skeletal pixels to provide higher accuracy.

In studies [29], a hybrid technique of hand segmentation utilizing depth and color data from the Kinect sensor has been suggested. In addition to relying on skeletal data, in the suggested technique, the image threshold was applied to the depth frame as a pixel segmentation technique to extract the hand from the color frame.

Several academics have proposed the use of a depth camera that offers three-dimensional geometric data about the item [30, 31]. This is due to the fact that the three-dimensional data from the depth camera directly reflects the depth field and is unaffected by lighting, shadows, and color, unlike a color image, which only comprises projection. However, the cost and accessibility of depth cameras will limit their application. In [32], they utilized Y-Cb-Cr, SkinMask, and HSV segmentation techniques (hue, saturation, and value). The SkinMask procedure is then subjected to binarization and color segmentation in order to identify pixels that match the color of the hand. Threshold masking determines the dominating characteristics in the HSV process (see Fig. 11).

Studies by [33–35] proposed a model that used 3D hands and objects using a single RGB image to understand interactions between them. [36–40] presented a method for tracing a complex deformable object by interacting with the hand based on the 3D position of the hand in single-depth images. Artificial Neural Networks (ANN), Fuzzy Clustering Algorithm, Graph-based Feature, Hidden Markov Model (HMM), Condensation Algorithm, and Finite State Machine (FSM) are all mentioned methods. In [41] as an effective method to recognize hand gestures.

Feature Extraction. The accuracy of the quality of any algorithm depends on the quality of extracted features, because these features, or rather important information, give a

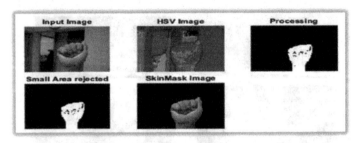

Fig. 11. Segmentation in [32]

complete impression of the classification or recognition process. Therefore, accurate information extraction from images must aid in the process of gesture recognition.

The Fourier descriptor, and fingertips, contour hand, motion gesture, or centroid, capture the basic structure. It can be considered a common method of feature extraction. Both contour hand and complex Alhzat are feature extractions used in [42]. In [43], employing Discrete Fourier-Transform (DFT) techniques on histograms, a method for extracting features was implemented (vertical and horizontal).

In [44], the wavelet feature is determined by enforcing the wavelet invariant moments of the hand region, and the distance feature is extracted by calculating the distance from the fingers to the hand centroid. Both of these features are determined by calculating the wavelet invariant moments of the hand region. After that, a feature vector is created, and it is made up of wavelet invariant moments and a distance feature. Last but not least, a support vector machine classifier that is based on the feature vectors.

The method that was proposed in [45] first processed the images after extracting a histogram of gradient features from the input data that was provided by a portable webcam. The portable webcam provides the proposed system with the input data, which comprises four different hand motions to be interpreted. After the image that was acquired has been processed using the data that was entered, the graph of the vector gradient features will be retrieved from the obtained image. Following this, the processed image is looked up in a database that contains images of gestures. The K-Nearest Neighbor method is used to perform the comparison and recognition of the image. The slide show is then controlled by the image that was initially detected.

American Sign Language was used in the study. [46] Images are collected from the webcam and preprocessed. The figure is divided into two parts by means of polygon approximation and convex decomposition approximation. Features are extracted by recording the unique features between the different convex parts of the hand. The resulting singularity was used as the extracted feature vector. This training includes features that are almost unique to various hand gestures.

This article [47] describes current machine learning approaches for recognizing hand gestures using detailed data from time-off light sensors. Experiments have shown that convolutional neural networks and long-term memory provide the most reliable results for implicitly extracted features. It is a method that uses image color statistics and also uses a "regional contrast" (RC)-based extraction algorithm for prominent objects.

[48] used a different technique to extract hand features, namely a histogram of oriented gradients (HOG) of oriented gradients (HOG) was used for image processing to extract characteristics of the hand. The Accurate End Point Identification method was implemented and applied to gesture images which were captured in varying backgrounds to detect edge points and branch points, and it was also applied to blurred images containing multiple objects.

[49] A three-dimensional convolutional neural network model for learning region-based spatiotemporal aspects of hand movements has been proposed. This model takes as its input a sequence of RGB frames that were taken by a straightforward camera. In order to extract the features from the full video sample, a 3DCNN was used, and a SoftMax layer was utilized in order to perform the classification. It acquired recognition rates of 84.38%, 34.9%, and 70% on the three datasets, respectively, by using three gesture datasets derived from color videos: KSU-SSL, ARSL, and ASL classes.

Higher-order local autocorrelation (HLAC) features are used to extract features in the novel method of feature extraction that is described in [50]. This method is a recent development in the field of feature extraction. Identifying the texture of the image of hands in relation to prospective location and the pixel product picked in white requires the extraction of features from grayscale images using a variety of masks. Then, based on the Mutual Information Quotient, the characteristics that hold the most valuable information are chosen for selection (MIQ). In order to categorize the various ways in which people use their hands, a multiple linear differentiation analysis (LDA) classifier was utilized. Experiments conducted on the dataset provided by NUS reveal that HLAC is superior to other feature extraction approaches in terms of its ability to recognize hand motions.

In each of the following works [51] and [52], several methods were used to extract specific features and apply them to gesture images. The first research focuses on the identification of accurate endpoints, which are applied to gesture images to detect edge points and branch points, as well as in blurry images that contain multiple objects. The second study presents a double-channel convolutional neural network (DC-CNN) in which the original image is preprocessed using canny detection to detect the edge of the hand before being given to the network. To categorize output results, each two-channel CNN has its own weight and SoftMax classifier.

In order to obtain the hand edge images, first the original gesture images must be preprocessed, and then edge detection must be done on those images. Second, the hand gesture images and the hand edge images are each chosen to serve as one of CNN's input channels in their respective orders. The number of convolutional layers and the other parameters are identical across all channels. However, each channel has its own unique weight. The final step is to execute feature fusion at the complete connection layer, and the output result is then classed using the SoftMax classifier. There are ten different gestures stored in the database.

In [53], depending on depth information, feature extraction was motion gesture and compared the motion patterns for 26 gestures. In [54], a Kinect camera depth sensor was used to capture the image. Euclidean distance and geodesic distance fingertip skeleton pixels were extracted. By using a depth camera, the feature extraction based on hand-skeletal joints' positions data set is dynamic hand gesture [55]. In [56], based on Kinect camera features, gestures were extracted by computing skeleton point clouds with a YOLOv3 algorithm, while [33, 34, 37, 38, 40] feature extraction depended on using 3D hand pose estimation.

Classification. There are many classification algorithms that can be used to identify different gestures, whether the gesture is dynamic, sign language, etc. The extracted features are sent to one of the classification methods, and the data is divided for testing and training the classification algorithm, through our survey of a number of researchers. The result was that the most used methods for classification are both Artificial Neural Networks (ANN), K-Nearest Neighbor (KNN), Naive Bayes (NB), Support Vector Machine (SVM), etc.

The study [57] provided an effective, fast, and easy method for dynamic hand gesture recognition based on two-line features extracted from two-line real-time video. The feature selection was used to represent the hand shape of the Kurdish Sign Language's dynamic word recognition. Features extracted in real-time from preprocessed manual objects were represented by optimized values for the captured binary frames. Finally, we used an artificial neural network classifier to recognize hand gestures.

[58] Hand gesture recognition algorithms for the elderly are offered. Using contour and rule-based algorithms, respectively, detection, feature extraction, and classification are the three main components of the procedure. The method relies on the vision-based recognition of six fixed hand gestures.

In [32], they used the segmentation methods of YCbCr, SkinMask, and HSV, then binarization. SoftMax classification is used to classify hand gestures where features are extracted through convolutional neural networks (CNN). While in [49], a SoftMax layer was used for classification. Using three gesture datasets from color videos: KSU-SSL, ARSL, and ASL classes, it obtained recognition rates of 84.38%, 34.9%, and 70% on the three datasets, respectively. Also, [52] used SoftMax for classification.

They were able to identify hand gestures in their research [59–62] by utilizing the Nearest Neighbor (KNN) classifier. The work that was presented in reference number [63] identified detections by employing a hybrid of the k-nearest neighbor (KNN) and decision tree classification methods. The classification of [64–68] gestures was also accomplished with the assistance of a Support Vector Machine (SVM). The gestures of [69] were organized into categories using a decision tree.

They employed a tweaked version of the deep forest algorithm in order to identify the pattern in [70]. The classification process in [71] was carried out using a random regression forest technique. The hand gesture is modeled and decomposed using the Gaussian mixture model and Hidden Markov Model, and the GMM is employed as a substrate of the HMM to decode the sEMG function of the gesture. This can be found in [72]. In addition, a hand gesture detection system was developed and implemented by introducing Bhattacharyya divergence into the Bayesian Sensing Hidden Markov Model (BSHMM). This research was published in [73].

Other. Far from using the segmentation algorithm, [74] proposed a real-time dynamic hand gesture detection system based on TOF. This system was designed to work in real-time. The act of identifying movement patterns based on hand motions captured as input depth images is referred to as "pattern recognition. The system works well overall, except that the depth of field of the TOF camera isn't good enough.

A new method is presented in [75] for RGB video recording of sign language based on extracted structural features, in addition to taking into account the difficulties in extracting accurate structural data due to obstruction. Using skeletal and depth data for a skeleton-based approach [76], a dynamic and recognizable hand gesture was introduced (see Fig. 12).

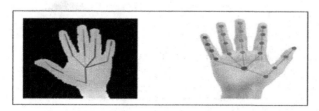

Fig. 12. Skeleton Dataset to Representation Hand Skeleton Model [76].

Using Kinect sensor depth metadata, a new dynamic hand gesture recognition technique was described in [77]. For classification and recognition, an orientation feature retrieved for segmentation (SVM) algorithm and HMM were used.

A three-part gesture recognition robot system was introduced [78]: an intelligent robot system, gesture recognition, and an Android app. Three independent discriminators contained in the gesture recognition system were verified to control gesture recognition based on the use of an algorithm based on feature extraction and template matching. The average rate of gesture recognition was 94.6%.

Principal Component Analysis (PCA) and classifiers such as the Support Vector Machine (SVM) and k-near-neighbor (k-NN) were used in addition to the recognition experiments. Reducing this similarity between frames is an important step in pattern recognition. The method was applied to the Irish Sign Language data set [79].

This article [80] focuses on a dynamic 3D gesture recognition system that uses hand location information. It uses the natural structure of the hand topology (later called hand skeletal data) to extract effective manual kinematic descriptors from a set of gestures. The descriptors are then encoded into statistical and temporal representations using the Fisher kernel and a multi-level time hierarchy, respectively. The proposed approach was applied to a three-handed gesture dataset, each containing 10, 14, and 25 gestures. Also, the proposed evaluation is from the perspective of hand gesture recognition and low-latency gesture recognition (see Fig. 13).

This work summarizes the technologies of the above works by surveying a number of artificial intelligence techniques for recognizing hand gestures (see Fig. 14).

3.2 ANN and DNN Techniques for Hand Gesture Recognition

Even if a related dataset is used to pre-train the network and take advantage of transfer learning, one of the primary challenges associated with deep learning-based image

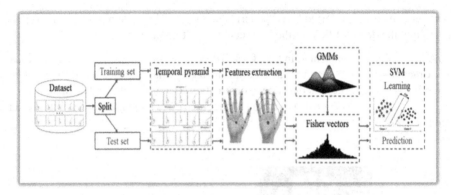

Fig. 13. Overview of The Approach in [80].

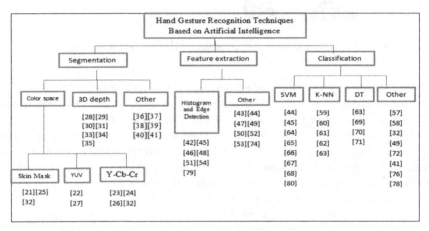

Fig. 14. Taxonomy of Artificial Intelligence Techniques based on Hand Gesture Recognition

recognition is the requirement for a vast amount of labeled data. In addition, there are other issues, such as design optimization, which can be difficult and time-consuming [81]. These challenges are one of the main problems with deep learning-based image recognition. (See Fig. 15) for the research and techniques that have been used recently to recognize hand gestures.

Method Based on CNN. In this paper [82], a standard dataset called IPN Hand is provided. This dataset contains more than 4,000 gesture samples and 800,000 RGB frames from 50 distinct targets for 13 different static and dynamic gestures focusing on interaction with non-touch screens based on 3D-CNN technologies.

Graph CNNs are employed in the study of [83] to create a 3D network of the hand surface. Hand segmentation and 3D hand position estimation, including skeletal constraints, can be learned using a CNN-based approach developed by [84]. Deep learning models using parallel convolutional neural networks (CNNs) to process the positions of hand skeleton joints have been introduced in [85] for the purpose of 3D hand gesture detection.

For classification, a network containing an RNN and additional accelerometer data was employed (CNN), and an RNN was used for the classification. [88] Hand motions were classified using the Deep Convolutional Neural Network. The Deep Convolutional Neural Network (ADCNN) feature from this paper was taken and used for hand categorization in this article. The experiment uses 100% training data, 99% test data, and a total run time of 15,598 s [90].

Another suggested method is to track hands using webcams. The background is then removed using the skin color (Y-Cb-Cr color space) and morphology approach. A kernel correlation filter (KCF) is also employed to monitor the ROI. The final images are sent to the Deep Convolutional Neural Network (CNN). It compared the performances of two modified models, AlexNet and VGGNet, using the CNN model. In [91], the recognition rates for training and test data are 99.90% and 95.61%, respectively.

A new method based on the Deep CNN feeds resized images directly to the network, ignoring segmentation and recognition levels and directly classifying hand gestures. The system operates in real-time, with a result of 97.1% for simple backgrounds and 85.3% for complex backgrounds [92].

The depth image generated by the Kinect sensor was used to segment the color image and then combined with a convolutional neural network that applied an error backpropagation algorithm to change the thresholds and weights of the neural network. Use skin-color modeling. An SVM classification algorithm has been added to the network to improve the results [93].

[94] Developed A 2-Channel Convolutional Neural Network (DCCNN) in another research paper, where the original images are preprocessed to detect the edges of the hand before being transmitted to the network. Each of the two-channel CNNs has its own weight, and the output is classified using the SoftMax classifier. The detection rate of the suggested system is 98.02.

RNN-Based Method. The author of [86] has developed two channels for dynamic hand gestures. The detection method uses a low-complexity recurrent neural network (RNN) algorithm for portable devices. It is initially based on video signals and uses convolutional neural networks. In contrast, [87] uses a bidirectional recurrent neural network (RNN) with skeletal sequence to enhance motion, and an RNN function was used.

In this paper [89], an improved recurrent neural network is proposed for skeletal-based dynamic hand gesture recognition. After finger movement and general movement features are extracted, they are fed into a bidirectional recurrent neural network (RNN) along with the extracted finger movement features to describe finger movements. This method is effective and superior to other art initiation methods.

The hand gesture recognition system successfully identifies 10 gestures in [96]. The entire system includes a signal processing part that produces a Range-Doppler Map

(RDM) sequence without clutter, and a machine learning part that is an LSTM (long-term memory) encoder for learning the temporal characteristics of the RDM sequence.

Hybrid Method. This study [95] proposes combining the capabilities of two deep learning technologies, a convolutional neural network (CNN) and a recurrent neural network (RNN), to automatically recognize hand gestures using depth and structure data. The purpose of this study is to use depth data and apply CNNs to extract important spatial information from images. Tandem CNN + RNN can recognize different gestures. It combines both skeletal and depth information to extract temporal and spatial information.

A proposed deep learning-based method for temporary 3D shape recognition issues [97] is primarily based on a combination of a convolutional neural network (CNN) and a long-term memory (LSTM) recurrent network. Introducing a two-level education method that focuses on CNN education at first and then changes the whole method (CNN + LSTM) at the second level.

This paper [98] affords a powerful deep structure for non-stop gesture recognition. First, continuous gesture sequences are broken up into remoted gesture times using the proposed temporally dilated Res3D community, which is mostly based on the 3-D convolutional neural community (3DCNN), the convolutional long-short-term-memory network community (ConvLSTM), and the 2-D convolutional neural community (2DCNN) for remoted gesture recognition.

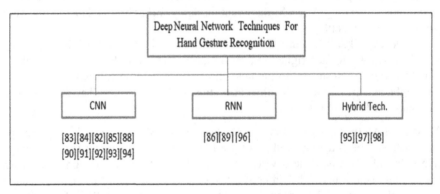

Fig. 15. Taxonomy of Deep Neural Network Techniques for Hand Gesture Recognition

4 Conclusion

There is no doubt that understanding various hand gestures, whether they are sign language or other expressions, is critical. Researchers have made great strides in hand gesture recognition because of its widespread practical applicability. In light of this, it is crucial to highlight the most cutting-edge technologies in use by conducting a comprehensive literature review on the subject of vision-based hand gesture recognition, with a particular focus on those based on the principles of artificial intelligence and deep learning techniques. The ability to use these technologies in a wide range of critical applications makes computer communication more natural. There are several factors that affect the interpretation of gestures, including the background, the source of light, and the skeletal structure of hand movement. The majority of studies have found that edge detection, depending on geometric features for fingers, is particularly useful for recognizing gestures when the fingers of the hand are extended but that recognition is more challenging when the hand is closed. Recently, deep learning has seen widespread application in a lot of research for hand gesture recognition with high accuracy. Through the comprehensive research survey, the associative memory network has not been used in any of the surveyed research. It is necessary to work on techniques based on neural networks or deep learning, which give better accuracy of results than other traditional methods.

References

1. Pisharady, K., Saerbeck, M.: Recent methods and databases in vision-based hand gesture recognition: a review. Comput. Vis. Image Underst. **141**, 152–165 (2015)
2. Yasen, M., Jusoh, S.: A systematic review on hand gesture recognition techniques challenges and applications. Peerj Comput. Sci. **5**, e218 (2019)
3. Camgoz, N.C.: Sign language transformers: joint end-to-end sign language recognition and translation. In: Proceedings of the IEEE/CVF Conference on Computer Vision And Pattern Recognition, pp. 10023–10033 (2020).
4. Tian, L.: Video big data in smart city: background construction and optimization for surveillance video processing. Future Gener. Comput. Syst. **86**, pp. 1371–1382 (2018).
5. Mei, T., Zhang, C.: Deep learning for intelligent video analysis. In: Proceedings of the 25th ACM International Conference on Multimedia, pp. 1955–1956 (2017).
6. Sarma, D., Bhuyan, M.K.: Methods, databases and recent advancement of vision-based hand gesture recognition for HCI systems: a review. SN Comput. Sci. **2**(6), 1–40 (2021)
7. Alsaffar, M., et al.: Human-computer interaction using manual hand gestures in real time. Comput. Intell. Neurosci. (2021)
8. Aumgartl, H., Sauter, D., Schenk, C., Atik, C., Buettner, R.: Vision-based hand gesture recognition for human-computer interaction using MobileNetV2. In: IEEE 45th Annual Computers. Software, and Applications Conference (COMPSAC), pp. 3–15. IEEE, Spain (2018)
9. Noroozi, F.: Survey on emotional body gesture recognition. IEEE Trans. Affect. Comput. **12**(2), 505–523 (2018)
10. Hisham, B., Hamouda, A.: Supervised learning classifiers for arabic gestures recognition using kinect V2. Appl. Sci. **1**(7), 1–21 (2019)
11. Premaratne, P., Nguyen, Q., Premaratne, M.: Human computer interaction using hand gestures. In: Huang, D.-S., McGinnity, M., Heutte, L., Zhang, X.-P. (eds.) ICIC 2010. CCIS, vol. 93, pp. 381–386. Springer, Heidelberg (2010). https://doi.org/10.1007/978-3-642-14831-6_51
12. Thórisson, K.R.: Simulated perceptual grouping: an application to human-computer interaction. In: Proceedings of the Sixteenth Annual Conference of the Cognitive Science Society, pp. 876–881. Routledge (2019)
13. Yun, Y., Ma, D., Yang, M.: Human–computer interaction-based decision support system with applications in data mining. Futur. Gener. Comput. Syst. **114**, 285–289 (2021)
14. Yuanyuan, S.H.I., Yunan, L.I., Xiaolong, F.U., Kaibin, M.I.A.O., Qiguang, M.I.A.O.: Review of dynamic gesture recognition. Virtual Reality Intell. Hardware **3**(3), 183–206 (2021)
15. Oudah, M., Al-Naji, A., Chahl, J.: Hand Gesture recognition based on computer vision: a review of techniques. J. Imaging **6**(8), 73 (2020)

16. Ahmed, M.A.: A review on systems-based sensory gloves for sign language recognition state of the art between 2007 and 2017. Sensors **18**(7), 2208 (2018)

17. Escalera, S., Athitsos, V., Guyon, I.: Challenges in multi-modal gesture recognition. Gesture Recogn., 1–60 (2017)

18. Pisharady, P.K., Saerbeck, M.: Recent methods and databases in vision-based hand gesture recognition: a review. Comput. Vis. Image Underst. **141**(152), 165 (2015)

19. Wang, P.: RGB-D-based human motion recognition with deep learning: a survey. Comput. Vis. Image Underst. **171**(118), 139 (2018)

20. Chalasani, T., Smolic, A.: Simultaneous segmentation and recognition: towards more accurate ego gesture recognition. In: Proceedings of the IEEE/CVF International Conference on Computer Vision Workshops, p. 0. IEEE (2019)

21. Hernández, I.: Automatic Irish Sign Language Recognition. University of Dublin, Trinity College (2018)

22. Shaik, K.B.: Comparative study of skin color detection and segmentation in HSV and YCbCr color space. Procedia Comput. Sci. **57**(41), 48 (2017)

23. Biswas, A.: Finger detection for hand gesture recognition using circular hough transform. In: Advances in Communication. Devices and Networking, pp. 651–660. Springer, Singapore (2018)

24. Perimal, M., Basah, S.N., Safar, M.J.A., Yazid, H.: Hand-gesture recognition-algorithm based on finger counting. J. Telecommun. Electron Comput. **10**(19), 24 (2018)

25. Huang, H.: Hand gesture recognition with skin detection and deep learning method. J. Phys. Conf. Ser. **1213**(2), 022001 (2019)

26. Ijawaryy, A., Malallah, L.: Real-time numerical 0–5 counting based on hand-finger gestures recognition. J. Theor. Appl. Inf. Technol. **95**(13), 34–41 (2017)

27. Prakash, J., Gautam, U.K.: Hand gesture recognition. Int. J. Recent Technol. Eng. (7), 54–59 (2019)

28. Zhang, F., et al.: Mediapipe hands: on-device real-time hand tracking. arXiv preprint arXiv (2006). 10214 (2020)

29. Karbasi, M., et al.: A hybrid method using Kinect depth and color data stream for hand blobs segmentation. Sci. Int. **71**, 515–519 (2017)

30. Ma, X., Peng, J.: Kinect sensor-based long-distance hand gesture recognition and fingertip detection with depth information. J. Sens. (2018)

31. Kim, M.S., Lee, C.H.: Hand gesture recognition for Kinect V2 sensor in the near distance where depth data are not provided. Int. J. Softw. Eng. Appl. (10), 407–418 (2016)

32. Tekin, B., Bogo, F., Pollefeys, M.: Unified Egocentric recognition of 3d hand-object poses and interactions. In: Proceedings of the IEEE Conference on Computer Vision And Pattern Recognition, pp. 4511–4520. IEEE, USA (2019)

33. Wan, C., Probst, T., Van Gool, L., Yao, A.: Self-supervised 3D hand pose estimation through training by fitting. In: Proceedings of the IEEE Conference on Computer Vision and Pattern Recognition, pp. 10853–10862. IEEE, USA (2019)

34. Ge, L., et al.: 3D hand shape and pose estimation from a single RGB image. In: Proceedings of the IEEE Conference on Computer Vision and Pattern Recognition, pp. 10833–10842. IEEE, USA (2019)

35. Taylor, J., et al.: Efficient and precise interactive hand tracking through joint, continuous optimization of pose and correspondences. ACM Trans. Graph. **35**, 1–12 (2017)

36. Tsoli, A., Argyros, A. A.: Joint 3D tracking of a deformable object in interaction with a hand. In: Ferrari, V., Hebert, M., Sminchisescu, C., Weiss, Y. (eds.) Computer Vision – ECCV 2018. LNCS, vol. 11218, pp. 504–520. Springer, Cham (2018). https://doi.org/10.1007/978-3-030-01264-9_30

37. Chen, Y., Tu, Z., Ge, L., Zhang, D., Chen, R., So-Handnet, Y.J.: Self-organizing network for 3D hand pose estimation with semi-supervised learning. In: Proceedings of the IEEE International Conference on Computer Vision, pp. 6961–6970. IEEE, Korea (2019)

38. Ge, L., Ren, Z., Yuan, J.: Point-to-point regression PointNet for 3D hand pose estimation. In: Ferrari, V., Hebert, M., Sminchisescu, C., Weiss, Y. (eds.) ECCV 2018. LNCS, vol. 11217, pp. 489–505. Springer, Cham (2018). https://doi.org/10.1007/978-3-030-01261-8_29

39. Wu, Xiaokun, Finnegan, Daniel, O'Neill, Eamonn, Yang, Yong-Liang.: HandMap: robust hand pose estimation via intermediate dense guidance map supervision. In: Ferrari, V., Hebert, M., Sminchisescu, C., Weiss, Y. (eds.) ECCV 2018. LNCS, vol. 11220, pp. 246–262. Springer, Cham (2018). https://doi.org/10.1007/978-3-030-01270-0_15

40. Cai, Y., Ge, L., Cai, J., Yuan, J.: Weakly-supervised 3D hand pose estimation from monocular RGB images. In: Ferrari, V., Hebert, M., Sminchisescu, C., Weiss, Y. (eds.) ECCV 2018. LNCS, vol. 11210, pp. 678–694. Springer, Cham (2018). https://doi.org/10.1007/978-3-030-01231-1_41

41. Ahmed, K.H., Al-Asadi, A.H.: Survey of hand gesture recognition systems. J. Phys. Conf. Ser., 042003(2019)

42. Abdul, R., Hafız, M.: CMSWVHG-control Ms windows via hand gesture. In: 2017 International Multi-Topic Conference (INMIC), pp. 1–7. IEEE. Pakistan (2017)

43. Zhou, W.: Real-time implementation of vision-based unmarked static hand gesture recognition with neural networks based on FPGAS. In: IEEE International Conference on Robotics and Biomimetics (ROBIO), pp. 1026–103. IEEE, Macao (2017)

44. Liu, X., Li, C.: Tian, L.: Hand gesture recognition based on wavelet invariant moments. In: IEEE International Symposium on Multimedia (ISM), pp. 459–464. IEEE, Taiwan (2017)

45. Salunke, T.P., Bharkad, S.D.: Power point control using hand gesture recognition based on hog feature extraction and K-NN classification. In: International Conference on Computing Methodologies and Communication (ICCMC), pp. 1151–1155. IEEE, India (2017)

46. Saha, H.N., Tapadar, S., Ray, S., Chatterjee, S.K., Saha, S.: A machine learning based approach for hand gesture recognition using distinctive feature extraction. In: 8th Annual Computing and Communication Workshop and Conference (CCWC), pp. 91–98. IEEE, USA (2018)

47. Zhang, Q.: Segmentation of hand gesture based on dark channel prior in projector-camera system. In: International Conference on Communications in China (ICCC), pp. 1–6. IEEE, China (2017)

48. Žemgulys, J.: Recognition of basketball referee signals from videos using histogram of oriented gradients (Hog) and support vector machine (Svm). Procedia Comput. Sci. **130**, 953–960 (2018)

49. Al-Hammadi, M.: Hand gesture recognition for sign language using 3DCNN. IEEE Access **8**, 79491–79509 (2020)

50. Bulugu, I., Ye, Zhongfu., B.J.: Higher-order local autocorrelation feature extraction methodology for hand gestures recognition. In: 2nd International Conference on Multimedia And Image Processing (ICMIP), pp. 83–87. IEEE, China (2017)

51. Ansar, H., Jalal, A., Gochoo, M., Kim, K.: Hand gesture recognition based on auto-landmark localization and reweighted genetic algorithm for healthcare muscle activities. Sustainability **13**(5), 2961 (2021)

52. Wu, X.Y.: A hand gesture recognition algorithm based on Dc-CNN. Multimedia Tools Appl. **79**(13), 9193–9205 (2020)

53. Molina, J., Pajuelo, J.A., Martínez, J.M.: Real-time motion-based hand gestures recognition from time-of-flight video. J. Sig. Process Syst. **86**, 17–25 (2017)

54. Xi, C., Chen, J., Zhao, C., Pei, Q., Liu, L.: Real-time hand tracking using Kinect. In: Proceedings of the 2nd International Conference on Digital Signal Processing, pp. 37–42. Tokyo, Japan (2018)

55. Devineau, G., Moutarde, F., Xi, W., Yang, J.: Deep learning for hand gesture recognition on skeletal data. In: Proceedings of the 13th IEEE International Conference on Automatic Face Gesture Recognition, pp. 106–113. IEEE, China (2018)

56. Mujahid, A., et al.: Real-time hand gesture recognition based on deep learning YOLOv3 model. Appl. Sci. **11**(9), 4164 (2021)

57. Mahmood, M.R., Abdulazeez, A.M., Orman, Z.: Dynamic hand gesture recognition system for Kurdish sign language using two lines of features. In: International Conference on Advanced Science and Engineering (ICOASE), pp. 42–47. IEEE, Iraq (2018)

58. Ganokratanaa, T., Pumrin, S.: Hand gesture recognition algorithm for smart cities based on wireless sensor. Int. J. Online Eng. **13**(6), 58–75 (2017)

59. Augustauskas, R,. Lipnickas, A.: Robust hand detection using arm segmentation from depth data and static palm gesture recognition. In: 9th IEEE International Conference on Intelligent Data Acquisition and Advanced Computing Systems: Technology and Applications (IDAACS), pp. 664–667. IEEE, Romania (2017)

60. Alksasbeh, M.Z., et al.: Smart hand gestures recognition using K-NN based algorithm for video annotation purposes. Indonesia J. Electron. Eng. Comput. Sci. **21**(1), 242–252 (2021)

61. Liao, S., et al.: Multi-object intergroup gesture recognition combined with fusion feature and KNN algorithm. J. Intell. Fuzzy Syst. **38**(3), 2725–2735 (2020)

62. Benalcázar, M.E., Motoche, C., Zea, J.A., Jaramillo, A.G.: Real-time hand gesture recognition using the MYO armband and muscle activity detection. In: Second Ecuador Technical Chapters Meeting ETCM, pp. 1–6. IEEE, Ecuador (2017)

63. Lian, K.Y., Chiu, C.C., Hong, Y.J., Sung, W.T.: Wearable armband for real time hand gesture recognition. In: International Conference on Systems Man and Cybernetics (SMC), pp. 2992–2995. IEEE, Canada (2017)

64. Zhu, Y., Jiang, S., Shull, B.: Wrist-worn hand gesture recognition based on barometric pressure sensing. In: 15th International Conference on Wearable and Implantable Body Sensor Networks (BSN), pp. 181–184. IEEE, USA (2018)

65. Sugiura, Y., Nakamura, F., Kawai, W., Kikuchi, T., Sugimoto, M.: Behind the palm: hand gesture recognition through measuring skin deformation on back of hand by using optical sensors. In: 56th Annual Conference of the Society of Instrument and Control Engineers of Japan (SICE), pp. 1082–1087. IEEE, Japan (2017)

66. Reshna, S., Jayaraju, M.: Spotting and recognition of hand gesture for Indian sign language recognition system with skin segmentation and SVM. In: International Conference on Wireless Communications, Signal Processing and Networking (WISPNET), pp. 386–390. IEEE, Indian (2017)

67. Tian, Z.: WICATCH: a Wi-Fi based hand gesture recognition system. IEEE Access (6), 16911–16923 (2018)

68. Sapienza, S.: On-line event-driven hand gesture recognition based on surface electromyographic signals. In: International Symposium on Circuits and Systems (ISCAS), pp. 1–5. IEEE, Italy (2018)

69. Shengchang, L., Haoyu, T., Wenshuang, Y.: A hand gesture recognition system based on 24 Ghz radars. In: International Symposium on Antennas and Propagation ISAP, pp. 1–2. IEEE, India (2017)

70. Zhao, J., Mao, J., Wang, G., Yang, H., Zhao, B.: A miniaturized wearable wireless hand gesture recognition system employing deep-forest classifier. In: Biomedical Circuits and Systems Conference, pp. 1–4. IEEE, Italy (2017)

71. Rishabh, S., Nutan, V., Prachi, R.: Interactive projector screen with hand detection using gestures. In: International Conference on Automatic Control and Dynamic Optimization Techniques ICACDOT, pp. 574–577. IEEE, India (2016)

72. Yang, J., Pan, J., Li, J.: sEMG-based continuous hand gesture recognition using Gmm-Hmm and threshold model. In: IEEE International Conference on Robotics and Biomimetics (ROBIO), pp. 1509–1514. IEEE, Macao (2017)
73. Chen, S.H., Hernawan, A., Lee, Y.S., Wang, J.C.: Hand gesture recognition based on Bayesian sensing hidden Markov models and Bhattacharyya divergence. In: International Conference on Image Processing (ICIP), pp. 3535–3539. IEEE, China (2017)
74. Molina, J., Pajuelo, J.A., Martínez, J.M.: Real-time motion-based hand gestures recognition from time-of-flight video. J. Sig. Process. Syst. **86**(1), 17–25 (2017)
75. Konstantinidis, D., Dimitropoulos, K., Daras, P.: Sign language recognition based on hand and body skeletal data. In: Conference: the True Vision-Capture, Transmission and Display of 3D Video (3DTV-CON), pp. 1–4. IEEE, Finland (2018)
76. De Smedt, Q., Wannous, H., Vandeborre, J.P., Guerry, J., Saux, B.: 3D hand gesture recognition using a depth and skeletal dataset: Shrec'17 Track. In: Proceedings of the Workshop on 3D Object Retrieval, pp. 33–38. Eurographics Association, Germany (2017)
77. Karbasi, M.: A hybrid method using Kinect depth and color data stream for hand blobs segmentation. Sci. Int. **29**, 515–519 (2017)
78. Guo, Y., He, Z., Xie, Q., Chen, K., Ni, W., Zou, E.: Development and application of gesture recognition system for intelligent robot. IOP Conf. Ser. Mater. Sci. Eng. **452**(042172) (2018)
79. Oliveira, M., Chatbri, H., Yarlapati, N., O'Connor, N. E., Sutherland, A.: Hand orientation redundancy filter applied to hand-shapes dataset. In: Proceedings of the 2nd International Conference on Applications of Intelligent Systems, pp. 1–5. Association for Computing Machinery, USA (2019)
80. De Smedt, Q., Wannous, H., Vandeborre, P.: Heterogeneous hand gesture recognition using 3D dynamic skeletal data. Comput. Visi. Image Underst. **181**, 60–72 (2019)
81. Oliveira, M., Chatbri, H., Little, S., Ferstl, Y., O'Connor, N. E., Sutherland, A.: Irish sign language recognition using principal component analysis and convolutional neural networks. In: International Conference on Digital Image Computing: Techniques and Applications (DICTA), pp. 1–8. IEEE, Australia (2017)
82. Benitez, G., Olivares, J., Sanchez, G., Yanai, K.: IPN hand: a video dataset and benchmark for real-time continuous hand gesture recognition. In: 25th International Conference on Pattern Recognition (ICPR), pp. 4340–4347. IEEE, Macao (2021)
83. Malik, J., Elhayek, A., Stricker, D.: Structure-aware 3D hand pose regression from a single depth image. In: Bourdot, P., Cobb, S., Interrante, V., kato, H., Stricker, D. (eds.) EuroVR 2018. LNCS, vol. 11162, pp. 3–17. Springer, Cham (2018). https://doi.org/10.1007/978-3-030-01790-3_1
84. Chen, J., Meng, J., Wang, X., Yuan, J.: Dynamic graph CNN for event-camera based gesture recognition. In: International Symposium on Circuits and Systems (ISCAS), pp. 1–5. IEEE, India (2020)
85. Sun, H., Ji, T., Zhang, B., Yang, K., Ji, R.: Research on the hand gesture recognition based on deep learning. In: 12th International Symposium on Antennas, Propagation and EM Theory (ISAPE), pp. 1–4. IEEE, China (2018)
86. Shin, S., Sung, W.: Dynamic hand gesture recognition for wearable devices with low complexity recurrent neural networks. In: International Symposium on Circuits and Systems (ISCAS), pp. 2274–2277. IEEE, Canada (2020)
87. Chen, X., Guo, H., Wang, G., Zhang, L.: Motion feature augmented recurrent neural network for skeleton-based dynamic hand gesture recognition. In: International Conference on Image Processing (ICIP), pp. 2881–2885. IEEE, China (2017)
88. Inujaim, I., Alali, H., Khan, F., Kim, Y.: Hand gesture recognition using input impedance variation of two antennas with transfer learning. IEEE Sens. J., 4129–4135 (2018)

89. Nguyen, S., Brun. L., Lézoray, O., Bougleux, S.: A neural network based on SPD manifold learning for skeleton-based hand gesture recognition. In: Proceedings of the IEEE Conference on Computer Vision and Pattern Recognition, pp. 12036–12045. IEEE, USA (2019)

90. Alnaim, N., Abbod, M., Albar, A.: Hand gesture recognition using convolutional neural network for people who have experienced a stroke. In: Proceedings of the 3rd international symposium on multidisciplinary studies and innovative technologies (ISMSIT), pp.1–6. Ankara, Turkey (2019)

91. Chung, H., Chung, Y., Tsai, W.: An efficient hand gesture recognition system based on deep CNN. In: Proceedings of the International Conference on Industrial Technology (ICIT), pp. 853–858. IEEE, Australia (2019)

92. Bao, P., Maqueda, A., Del-Blanco, R., García, N.: Tiny hand gesture recognition without localization via a deep convolutional network. IEEE Trans. Consum. Electron. 63(3), 251–257 (2017)

93. Li, G., et al.: Hand gesture recognition based on convolution neural network. Cluster Comput. 22(2), 2719–2729 (2019)

94. Wu, X.Y.: A hand gesture recognition algorithm based on Dc-CNN. Multimedia Tools Appl. 79(13), 1–13 (2019)

95. Lai, K., Yanushkevich, S.N.: CNN+RNN depth and skeleton based dynamic hand gesture recognition. In: International Conference on Pattern Recognition (ICPR), pp. 3451–3456. IEEE. China (2018)

96. Choi, W., Ryu, S., Kim, J.: Short-range radar based real-time hand gesture recognition using Lstm encoder. IEEE Access 7 (2019)

97. Nunez, J.C., Cabido, R., Pantrigo, J.J., Montemayor, A.S., Velez, J.F.: Convolutional neural networks and long short-term memory for skeleton-based human activity and hand gesture recognition. Pattern Recogn. 76, 80–94 (2018)

98. Zhu, G., Zhang, L., Shen, P., Song, J., Shah, S.A., Bennamoun, M.: Continuous gesture segmentation and recognition using 3DCNN and convolutional LSTM. IEEE Trans. Multimedia 21(4), 1011–1021 (2018)

A Comprehensive Review in Using the Advances of Deep Learning in the 3D Race Classification

Noor H. Reda[1]([✉])([iD]) and Hawraa Abbas[2]

[1] Babylon University, Babylon, Iraq
nhredha@gmail.com
[2] School of Engineering, Kerbala University, Kerbala, Iraq
Hawraa.h@uokerbala.edu.iq

Abstract. Human faces can reveal not just the human identity, but even demographic characteristics such as ethnicity and gender. Recently, the researchers get the advantages of Deep Learning techniques in developing face recognition systems implemented on both 2D and 3D face datasets. However, the usefulness of Deep learning in analyzing facial features of 3D faces gender, and ethnicity are examined in literature with only three main perspectives: data representation, augmentation, and comparison using the several commonly used format of 3D face representation such as depth images, point clouds, normal maps, triangular mesh, and horizontal disparity images. Many algorithms are implemented by authors on popular 3D datasets including FRGC v2, 3D-Texas, and BU3D-FE. In this work, we highlight the advantages of using the deep learning 3D representation in "race recognition" approaches and refer the researchers to the important related works in this field by comparing them according to their distinguishing metrics and invariant conditions support and the used techniques and datasets.

Keywords: Race Classification · Deep Learning · 3D face Recognition

1 Introduction

1.1 Face Morphology and Computer Vision

The biological system of the human body is a complex composition in which many details and information can be reflected via the superficial layer of the skin. Body parts' appearance and pattern, shape, color, local and general characteristics can tell information about the human age, gender, disease, ethnicity, and more. The human face is a very important part of the human body that can tell many details to the physician, specialists, and devices' sensors. The morphology of the skull, color, iris, lips, under-bones concavities, muscle shape, skin pattern, and fat distribution reflect different biological and social signs about the human.

Facial muscle motion and actions also can reveal more information about biological health and diagnose many types of negative and positive signs of health state such as; partial loss of muscle activity, involuntary movements, and muscle shape abnormality.

A. M. Al-Bakry et al. (Eds.): NTICT 2022, CCIS 1764, pp. 77–106, 2023.
https://doi.org/10.1007/978-3-031-35442-7_5

In general, the images of human faces with their global appearance and their local segmented parts can be translated or mapped into good facial information. Face photo can be segmented into different areas of interest (AOI), face photo is used to maintain different types of information via extracting face features that are mapped into their corresponding values and more.

The human face plays an important role in multi-disciplinary research as it reflects a bank of information and demographical attributes such as gender, ethnicity, expression, age, social signals, emotions, and more [1].

Computer vision is one of many scientific fields that got many advantages in face morphology analysis and recognition. It allows the researchers and specialists to focus on their required interest areas and face features and enables them to study specific cases and conditions via image processing, data mining, artificial intelligence, computer training, and fast learning abilities. Distinct anatomical areas of face image are used as "face landmarks" to support researchers and daily life applications. By applying some pre-processing, object and edge detection, extraction, and recognition techniques, it becomes possible to analyze the lips, eyes, iris, nose, mouth, and contours to classify, detect, verify, authenticate, recognize, and serve different today's scientific and industrial applications.

Face description is usually performed by collecting the information of the visual attributes such as; soft biometrics (gender, race, age), in addition to the physical characteristics such as lips shape, and other environmental related aspects (lighting, shadow, head pose). In the face recognition step, the means of several attributes can be considered to avoid restricting the recognition to the overwhelming biometric comparison. However, considering a single local feature might support the global or multiple features in the comparison or classification tasks and enhance the accuracy.

Researchers marked several issues in the face recognition and classification field such as; variability of data (facial expressions for example can vary with the degree of expressiveness, age, personality, or race. The head pose also affects the recognition during capturing the face image. In addition, illumination conditions of capturing environment are worthy to be considered as an affecting factor in facial features recognition.

Gabor-based [2] and several alternative HOG and LBP-based techniques used handcrafted or some enhanced selected face features to avoid degrading the accuracy via this variability [3]. Although such traditional features learning tackled some variability limitations, the huge data variability defined another challenge. Recent deep learning-based approaches performed better with large variability and achieved higher accuracy in face morphology recognition and human groups' classification.

1.2 Using the Facial Features to Analyze the Human Face

Computer vision tries to simulate the human visual perception system as an initial step to collect meaningful descriptions of the required facial features of different applications. Some classic approaches derived the color texture and superficial shape (geometrical) in what is called appearance-based approaches. The extracted face descriptions in this type are supported by the good abilities of both machine learning and pattern recognition to achieve an acceptable accuracy in extraction and recognition based on the fast comparison. However, these approaches sometimes miss the linearity of following the face precepting mechanism that is used in the human visual system. In addition, image manipulation (such as; scale variation), data variation, and illumination variation represented essential degradation factors of such approaches' accuracy. "Feature-based" approaches considered both configural and shape features to enhance the recognition accuracy and avoid the previous limitations. Some examples of existing approaches that used Local features are; a classification approach [4] that used the Lip shape and its color to recognize the gender. This work analyzed the "Lip Feature" which is an important human face local feature that usually differs from person to person. Another existing work [5] discuss the robustness of using the "Iris" area and its random tissues and unique properties in extraction and classification tasks. "Nose feature" and especially "nose tip" was reported in the literature as a distinctive region of a human face that has a property of stability even during face expressions changes.

Furtherly to achieve different tasks, Face data might be processed at various levels, the feature might be integrated, and multiple features are studied together to learn how they are relating to each other and how to influence each other. Generally, two types of detection approaches are examined: "feature-based" and "image-based". The first approach extracts important features from the human face and matches them against a gallery or a saved knowledge of the facial features. However, the image-based approach obtains directly the best match between the testing images and the training images [6].

A common local features-based type of classifier finds the minimum distance and labels the testing sample to the mean associated class, while the nearest neighbor classifier assigns the testing samples to the class that has the nearest neighbor. More specifically, the k-nearest neighbor (KNN) classifier assigns the testing images to the nearest neighbor by the first k searched neighbors. Machine learning algorithms such as CNN also is commonly used as classifiers, identifiers (comparing to many), and authenticators (comparing to one) of 2D and 3D facial image representations. Several commonly used features in Literature are summarized below:

Gabor Filters (Commonly Used)

Gabor Filters is a processing tool to extract the feature from images and obtain information about it. This tool implements neural network algorithms that could be trained by the obtained features of this filter. Scaling RMS contrast and presenting fuzzily skewed filtering is an innovative approach used in this technique. The source photos are first transformed into gray-level images before being cropped into (100 x 100) pixel images. The face images are rotated by calculating the center of the two eyes for each face. Contrast and illumination equalization, histogram equalization, and fuzzy filtering are the three steps in the pre-processing phase of the related approach. A model of ethnic classification of a person from face images is proposed by Momin [7] to detect the facial landmarks and then applies Gabor filters to each component to extract key facial features. It showed that the mouth and the nose outperform the eyes in the characterization of ethnicity. Jae Choi [8] employed Gabor DCNN (GDCNN) to improve the face analysis and performed extensive experiments on four public face databases. Ahmed [9] in

2021 implemented Gabor wavelet transform for feature extraction on ORL and YALE databases and used the CNN deep learning to achieve 85.42% and 92% respectively.

Statistical Principal Component Analysis (PCA)
PCA also called "Eigenface" extracts the standard features from the human face photos to be assigned with unique features resulting using the subtraction of the average vector from the face vector. It is a type of template matching step to directly compare the pixel intensity values obtained from facial images. Then, the eigenvectors are obtained mathematically from a covariance with a step of dimensionality reduction to avoid memory issues.

PCA Advantages: (1) Easy to compute based on linear algebra), (2) By using PCA beforehand to lower the dimensions of the training dataset, it prevents the predictive algorithms from overfitting.

PCA Disadvantages: (1) It is difficult to tell which are the most important features in the dataset after computing principal components. (2) A trade-off between information loss and reducing the dimensionality of the discriminative feature vector.

PCA is combined with deep learning by Sunitha [10] to employ feature reduction.

on the high-dimensional retrieved features in addition to using an optimal kernel extreme learning machine (KELM) with parameter tuning to enhance the performance.

Linear Discriminant Analysis (LDA)
LDA also called "Fisher's Discriminant Analysis" that collects images and classifies them, then calculates the vector of the classes via maximizing the inter-class matrix in addition to minimizing the intra-class matrix. Calculating the Eigenvector is also used in this extraction approach. However, choosing a single feature for analysis might cause overlapping in this classification thus, using multiple features usually leads to better classification.

Sahan [11] in 2021 generated a type of one-dimensional face feature set using the LDA from the original image database to train one dimension classifier (1D-DCNN) and implemented it on the MCUT dataset with a near-optimal achieved accuracy. The efficiency and performance of combining the Deep Learning and LDA are also tested by Bajrami [12] on labeled faces in the wild LFW dataset. The author showed that the Deep learning method achieves better recognition accuracy and recognition time is much faster than the LDA method in large-scale datasets.

Independent Component Analysis (ICA)
Similar to the PCA (a generalization of the PCA), ICA uses a subspace to reduce the dimensionality. PCA treats the images as random variables of a Gaussian distribution, then minimizes the second-order statistics. However, ICA is also generalized to non-Gaussian distributions and is used to find the nature of the data statistical dependency. An initial hybridization in filter banks [13] is generated by a fusion of PCA and ICA filters and is used by Dutta by employing the DCNN to improve the face classification on Frav-3D, Gavab-DB, and Casia-3D datasets. The author called the proposed approach

(PICANet) which consists of different layers: convolutional layer, nonlinear processing layer, pooling layer, and classification layer.

Local binary patterns (LBP)

LBP is an image operator that converts an image into an array of integer labels that represent the image's small-scale appearance. It converts the greyscale image of each pixel's (3 by 3) neighbors into a binary image using the middle pixel value. The difference between the center and the points around it is then calculated by the LBP (greater than zero a one is assigned, otherwise it remains zero). Furthermore, LBP can use the histogram of labels to construct a texture description. LBPNet approach is proposed by Xi [14] to extract and compare features in multilayer hierarchy which retains the CNN topology with modified trainable kernels on FERET and LFW datasets. Another work to combine the LBP and CNN in face analysis also is presented by Zhang [15].

Dynamic link architecture (DLA)

The DLA's main concept is to exploit synaptic plasticity, which is already present on the time scale of information processing and not just for memory acquisition, to quickly combine groupings of neurons into higher symbolic units.

Elastic Bunch Graph Matching (EBGM)

EBGM can only be used on objects that share a common structure, such as frontal faces with a common set of "landmarks" such as the tip of the nose or the corner of an eye. A Gabor wavelet convolution is used to characterize the characteristics. The EBGM's fundamental flaw is that the initial stage of the recognition process requires manual landmark selection of the facial image [16].

Geometric feature matching (GFM)

Face recognition performance cannot be ideal and will generally not be as good as appearance-based models that leverage substantially more information encoded in a face image since a face is described by just a limited number of biologically important landmarks. The study of geometry-based facial recognition, on the other hand, will help to promote the development of hybrid and speedier approaches. Even if the intricacies of the face's key characteristics are not resolved, GFM can recognize the image. The remaining data is simply geometrical and represents the remaining data at a very coarse resolution (i.e., loss of image pixels). The goal, however, is to obtain informative elements such as the chin and other significant facial features. The correlation coefficients are obtained using a collection of training face images to locate the eye position in the image. It then compares this to the test image and looks for the highest values [17].

Histograms of Orientated Gradient (HoG) Features

A feature descriptor that is used in computer vision and image processing to detect objects. The method counts the number of times a gradient orientation appears in a localized area of an image. This method is comparable to edge orientation histograms, scale-invariant feature transform descriptors, and shape contexts, but it is distinguished by the fact that it is computed on a dense grid of evenly spaced cells and employs overlapping local contrast normalization for increased accuracy [18].

Scale Invariant Feature Transform (SIFT) Features

SIFT is a computer vision technique for detecting, describing, and matching local features in images. A set of reference photos is used to extract SIFT key points of objects, which are then saved in a database. An object in a new image is recognized by comparing each feature from the new image to this database individually and discovering candidate matching features based on the Euclidean distance of their feature vectors. Subsets of important points that agree on the item and its location, scale, and orientation in the new image are identified from the whole set of matches to filter out good matches. Using an efficient hash table implementation of the generalized Hough transform, consistent clusters can be determined quickly. Outliers are removed after each cluster of three or more features that agree on an object and its pose is subjected to more extensive model testing. Finally, given the precision of the fit and the number of likely false matches, the likelihood that a certain set of features indicates the presence of an object is calculated. Object matches that pass all of these checks can be confidently identified as the correct ones [19].

WLD Features

WLD is based on the concept that human pattern perception is influenced not only by the change in a stimulus (such as sound or illumination) but also by the stimulus's original intensity. Differential excitation and orientation are the two components that makeup WLD. The ratio between two terms determines the differential excitation component: One is the relative intensity differences between a current pixel and its neighbors, while the other is the current pixel's intensity. The gradient orientation of the current pixel is represented by the orientation component. It constructs a concatenated WLD histogram for a given image using the two components [20].

In summary, methods that use a combination of features or multiple features would have high dimensionality, computational complexity, and reduced speed. However, Feature Selectivity, Feature Fusion Techniques, or Dimensionality Reduction can be employed to avoid these limitations.

Methods based on appearance can be holistic (global) or local. Local approaches use local neighbor-hood of small size for feature extraction, whereas holistic methods extract the feature from the query image worldwide. The shape of the face is well represented by global features, but the texture of the face is well represented by local features. Shape-based features are good for coarser recognition and representation of a face, but they fall short when compared to appearance-based techniques in capturing delicate details like wrinkles and bulges. Using a few spatial locations on the face to represent features is not as successful as using appearance-based feature representation [21]. A list of some existing face feature extraction approaches and techniques is summarized in (Table 1).

1.3   Face Features Representation

Face Space Theory, A Representation Example

Face space Theory is one of the well-known traditional approaches that is suggested by

Table 1. The Basic methods and algorithms of face feature extraction

Feature Extraction Approach
LBP [22]
Eigen Light Field [23]
Gabor Wavelet [24]
LTP [25]
PCA Eigenfaces [26]
SIFT [27]
3D Morphable Model [28]
PDBNN [29]
Modular Eigenfaces [30]
LDA Fisher faces [31]
ICA [32]
SURF [33]
APM [34]
DLA [35]
AAM [36]
ASM [37]
Genetic Algorithm Evolutionary Pursuit (EP) [38]
Wavelet Packet Analysis (WPA) [39]
EBGM [40]
Trace Transform (TT) [41]
Kernel Methods [42]
Simulated Annealing for 3D Face Recognition [43]
Partial Least Squares (PLS) [44]
Discriminant Face Descriptor [45]
Hybrid Deep Learning (HDL) [46]
Arc Face [47]
Large margin cosine loss (LMCL) [48]
CNN and Bag-of-visual-words (BOVW) [49]

Valantine, it represented the human face using a multidimensional space. Each dimension represents a facial feature, each face is represented by a point in space (a feature vector), and each vector value reflects a feature magnitude on its scale. The "facial space distances" between feature vectors corresponding to perceptual differences between human faces were assessed using this theory.

Additionally, this assumes that taking up a subspace per identity including the different appearances of each identity resulted from the variation of head pose, illumination, aging, and expression [50]. The face space theory can be summarized with the following:

Faces: multidimensional space.

Face: feature vector (a point in multidimensional space).

The magnitude of the descriptive feature per its corresponding unique scale: value in the feature vector.

perceptual differences between faces: inter feature vectors distances (face space distances).

Identity: a subspace of total space (contains its different appearances).

The critical face features that when changed could classify the human face into other different subspaces (change in identity).

Face space theory is followed by many extensions or improved approaches based that supposed some enhancements in face recognition fields such as; a reverse engineering technique by Abudarham [51] that discuss the problem of identification of critical features. It defined the "critical features" for identification as that feature that when changed would move the face outside its subspace and cause a change in identity. On other hand, "not critical features" are those when changed would not move the face outside its subspace features and do not affect the identity recognition of a face, as described in (Fig. 1) [51].

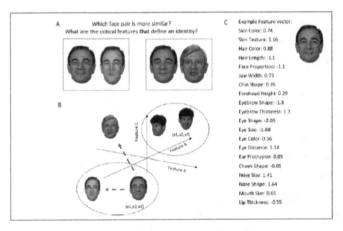

Fig. 1. Critical and non-Critical Face Features

This work modified one or more of the 20 features of human faces using a computer application and examine how changing each of these features affects the identification based on human perception ability. It implemented several experiments to identify the critical features and sort the 20 features according to their importance and effect on the identification process. Furthermore, the initial selectivity of critical features is also considered a dimensionality reduction step (preprocessing step) in the face recognition field.

2   Classifying the Human Faces According to Their Features

Template Matching
Each face image is described by a feature vector in the computer vision world and stored in computers as matrices, the least distance between two matrices (two faces) reflects the most similarity. In template matching, the classification might base on calculating the distance (such as; Euclidean, Squared Euclidean, City-Block, Canberra, Hausdorff, Quadratic Form, and Chi-square Statistic).

Machine Learning
ML starts with training the model using training data (examples) and their related class labels (supervised learning). The classifier then separates data into classes. Machine learning such as; SVM, KNN, Naïve Bayes algorithm (NB), or ANN are used for classification separately or in a cascaded manner.

Artificial Neural Network (ANN)
A network of artificial neurons that can communicate with one another and learn from their experiences. The numeric weights of linked neurons are modified throughout the training stage. The initial layer recognizes a set of provided inputs, whereas successive levels identify "patterns of patterns" detected by the preceding layers [52, 53].

Convolutional Neural Network (CNN)
The convolutional layer, pooling layer, nonlinear layers, and fully connected layers are all layers in the CNN architecture. The convolution and pooling layers function as a neural network that extracts features, whilst the fully connected layers function as a classification neural network that functions based on picture features and produces an output [54]. When compared to standard NN designs, the CNN automatically learns local feature extractors and implements the weight-sharing principle, allowing for a reduction in the number of free parameters and therefore increasing performance capacity [54].

2.1   Some Issues and Challenges of the Face and Race Classification

Uncontrolled Illumination
In contrast to the human perception systems, face recognition and classification approaches in the computer vision field might misclassify human faces due to vary-ing light during photo capturing. Illumination might tell faked information about the skin color features or even the shape-related features and cause labeling them with the wrong class, see (Fig. 2).

The extraction of illumination invariant characteristics, which is required for a strong face recognition system, is still hampered by illumination. The impacts of illumination on an image include changes in location, shadow shape, and the reversal of contrast gradients [55].

Training level and testing level are also degraded accuracy prone while the learning process is also sensitive to varying illumination. Using image processing techniques is a

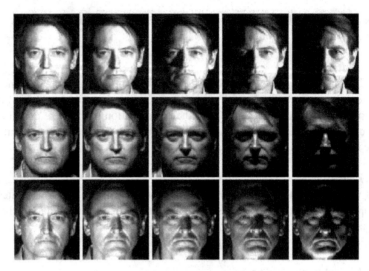

Fig. 2. Illumination Invariant Effect

commonly experienced solution in literature, normalizing the captured 2D images of various light conditions such as; Single scale retinex (SSR), Multiscale retinex (MR), Self-quotient image (SQI), Discrete cosine transform (DCT)-based Normalization, Wavelet transform-based, Tan and Triggs normalization (TT), Weber faces Retina model, histogram equalization, Gamma correlation, logarithms transform, and using only specific parts of faces that are less sensitive to the lighting environment. However, 3D face approaches have been showing better robustness for illumination issues with limitations of training samples cost and implementation complexity. For more details about the illumination issues, we recommend the reader to see these references: [56–61]. Some examples of faces data sets that (support/don't support) the illumination variation are summarized in (Table 2).

Facial Expression
In contrast to the static mode of the human face, facial expressions variation is used to reflect different emotions and translate many mental states of people such as; sadness, happiness, and more. This expression is usually used in medical applications in which each facial expression can be combined with a specific ailment. In the year 2017, Savran [79] conclude that an individual expresses and passes 7% of information to others via language, 38% via speech representation, and 55% via facial expression. In general, the facial expression is reflected by a change in the facial appearance and face parts' geometry and might lead to degrading the face classification and recognition algorithms. A related work [80] tried to solve this issue using some specific preprocessing steps to distinguish only the expression-specific features from the face and treat them separately. Producing 3D disparity maps is also proposed by Mi [81] through which a biological-based disparity energy model is used to identify and verify human faces with different facial expressions. Sharp variances [82] in the facial convex regions are also studied as a 3D model and linked to the bone structure by Li [82]. The extraction of illumination

Table 2. Illumination Invariant Support in the Existed Datasets

Support Illumination Variation	Doesn't Support Illumination Variation
Multi-PIE [62]	LFW [63]
GBU [64]	CASIA-Webface [65]
FRGC v2.0 [66]	FaceScrub [67]
CASIA-3D FaceV1 [68]	IJB-A [69]
UHDB11 [70]	VGG-Face [69]
UHDB3 [56]	MegaFace [71]
	MS-Celeb-1M [72]
	MF2 [73]
	SCface [74]
	ND-2006 [74]
	Bosphorus [75]
	3D-TEC [76]
	UMB-DB [77]
	Florence Faces [78]

invariant elements remains a challenge for robust face recognition systems. The effects of illumination on an image include changes in position, shadow shape, and contrast gradient reversal.

Gradual Modification by Ageing

Classification algorithms can result in two different classes for the same individual face during two iterations that are separated by several years period. Typically, aging variation can significantly affect the human face structure. A massive time gap between the average age of human faces that are used in training and faces that are intended to be checked as input images. An example of a model based on age partial spaces learning from appearance-age labels is studied by Zhou [83] using probabilistic linear discriminant analysis. Appearance-age labels are used in this work to train the aging subspace, to be followed by using the expectation-maximization algorithm and experimenting with the proposed algorithm on the FGNET, and MORPH datasets. In literature, solving the aging issue sometimes is motivated by the fact that aging effects on human faces are a nonlinear modification that defers even within the same class of faces. However, aging is usually a smooth transformation in the face parts' appearance.

Medical Modification of Face Appearance

The face image of an individual might be entirely changed by Plastic surgery that can change the skin texture, face parts size and shape, and more. Hence, face features and even the holistic appearance of the human face can be severely changed and lead the recognition algorithm to make the wrong decision or wrong resulting class. The challenge of plastic surgery is studied on a specific face dataset by Sable [84] via applying entropy-based volume SIFT face recognition. This work extracted the important regions and amounts of the scale-space structure and considered the entropy as a high-order statistical feature that is slightly affected by medical modification and alterations in the human face. A recent review by Bouguila [85] concluded that:

1) The quality and comprehensiveness of training data sets will have a significant impact on the accuracy of future facial recognition systems.
2) Facial recognition training databases featuring patients who have had facial treatments should be increased and balanced to include more photographs of people of various ages, races, and surgeries.
3) To account for cumulative effects during algorithm training, patients who have undergone various procedures at the same time would be useful.
4) Efforts must be made to offer scientifically rigorous data on facial biometric identification following facial cosmetic surgery, as well as to incorporate these concepts into the usual consultation or consent process for patients seeking aesthetic facial surgery.

Occlusion and Covered Parts

Occlusion can be described by the blockage of a limited part/parts of a face image that is covered or obstructed. Criminal people and thieves usually occlude parts of their faces to avoid recognizing their identity. Scarves, Sunglasses, and hats can hide some important information for recognition applications. Hence, face recognition systems need to be robust to occlusion. Zeng [86] in 2020 mentioned five widely used testing scenarios in studying the occlusion face recognition, ranging from most to least realistic representations:

Real occlusions: Faces are occluded by realistic pictures such as sunglasses or a scarf in gallery photographs, while faces are occluded by realistic images such as sunglasses or a scarf in probe images.

1) Partial faces: gallery images are occlusion-free mugshots, whereas test face images are only partial faces.
2) Synthetic occlusions: gallery photographs are real-life faces captured in uncontrolled situations, whereas probe faces are occluded with synthetic occlusions to replicate real-life occlusions.
3) Occluding rectangle: gallery images are mugshots with no occlusion, whereas test face images are occluded with a rectangle, such as white or black rectangles.
4) Occluding irrelevant photos: gallery images are un-occluded mugshots, whereas test face images are occluded with unrelated images like a baboon or a non-square image.

Two-dimensional images of the human face can describe many important features, several examples of such common traditional features are described in (Table 3).

Table 3. Several Traditional Features of Face Classification

Feature	Description
Skin color	Light-Dark
Skin texture	arks, scars, freckles, wrinkles
Hair Color	Red, Blond, Black, ...
Hair length	Bald-long hair
Face proportion:	The ratio between length (top to bottom) and width
Jaw width	Narrow–wide
Chin shape	Pointed–rounded–flat (square)
Forehead height	Distance between the eyebrows and the hairline (Short–long)
Eyebrow shape	Rounded–straight
Eyebrow thickness	Thin–thick
Eye shape	Narrow–round
Eye size	Small-large
Eye color	Light–dark
Eye distance	Small-large
Ear protrusion	Flat on the skull or protruding outward (Adjacent to the skull–protruding outward)
Cheek shape	Sunken and skinny cheeks or full and puffy (Sunken–puffy)
Overall Nose size	Small–Large
Nose shape	Pointed and thin - flat and wide
Mouth size	width from left to right (Small–Large)
Lip thickness	Thin–Thick

3   Race Classification

3.1   Race Recognition Based on Face Morphology

A race is a grouping of individuals into groups that are generally considered separate within a society, based on similar physical or social characteristics [87]. The human faces contain important information that could be used to collect useful demographics and enhance face recognition tasks in computer vision systems. Naturally, humans utilize information from various visual cues for face recognition and particularly people who are related to the same race are more accurate at recognizing faces of their race than stranger races. Hence, focusing on race information could be also used to concentrate the algorithms' search towards a more feasible space during the matching process of unseen faces and to optimize face recognition algorithms.

In reality, "heritable, phenotypic features, geographic ancestry, physical appearance, ethnicity, and social status are used to categorize humans into huge and distinct populations or groupings". A high concurrency was defined for creating race recognition systems based on this concept [88].

In recent years, race-based face recognition has emerged as a fascinating topic for a variety of applications, including enhancing security systems and preserving various types of multimedia data privacy and lawful user identification, as well as managing industrial systems [89]. Facial morphometry describes how the form of a person's face evolves. It's also excellent for allowing variations between races, ethnic groupings, sexes, and even family members. Artists and plastic surgeons alike are fascinated by the morphology of the face. The face criteria are beneficial in a variety of situations, including looking for a missing person, identifying a criminal, and locating a person in unfortunate circumstances such as a car accident, burn, or natural catastrophe. Face parameters can be used to treat congenital and post-traumatic facial deformities [90].

In Inter person interaction, the face plays an essential role in carrying the identification information. The unique information of each individual's face helps others to identify him in daily life communication and interaction. Computer vision uses the features of the face like cutaneous, bones, subcutaneous layers, and muscle shapes to distinguish the unique morphological attributes of every single person. Many scientific, medical, and art fields used, measured, and reproduced some facial characteristics to study, analyze, and recognize individuals. In literature, an example of an interesting facial topic was the face contour that is used by plastic surgeons, anatomists, anthropologists, and even artists to identify individuals' race.

Racial information analysis includes the initial face detection level, images' preprocessing level, the extraction of race-discriminative features of human faces level, and the final level of finding a specific representation of the face by which the relevant race can be grouped or classified based on their shared distinctive information. Face detection is used to confirm the existence of a face in an image or video. The image is pre-processed after detection to acquire the region of interest and improve image quality. Another type of pre-processing technique is normalization, which involves transforming and mapping diverse scales of face images into the same scale. Another preprocessing method is face alignment, which is the process of locating fiducial points such as the mouth, eyes, chin, and nose [91].

Calder [92] distinguished human faces by their face-specific cues with a range graduated from the basic global level to the detailed face feature, till the final individual identification based on both levels. Many recent types of research required some knowledge of second-order level features to integrate their race categorization and recognition tasks.

In the year 2014, Fu [93] qualitatively classified the representative feature extraction methods into; Chromatic, Global feature, and Local feature descriptor representation.

"Chromatic Representation" such as skin color tones to represent the primary face features required to classify the faces according to their race into Asian/ Non-Asian, or Caucasian/ Non-Caucasian [94–96]. Although the fusion of skin tone with some facial metrics can perform well in racial comparison, several clear drawbacks are experienced such as; (1) intra-groups skin color sharing (for instance, two different races such as;

Southern Indians and Africans can be classified together based on their dark-skin tones). (2) In an uncontrolled illumination environment, color is highly sensitive to light variation. (3) several psychological studies demonstrated that skin tone has not a virtual relationship to the human race perception system [97].

The second representation is "Global feature representation" (AKA Holistic representation) performed well in race recognition for its capability of preserving the interrelations among facial parts descriptions. PCA-based statistical feature extraction approaches [98–100] are commonly used examples of accurate and reliable extracting and recognizing facial cues.

Holistic features-based classification is often used to establish a "baseline" for comparisons, GHULAM [101] is an example of such use of PCA features where these global features are extracted and used in comparing between training and test images of the dataset.

"Local Feature Descriptor Representation" Compared to global had several advantages of lower processing time, reliability, minimizing noise, elimination the irrelevant information to reduce the used memory, and additionally it is robust to face geometry, face rotation aging, and pose variation. Gabor [102] wavelet representation is one of the commonly used techniques in race categorization applications. However, its feature vector's high dimensionality forces a need for associated dimension reduction techniques. Some other existing examples of local features' representation are Adaboost, optimal decision-making rules, Quad-Tree clustering, independent component analysis (ICA-based), wavelet, weber local descriptors, and local binary patterns LBP.

The periocular region contains many different racial traits, such as eyelids and canthus. These fundamental characteristics cannot be highlighted in methods for dealing with periocular region texture as a whole. It can obtain detailed texture and geometrical features in some fascinating local regions by examining geometrical structures in the periocular area based on facial landmarks [103].

A related work [104] in 2017, considered that there are three main methods of race classification; Holistic face, local feature, and 3D methods. 3D-based classification outperforms the 2D models via its essential craniofacial features and robustness against the variant face poses and expressions and variant illumination. Several recent contributing works [103, 105] used the 3D face features with some limitations of complicated feature extraction steps.

Human faces can be classified into a variety of features. However, classifying faces based on expression, age, and gender in large datasets can cause an accuracy reduction. Alternatively, race-based classification provides the dominant personal feature that cannot be easily hidden behind the face traits and appearances like gender and age can. Similar to face recognition, typical race classification systems usually normalize the input faces and prepare the images for extracting the discriminant features of the fact based on these selected features, the race classifier recognizes the race of the input face image and labels them into Asian, African, European, …etc. globally, the World population is classified into the most studied and popular racial groups Caucasian, East Asian, African/African American, Pacific Islander, Asian Indian, Native American/American Indian, and Hispanic/Latino. However, building a robust and accurate race classifier might be a challenge while using huge face databases. Such a classifier also needs to be trained well on suitable multiple-race face datasets to avoid later overfitting by the new unseen examples. Face segmentation and investigation of salient face features is an essential step in race recognition to avoid processing all the faces traditionally and increase the data dimensionality. In literature, most race classifiers either use landmark localization or a one-dimensional feature vector to describe the face. Although landmarks localization usually outperforms one-dimensional approaches, changes in face rotation, lighting conditions, and capturing distance might degrade its performance. Traditional classifier usually uses machine learning methods to classify the faces in two general steps; extracting artificially designed features and training a proper classifier with these features.

A commonly used direction in race classification literature is the anthropometric (shape-based) methodology that is usually proposed to tackle the race estimation problem. Many proposed 3D models depend on anthropometric statistics to categorize human faces according to their race where they reconstruct the facial geometrical structure by using 3D face models from the faces' images. Although their high computational cost, 3D models can perform well. However, some distances between landmark points in 2D images also can be used as geometric invariants in 3D models to simplify these approaches.

Becerra [106] proposes a simpler way of describing face photos by merging local appearance and geometry traits and exploiting race information from distinct face sections using a component-based methodology in 2018. The experimental results of this work are obtained in the FERET subset from the EGA database with traditional but effective classifiers like Random Forest and Support Vector Machines. These results are extremely similar to those obtained with a recent deep learning approach, according to the author. 68 landmark points (control points) are scattered around the face in this work in the following manner: 17 points for face contour, 12 points for eyes, 10 points for brows, 9 points for nose, and 20 points for the mouth. It computed the ratio of distances of all conceivable combinations of four and five non-coplanar or collinear control points using the 2D/3D invariant measures defined in prior similar work for the case of 2D images. As a result, we ended up with a high-dimensional vector, which we decreased using Principal Components Analysis (PCA). Some configurations (distances or ratios) are more significant than others, and some of them may be redundant, therefore this allows for the optimum invariants to be found for the situation. The geometric depiction of this work's invariant distances is shown in (Fig. 3).

The face image is divided into 10 interest regions (see Fig. 4) to explore the impact separately following the approach that includes hair and contour components due to its proven importance for attribute categorization in the state of art.

3.2   Race Classification, A Literature Review

One of the most basic and simple ways of characterizing a face is through visual features. Soft biometrics, such as demographic data (age, gender, race), facial signs, and specific face traits, as well as other contextual factors, are examples. Because of its numerous implementations in fields such as biometrical authentication, control of the individual's access, buildings' surveillance, and security systems, visual attribute estimation has been a hot study topic in last years. Soft biometrics could be implemented in a variety of

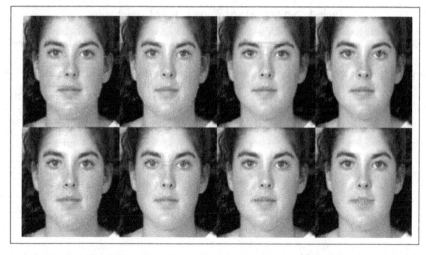

Fig. 3. Invariant distances for geometric representation

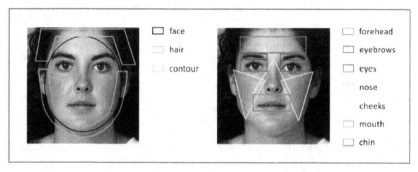

Fig. 4. The 10 regions of interest

ways, including performing identification using a set of face information, narrowing the search area of hard biometrics by comparing it to those that fit a specific soft biometric description, and supplementing hard biometric feature evidence. Some existing related works of race classification are shown in (Table 4).

Table 4. Several Related Works in Race Classification

Authors	Year	Datasets	Datasets Description	Supported Races	Used Techniques
Becerra et al. [106]	2018	EGA	integrates different single-race datasets (FERET, FRGC, CASIA-Face V5, FEI, JAFFE, and Indian Face), containing 2 345 faces of three age groups and five races	Asian, Indian, African-American, Caucasian, and Latin	subdivides the faces into ten regions, uses multiple 2D/3D geometric invariants, using both the SVM and RF classifiers
GHULAM MUHAMMAD et al. [101]	2012	FERET	Support five races from FERET, each containing more than 50 subjects	Asian, Black-or-African-American, Hispanic, Asian-Middle-Eastern, White	Kruskal-Wallis as a feature selector. Combines the LBP, WLD, and City-block distance
Hengxin Chen et al. [104]	2017	OFD, FERET	selected 200 East Asian face images from (OFD), selected 200 Caucasian face images from FERET	East Asian, Caucasian	STASM landmarks extraction, Fused Adaboost training, Periocular Features of five local features
Lu et al. [107]	2004	Asian PF01, NLPR, AR and Yale	2630 faces	Asian and Non-Asian	Gaussian, LDA
Ou et al. [108]	2005	FERET		Asian and Non-Asian	PCA, ICA, SVM
Manesh et al. [109]	2010	FERET, CAS-PEAL	1691 faces	Asian and Non-Asian	Segmentation, Gabor, SVM
Roomi et al. [95]	2011	Yale, FERET	Faces of 250 subjects	Caucasian, Asian, African, American	Skin color feature, Adaboost
Xie et al. [94]	2012	MBGC	40000 faces	Caucasian, Asian, African,	Color feature, KCFA
Chen and Ross [88]	2013	MORPH, CAS-PEAL	750 faces	Caucasian, Asian, African,	Local gradient, Gabor
Salah et al. [110]	2013	EGA	746 faces	Caucasian, Asian, African, American	PCA, LBP, HaaR, KNN
Han et al. [111]	2014	MORPH2, PCSO	178219 faces	Black, white	inspiring features Biologically
Momin and Tapamo [112]	2016	MORPH, Indian faces	484 faces	Asian vs. Non-Asian	Gabor, K-mean, NB, SVM, MLP

(continued)

Table 4. (*continued*)

Authors	Year	Datasets	Datasets Description	Supported Races	Used Techniques
Anwar Naeem [113]	2017	Tested with multiple datasets	13394 faces	Caucasian, Asian, African, American	CNN for features extraction, SVM classifier
Masood et al. [114]	2018	) FERET	447 faces	Caucasian, Mongolian, Negroid	CNN and ANN
Mezzoudj Saliha et al. [89]	2018	CAS-PEAL, FERET	(34214 faces)	Asian / Non-Asian	LBP, Logistic regression
Khalil Khan et al. [115]		CAS-PEAL, FERET			Segmentation, DCNN
Muhammed et al. [116]		FERET		Eastern/Middle Asian, Hispanic Caucasian, African American	LBP and KNN
Roomi et al. [95]		FERET		Caucasian, Asian, African, American	skin information and Adaboost
Vo et al. [117]		VNFaces		Vietnamese and others	DCNNs
Darabant et al. [1]	2021		175,000 facial images	Afro-American, Asian, Caucasian, and Indian subjects	(up to 19 layers) of CNN
Khan et al. [115]	2021	-FERET -CAS-PEAL -VN Face -VMER	- 1199 - 99, 594 - 6100 - 3.3 million	-Asian, Non-Asian, Caucasian, African, and some sub-ethnic groups	DCNN with classes of (nose, hair, back, eyes, brows, skin, and mouth
Greco et al. [118]	2020	VMER	3,000,000 face images	East Asian, African American, Asian Indian, and Caucasian Latin	ResNet-50, Mobile Net v2VGG-16, and VGG-Face
Ahmed et al. [119]	2020	BUPT Equalised Face dataset for training -UTK and CFD for testing	1.3 M images	Caucasian, African, Asian and Indian	Six-layer CNN and VGG
AlBdairi et al. [120]	2020	-CASIA -LFW	3141 images	Chinese, Pakistan, Russian	CNN(12 layers)compared with VGG and v3
Pratama et al. [121]	2020		48 images	Indonesian Races	SVM K-Nearest
Masood et al. [114]	2018	) FERET	447 faces	Caucasian, Mongolian, Negroid	CNN and ANN
Mezzoudj Saliha et al. [89]	2018	CAS-PEAL, FERET	(34214 faces)	Asian / Non-Asian	LBP, Logistic regression
Anwar Naeem [113]	2017	Tested with multiple datasets	13394 faces	Caucasian, Asian, African, American	CNN for features extraction, SVM classifier
Momin and Tapamo[112]	2016	MORPH, Indian faces	484 faces	Asian and. Non-Asian	Gabor, K-mean, NB, SVM, MLP
Han et al. [111]	2014	MORPH2, PCSO	178219 faces	Black, white	inspiring features Biologically
Chen and Ross [88]	2013	MORPH, CAS-PEAL	750 faces	Caucasian, Asian, African,	Local gradient, Gabor

(*continued*)

Table 4. *(continued)*

Authors	Year	Datasets	Datasets Description	Supported Races	Used Techniques
Salah et al. [110]	2013	EGA	746 faces	Caucasian, Asian, African, American	PCA, LBP, HaaR, KNN
Xie et al. [94]	2012	MBGC	40000 faces	Caucasian, Asian, African,	Color feature, KCFA
Ghulam Muhammad et al. [101]	2012	FERET			A combination of LBP and WLD, Kruskal-Wallis face features selection algorithm, City-block distance for classification
Roomi et al. [95]	2011	Yale, FERET	Faces of 250 subjects	Caucasian, Asian, African, American	Skin color feature, Adaboost
Manesh et al. [109]	2010	FERET, CAS-PEAL	1691 faces	Asian and Non-Asian	Segmentation, Gabor, SVM
Ou et al. [108]	2005	FERET		Asian and Non-Asian	PCA, ICA, SVM
Lu et al. [107]	2004	Asian PF01, NLPR, AR and Yale	2630 faces	Asian and Non-Asian	Gaussian, LDA
Khalil Khan et al. [115]		CAS-PEAL, FERET			Segmentation, DCNN
Muhammed et al. [116]		FERET		Eastern/Middle Asian, Hispanic Caucasian, African American	LBP and KNN
Roomi et al. [95]		FERET		Caucasian, Asian, African, American	skin information and Adaboost
Vo et al. [117]		VN-Faces		Vietnamese and others	DCNNs

3.3   3D Face Analysis and Racial Face Classification

Recent advances in three-dimensional (3D) picture-capturing technologies have piqued interest in developing 3D image processing and analysis tools to go along with them. One such area of study is three-dimensional human face recognition, which has a broad range of applications, including automated subject identification, security, and human-computer interaction. Three-dimensional (3D) face recognition has an advantage over two-dimensional (2D) face recognition in that 3D facial images are more resistant to changes in facial position and ambient lighting conditions than 2D images. Human ethnicity characteristics give valuable information for anthropology research and auto-mated facial data analysis. When it comes to recognizing ethnicity, most people rely on their vision. When employing 2D photos, however, ethnicity classification in an auto-mated system is difficult. This is because the ethnicity classification process based on 2D imaging is influenced by a variety of elements such as lighting, make-up, and head postures. An ethnicity classification process based on 3D facial data, on the other hand, can produce more accurate findings. It is resistant to changes in texture.

With the advancements in 3D imaging technology, Liu [122] has presented an integration approach that uses both registered range images that characterize the surface shape and intensity images for ethnicity identifications (see Fig. 5). The author achieved 96.8% accuracy by using an SVM classifier to classify the faces. The proposed techniques are evaluated using a combination of two frontal 3D face databases.

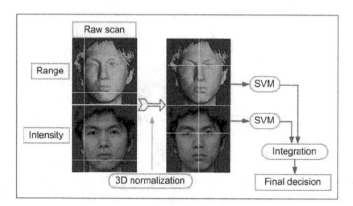

Fig. 5. Integration scheme of both range and intensity

Toderici et al. [103] proposed a subject retrieval using a metric function (Harr wavelet and CW-SSIM (structure similarity)) on deformed 3D meshes (only global shape information). Four classifiers are proposed in this work; KNN, kernelized KNN, multidimensional scaling (MDS), and learning based on wavelet coefficients. These classifiers are examined on FRGC v2.0 and achieved approximately 99% mean accuracy. Ocegueda et al. [105] provides measuring metrics to calculate the probability per vertex in 3D mesh being "discriminative" or "non-discriminative". This work used Gauss-Markov posterior marginals (GMPM) to find the most discriminative regions of the face (the estimated probabilities as feature scoring) and implement the proposed approach on only Asian and White from BU-3DFE and FRGC v1 databases. The author compared his results with Toderici et al. [103] to defend his achieved accuracy. Zhong et al. [124] firstly used Gabor features and learned the visual codebook (LVC) method to compute the visual codes for eastern and western people, then measured both the merging and mapping distances (by calculating the max distance function). In the second level, the author proposed a "membership function" to calculate the membership degree of both eastern and western groups for the used faces from the FGRC v2 dataset. Ding et al. [125] combined the use of 3D shape and the Boosted Local Texture) to enhance the race-based classification. To extract the local texture, the author used the Oriented Gradient Maps (OGMs) to highlight ethnicity-related local texture and used Adaboost to add an associated weight for individuals. Experiments are implemented on the FRGC v2 dataset to categorize Asians and Non-Asians with an accuracy of 98.3%. Berretti et al. [126] models the 3D faces of nose tip centered multiple stripes, where most of the points of each stripe remain within the same stripe though the facial expression changes. The author used nine stripes of (1 cm) width as a discriminative region between different individuals. To accommodate the expression deformation, the author furtherly segments each stripe into; lower (L), upper-left (UL), and upper-right (UR) concerning the coordinates of the nose tip (See Fig. 6). This work used 3D Weighted Walkthroughs (3DWW) approach to measure the (inter-stripe 3DWW) and (intra-stripe 3DWW) distances, it implemented the proposed measuring on (SHREC 2008) dataset and the FRGC v2 dataset and calculated the spatial displacement of these iso-geodesic stripes).

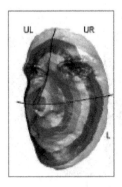

Fig. 6. The three parts of the face stripe

Some advantages of implementing the 3D model in race classification are summarized by the following essential point:

- The key benefit of using a 3D model is that it keeps all of the information about the face geometry [126].
- In a 3D face model, facial features are represented by local and global curvatures, which can be considered a person's true signature [126].
- 3D face recognition systems could accurately recognize human face details even under dim lights and with variant facial positions, occlusion, and expressions.
- Because a more precise representation of the facial features leads to a possibly stronger discriminating power, 3D face recognition is also growing to be a further evolution of the 2D recognition challenge [126].
- 3D face recognition can achieve better accuracy by measuring the geometrical characteristics of rigid features on the face.
- 3D face recognition can easily transform the head pose into a known view.
- 3D face recognition can deform the face shape while keeping its appearance and texture.
- 3D registration can help to predict and build the missed parts of the human face based on face symmetry.
- The majority of 3D scanners capture both a 3D model and the texture associated with it. This enables the output of pure 3D matches to be combined with the output of more traditional 2D face recognition algorithms (Table 5).

3.4 Deep Learning Advances in Race Recognition

For effective ethnicity recognition and categorization, machine learning and deep learning technologies have proven to be beneficial. In the face recognition literature, there

Table 5. Several Existed 3D Race Classification

Author	Features	Classifier	Accuracy	Dataset	Races
Lu et al. [122]	Holistic: Registered Range and Intensity	Two SVMs	96.8%	Combination of UND and MSU	Asian, Non-Asian
Toderici et al. [103]	A metric function (Harr wavelet and structure similarity	KNN, kernelized KNN, MDS, and learning based on wavelet coefficients	99.5%	FRGC 2.0	Eastern, Western, Asian, Non-Asian
Ocegueda et al.	the estimated probabilities as feature scoring	The linear classifier LIBLINEAR	Relatively high	Only Asian and White from BU-3DFE and FRGC v1	Asian and White
Zhong et al. [123]	extracted intrinsic discriminative data from 3D faces using Gabor filters and builds the LVC	(1) K-means clustering (2) Comparing the Gabor feature to the learned codes	89.65	FRGC v2	Eastern, western
Ding et al. [124]	Combination of (Holistic Shape and Texture) using OGMs and Adaboost to extract the texture	Decision Tree	98.3%	Experimented on FRGC v2, and validated on BU-3DFE	Asian, Non-Asian
Berretti et al. [125]	Graph model: Reginal segmentation into multiple stripes	3D Weighted Walkthroughs (3DWW) and measuring the distance between iso-geodesic stripes		(SHREC 2008) and (FRGC v2)	None (analysis work)

are two types of methods: local and global methods. A literature direction suggested training a model that parses each facial part individually, such as the lips, nose, and skin. On the other hand, several other studies linked independent CNNs by first finding face sections and then transferring data in both coarse and fine directions. Furthermore, many researchers have recently shifted their focus away from popular race groups like African Americans, Caucasians, and Asians and toward sub-ethnic groups like Koreans and Japanese, motivating them to investigate the advanced abilities of recent Deep Learning to accurately detect race in realistic situations. During disasters, Deep Neural Networks (DNNs) were trained online using a new learning process called stochastic gradient descent. Deep learning-based smart platforms can efficiently gather, handle, mine, and analyze huge volumes of data, as well as automatically create good representations from raw data, thanks to their multilayers. Deep learning's breakthroughs also pique the interest of researchers due to its multiple applications in computer vision, natural language processing, and speech processing. CNN's, which are a type of deep learning model, has recently produced some promising results in large-scale image and video recognition. Because of its exceptional performance on ImageNet data, the VGG model, which was first proposed in 2015, has been frequently used in computer vision studies.

4   Conclusion

This work investigates the deep learning applicability in 3D facial features analysis to recognize the human gender and ethnicity features. We discussed the issues and motivations in race perception, as well as the conceptual details of the racial processing of human faces. Then, inside the unified learning scenario, several categorizing tables are presented to summarize the models of representing the face features, compare its performance metrics, and investigate the existing racial databases. Finally, we highlight the opportunities and existing obstacles, as well as potentially relevant cross-cutting topics and research directions, and issues of learning the race from the human face to motivate future study in this field. Tasks involving biometric recognition and computer vision, such as 3D face recognition, are processed by the deep learning-based 3D face recognition approaches over various 3D face forms such as depth images, normal maps, mesh, and more. The pre-trained VGG-16 is one of the best Deep Learning to mitigate some limitations of traditional neural learning approaches and it shows a good example to learn discriminative features that are effective for distinguishing different individuals according to their race and gender.

References

1. Darabant, A.S., Borza, D., Danescu, R.: Recognizing human races through machine learning—a multi-network, multi-features study. Mathematics 9(2), 195 (2021). https://doi.org/10.3390/math9020195
2. Lyons, M., et al.: Coding facial expressions with gabor wavelets. In: Proceedings Third IEEE International Conference on Automatic Face and Gesture Recognition. IEEE (1998)

3. Mayer, C., Eggers, M., Radig, B.: Cross-database evaluation for facial expression recognition. Pattern Recognit Image Anal. **24**(1), 124–132 (2014). https://doi.org/10.1134/S10546 61814010106
4. Bakshi, S., Raman, R., Sa, P.K.: Lip pattern recognition based on local feature extraction. In: 2011 Annual IEEE India Conference. IEEE (2011)
5. Barpanda, S.S., Majhi, B., Sa, P.K.: Region based feature extraction from non-cooperative iris images using triplet half-band filter bank. Optics Laser Technol. **72**, 6–14 (2015)
6. Kumar, A., Kaur, A., Kumar, M.: Face detection techniques: a review. Artif. Intell. Rev. **52**(2), 927–948 (2019). https://doi.org/10.1007/s10462-018-9650-2
7. Momin, H., Tapamo, J.-R.: A comparative study of a face components based model of ethnic classification using gabor filters. Appl. Math. Inf. Sci. **10**(6), 2255–2265 (2016)
8. Choi, J.Y., Lee, B.: Ensemble of deep convolutional neural networks with Gabor face representations for face recognition. IEEE Trans. Image Process. **29**, 3270–3281 (2020). https://doi.org/10.1109/TIP.2019.2958404
9. Ahmed, S., et al.: Optimum feature selection with particle swarm optimization to face recognition system using Gabor wavelet transform and deep learning. BioMed Res. Int. **2021**, 1–13 (2021). https://doi.org/10.1155/2021/6621540
10. Sunitha, G., et al.: Intelligent deep learning based ethnicity recognition and classification using facial images. Image Vision Comput. **121**, 104404 (2022)
11. Sahan, J.M., Abbas, E.I., Abood, Z.M.: A facial recognition using a combination of a novel one dimension deep CNN and LDA. Mater. Today: Proc. (2021)
12. Bajrami, X., Gashi, B., Murturi, I.: Face recognition performance using linear discriminant analysis and deep neural networks. Int. J. Appl. Pattern Recogn. **5**(3), 240–250 (2018)
13. Dutta, K., et al.: 3D face recognition using a fusion of PCA and ICA convolution descriptors. Neural Process. Lett. **54**, 1–21 (2022)
14. Xi, M., et al.: Local binary pattern network: a deep learning approach for face recognition. In: 2016 IEEE International Conference on Image Processing (ICIP). IEEE (2016)
15. Zhang, H., et al.: A face recognition method based on LBP feature for CNN. In: 2017 IEEE 2nd Advanced Information Technology, Electronic and Automation Control Conference (IAEAC). IEEE (2017)
16. Lahasan, B.M., et al.: Recognizing faces prone to occlusions and common variations using optimal face subgraphs. Appl. Math. Comput. **283**, 316–332 (2016)
17. Brunelli, R., Poggio, T.: Face recognition: features versus templates. IEEE Trans. Pattern Anal. Mach. Intell. **15**(10), 1042–1052 (1993)
18. https://en.wikipedia.org/wiki/Histogram_of_oriented_gradients
19. Lowe, D.G.: Distinctive image features from scale-invariant keypoints. Int. J. Comput. Vision **60**(2), 91–110 (2004)
20. Chen, J., et al.: WLD: a robust local image descriptor. IEEE Trans. Pattern Anal. Mach. Intell. **32**(9), 1705–1720 (2009)
21. Payal, P., Goyani, M.M.: A comprehensive study on face recognition: methods and challenges. Imaging Sci. J. **68**(2), 114–127 (2020)
22. Ojala, T., Pietikäinen, M., Harwood, D.: A comparative study of texture measures with classification based on featured distributions. Pattern Recogn. **29**(1), 51–59 (1996)
23. Gross, R., Matthews, I., Baker, S.: Appearance-based face recognition and light-fields. IEEE Trans. Pattern Anal. Mach. Intell. **26**(4), 449–465 (2004)
24. Smith, R.S., Windeatt, T.: Facial expression detection using filtered local binary pattern features with ECOC classifiers and platt scaling. In: Proceedings of the First Workshop on Applications of Pattern Analysis. PMLR (2010)
25. Tan, X., Triggs, B.: Enhanced local texture feature sets for face recognition under difficult lighting conditions. IEEE Trans. Image Process. **19**(6), 1635–1650 (2010)

26. Turk, M., Pentland, A.: Eigenfaces for recognition. J. Cogn. Neurosci. **3**(1), 71–86 (1991). https://doi.org/10.1162/jocn.1991.3.1.71
27. Susan, S., et al.: Fuzzy match index for scale-invariant feature transform (SIFT) features with application to face recognition with weak supervision. IET Image Process. **9**(11), 951–958 (2015)
28. Blanz, V., Vetter, T.: A morphable model for the synthesis of 3D faces. In: Proceedings of the 26th Annual Conference on Computer Graphics and Interactive Techniques (1999)
29. Lin, S.-H., Kung, S.-Y., Lin, L.-J.: Face recognition/detection by probabilistic decision-based neural network. IEEE Trans. Neural Netw. **8**(1), 114–132 (1997)
30. Pentland, A., Moghaddam, B., Starner, T.: View-based and modular eigenspaces for face recognition, pp. 16–30 (1994)
31. Belhumeur, P.N., Hespanha, J.P., Kriegman, D.J.: Eigenfaces vs. fisherfaces: recognition using class specific linear projection. IEEE Trans. Pattern Anal. Mach. Intell. **19**(7), 711–720 (1997)
32. Bartlett, M.S., Movellan, J.R., Sejnowski, T.J.: Face recognition by independent component analysis. IEEE Trans. Neural Netw. **13**(6), 1450–1464 (2002)
33. Bay, H., Tuytelaars, T., Van Gool, L.: Surf: speeded up robust features. In: Leonardis, A., Bischof, H., Pinz, A. (eds.) Computer Vision – ECCV 2006: 9th European Conference on Computer Vision, Graz, Austria, May 7-13, 2006. Proceedings, Part I, pp. 404–417. Springer, Heidelberg (2006). https://doi.org/10.1007/11744023_32
34. Yin, Q., Tang, X., Sun, J.: An associate-predict model for face recognition. In: CVPR 2011. IEEE (2011)
35. Konen, W., von der Malsburg, C.: Learning to generalize from single examples in dynamic link architecture. In: Buzsáki, G., Llinás, R., Singer, W., Berthoz, A., Christen, Y. (eds.) Temporal Coding in the Brain, pp. 205–219. Springer, Heidelberg (1994). https://doi.org/10.1007/978-3-642-85148-3_12
36. Cootes, T.F., Walker, K., Taylor, C.J.: View-based active appearance models. In: Proceedings Fourth IEEE International Conference on Automatic Face and Gesture Recognition (Cat. No. PR00580). IEEE (2000)
37. Tu, J., Zhang, Z., Zeng, Z., et al.: Face localization via hierarchical condensation with fisher boosting feature selection. In: Proceedings of the 2004 IEEE Computer Society Conference on Computer Vision and Pattern Recognition, vol. 2, p. II (2004)
38. Liu, C., Wechsler, H.: Face recognition using evolutionary pursuit. In: European Conference on Computer vision. Springer, Heidelberg (1998). https://doi.org/10.1007/BFb0054767
39. Sheikh, Z.G., Thakare, V.M.: Wavelet based feature extraction technique for face recognition and retrieval : a review (2016)
40. Wiskott, L., et al.: Face recognition by elastic bunch graph matching. IEEE Trans. Pattern Anal. Mach. Intell. **19**(7), 775–779 (1997)
41. Srisuk, S., et al.: Face authentication using the trace transform. In: 2003 IEEE Computer Society Conference on Computer Vision and Pattern Recognition, 2003. Proceedings, vol. 1. IEEE (2003)
42. Yang, M.-H.: Kernel eigenfaces vs. kernel fisherfaces: face recognition using kernel methods. Fgr **2** (2002)
43. Queirolo, C.C., et al.: 3D face recognition using simulated annealing and the surface interpenetration measure. IEEE Trans. Pattern Anal. Mach. Intell. **32**(2), 206–219 (2009)
44. Liu, M., et al.: Partial least squares regression on grassmannian manifold for emotion recognition. In: Proceedings of the 15th ACM on International Conference on Multimodal Interaction (2013)
45. Lei, Z., Pietikäinen, M., Li, S.Z.: Learning discriminant face descriptor. IEEE Trans. Pattern Anal. Mach. Intell. **36**(2), 289–302 (2013)

46. Akhtar, Z., Rattani, A.: A face in any form: new challenges and opportunities for face recognition technology. Computer **50**(4), 80–90 (2017)
47. Deng, J., et al.: Arcface: additive angular margin loss for deep face recognition. In: Proceedings of the IEEE/CVF Conference on Computer Vision and Pattern Recognition (2019)
48. Wang, H., et al.: Cosface: Large margin cosine loss for deep face recognition. In: Proceedings of the IEEE Conference on Computer Vision and Pattern Recognition (2018).
49. Georgescu, M.-I., Ionescu, R.D., Popescu, M.: Local learning with deep and handcrafted features for facial expression recognition. IEEE Access **7**, 64827–64836 (2019)
50. Lewis, M.: Face-space-R: towards a unified account of face recognition. Vis. Cogn. **11**(1), 29–69 (2004)
51. Abudarham, N., Yovel, G.: Reverse engineering the face space: discovering the critical features for face identification. J. Vis. **16**(3), 40 (2016)
52. Le, Q.V.: Building high-level features using large scale unsupervised learning. In: 2013 IEEE International Conference on Acoustics, Speech and Signal Processing, pp. 8595–8598 (2013).https://doi.org/10.1109/ICASSP.2013.6639343
53. Rehman, A., Saba, T.: Neural networks for document image preprocessing: state of the art. Artif. Intell. Rev. **42**(2), 253–273 (2012). https://doi.org/10.1007/s10462-012-9337-z
54. Kim, P.: Convolutional neural network MATLAB deep learning, pp. 121–147. Apress, Berkeley (2017)
55. Zhuang, L., et al.: Sparse illumination learning and transfer for single-sample face recognition with image corruption and misalignment. Int. J. Comput. Vision **114**(2), 272–287 (2015)
56. Le, H.A., Kakadiaris, I.A.: UHDB31: a dataset for better understanding face recognition across pose and illumination variation. In: Proceedings of the IEEE International Conference on Computer Vision Workshops (2017)
57. Han, H., et al.: A comparative study on illumination preprocessing in face recognition. Pattern Recogn. **46**(6), 1691–1699 (2013)
58. Ochoa-Villegas, M.A., et al.: Addressing the illumination challenge in two-dimensional face recognition: a survey. IET Comput. Vision **9**(6), 978–992 (2015)
59. Yu, Y.-F., et al.: Discriminative multi-layer illumination-robust feature extraction for face recognition. Pattern Recogn. **67**, 201–212 (2017)
60. Wang, J.-W., et al.: Illumination compensation for face recognition using adaptive singular value decomposition in the wavelet domain. Inf. Sci. **435**, 69–93 (2018)
61. Liu, H.-D., et al.: Local histogram specification for face recognition under varying lighting conditions. Image Vision Comput. **32**(5), 335–347 (2014)
62. Gross, R., et al.: Multi-pie. Image Vision Comput. **28**(5), 807–813 (2010)
63. Huang, G.B., et al.: Labeled faces in the wild: a database for studying face recognition in unconstrained environments. In: Workshop on faces in'Real-Life'Images: Detection, Alignment, and Recognition (2008)
64. Lui, Y.M., et al.: Preliminary studies on the good, the bad, and the ugly face recognition challenge problem. In: 2012 IEEE Computer Society Conference on Computer Vision and Pattern Recognition Workshops. IEEE (2012)
65. Yi, D., et al.: Learning face representation from scratch(2014).. arXiv preprint arXiv:1411.7923
66. Phillips, P.J., et al.: Overview of the face recognition grand challenge. In: 2005 IEEE Computer Society Conference on Computer Vision and pattern Recognition (CVPR 2005), vol. 1. IEEE (2005)
67. Ng, H.-W., Winkler, S.: A data-driven approach to cleaning large face datasets. In: 2014 IEEE International Conference on Image Processing (ICIP). IEEE (2014)

68. Chinese Academy of Sciences Institute of Automation. CASIA-3D FaceV1 (2008). http://biometrics.idealtest.org

69. Klare, B.F., et al.: Pushing the frontiers of unconstrained face detection and recognition: Iarpa janus benchmark a. In: Proceedings of the IEEE Conference on Computer Vision and Pattern Recognition (2015)

70. Toderici, G., Evangelopoulos, G., Fang, T., Theoharis, T., Kakadiaris, I.A.: UHDB11 database for 3D-2D face recognition. In: Klette, R., Rivera, M., Shin'ichi S. (eds.) Image and Video Technology, pp. 73–86. Springer, Heidelberg (2014). https://doi.org/10.1007/978-3-642-53842-1_7

71. Kemelmacher-Shlizerman, I., et al.: The megaface benchmark: 1 million faces for recognition at scale. In: Proceedings of the IEEE Conference on Computer Vision and Pattern Recognition (2016)

72. Guo, Y., et al.: Ms-celeb-1m: challenge of recognizing one million celebrities in the real world. Electron. Imag. 2016(11), 1–6 (2016)

73. Nech, A., Kemelmacher-Shlizerman, I.: Level playing field for million scale face recognition. In: Proceedings of the IEEE Conference on Computer Vision and Pattern Recognition (2017)

74. Grgic, M., Delac, K., Grgic, S.: SCface–surveillance cameras face database. Multimedia tools Appl. 51(3), 863–879 (2011)

75. Savran, A., et al.: Bosphorus database for 3D face analysis. In: Schouten, B., Juul, N.C., Drygajlo, A., Tistarelli, M. (eds.) Biometrics and Identity Management, pp. 47–56. Springer, Heidelberg (2008). https://doi.org/10.1007/978-3-540-89991-4_6

76. Vijayan, V., Bowyer, K., Flynn, P.: 3D twins and expression challenge. In: 2011 IEEE International Conference on Computer Vision Workshops (ICCV Workshops). IEEE (2011)

77. Colombo, A., Cusano, C., Schettini, R.: UMB-DB: a database of partially occluded 3D faces. In: 2011 IEEE International Conference on Computer Vision workshops (ICCV Workshops). IEEE (2011)

78. Bagdanov, A.D., Del Bimbo, A., Masi, I.: The florence 2d/3d hybrid face dataset. In: Proceedings of the 2011 Joint ACM Workshop on Human Gesture and Behavior Understanding (2011)

79. Savran, A., Sankur, B.: Non-rigid registration based model-free 3D facial expression recognition. Comput. Vis. Image Underst. 162, 146–165 (2017)

80. Lopes, A.T., et al.: Facial expression recognition with convolutional neural networks: coping with few data and the training sample order. Pattern Recogn 61, 610–628 (2017)

81. Mi, J.-X., Liu, T.: Multi-step linear representation-based classification for face recognition. IET Comput. Vision 10(8), 836–841 (2016)

82. Li, Y., et al.: Expression-insensitive 3D face recognition by the fusion of multiple subject-specific curves. Neurocomputing 275, 1295–1307 (2018)

83. Zhou, H., Lam, K.-M.: Age-invariant face recognition based on identity inference from appearance age. Pattern Recogn 76, 191–202 (2018)

84. Sable, A.H., Talbar, S.N., Dhirbasi, H.A.: Recognition of plastic surgery faces and the surgery types: an approach with entropy based scale invariant features. J. King Saud Univ.-Comput. Inf. Sci. 31(4), 554–560 (2019)

85. Bouguila, J., Khochtali, H.: Facial plastic surgery and face recognition algorithms: interaction and challenges. a scoping review and future directions. J. Stomatol. Oral Maxillofacial Surg. 121(6), 696–703 (2020)

86. Zeng, D., Veldhuis, R., Spreeuwers, L.: A survey of face recognition techniques under occlusion (2020). arXiv preprint arXiv:2006.11366

87. Barnshaw, J.: Race. In: Schaefer, R.T. (ed.) Encyclopedia of Race, Ethnicity, and Society, vol. 1,pp. 1091–1093 SAGE Publications (2008). ISBN 978–1-45-226586-5

88. Chen, C., Ross, A.: Local gradient Gabor pattern (LGGP) with applications in face recognition, cross-spectral matching, and soft biometrics. In: Biometric and Surveillance Technology for Human and Activity Identification X, vol. 8712. International Society for Optics and Photonics (2013)
89. Saliha, M., Ali, B., Rachid, S.: Towards large-scale face-based race classification on spark framework. Multimedia Tools Appl. **78**(18), 26729–26746 (2019). https://doi.org/10.1007/s11042-019-7672-7
90. Sharma, K., Khanal, K., Mansur, D.I.: Variations in total facial index among students of Kathmandu University School of Medical Sciences. Nepal Med. Coll. J. **16**(2–5), 173–176 (2014)
91. Oloyede, M.O., Hancke, G.P., Myburgh, H.C.: A review on face recognition systems: recent approaches and challenges. Multimedia Tools Appl. **79**(37–38), 27891–27922 (2020). https://doi.org/10.1007/s11042-020-09261-2
92. Calder, A.J., Young, A.W.: Understanding the recognition of facial identity and facial expression. Nat. Rev. Neurosci. **6**(8), 641–651 (2005)
93. Fu, S., He, H., Hou, Z.-G.: Learning race from face: a survey. IEEE Trans. Pattern Anal. Mach. Intell. **36**(12), 2483–2509 (2014)
94. Xie, Y., Luu, K., Savvides, M.: A robust approach to facial ethnicity classification on large scale face databases. In: 2012 IEEE Fifth International Conference on Biometrics: Theory, Applications and Systems (BTAS). IEEE (2012).
95. Roomi, S.M.M., et al.: Race classification based on facial features. In: 2011 Third National Conference on Computer Vision, Pattern Recognition, Image Processing and Graphics. IEEE (2011)
96. Tariq, U., Hu, Y., Huang, T.S.: Gender and ethnicity identification from silhouetted face profiles. In: 2009 16th IEEE International Conference on Image Processing (ICIP). IEEE (2009)
97. Yin, L., Jia, J., Morrissey, J.: Towards race-related face identification: research on skin color transfer. In: Sixth IEEE International Conference on Automatic Face and Gesture Recognition, Proceedings. IEEE (2004)
98. Natu, V., Raboy, D., O'Toole, A.J.: Neural correlates of own-and other-race face perception: Spatial and temporal response differences. Neuroimage **54**(3), 2547–2555 (2011)
99. Tin, H.H.K., Sein, M.M.: Race identification for face images. ACEEE Int. J. Inform. Tech **1**(02), 35–37 (2011)
100. Awwad, A., Ahmad, A.: Arabic race classification of face images. Int. J. Comput. Technol. **4**(2a1), 234–239 (2013)
101. Muhammad, G., et al.: Race classification from face images using local descriptors. Int. J. Artif. Intell. Tools **21**(05), 1250019 (2012)
102. Shen, L., Bai, L.: A review on Gabor wavelets for face recognition. Pattern Anal. Appl. **9**(2), 273–292 (2006)
103. Toderici, G., et al.: Ethnicity-and gender-based subject retrieval using 3-D face-recognition techniques. Int. J. Comput. Vision **89**(2), 382–391 (2010)
104. Chen, H., et al.: A novel race classification method based on periocular features fusion. Int. J. Pattern Recogn. Artif. Intell. **31**(08), 1750026 (2017)
105. Ocegueda, O., et al.: 3D face discriminant analysis using Gauss-Markov posterior marginals. IEEE Trans. Pattern Anal. Mach. Intell. **35**(3), 728–739 (2012)
106. Becerra-Riera, F., Llanes, N.M., Morales-González, A., Méndez-Vázquez, H., Tistarelli, M.: On combining face local appearance and geometrical features for race classification. In: Vera-Rodriguez, R., Fierrez, J., Morales, A. (eds.) CIARP 2018. LNCS, vol. 11401, pp. 567–574. Springer, Cham (2019). https://doi.org/10.1007/978-3-030-13469-3_66
107. Lu, X., Jain, A.K.: Ethnicity identification from face images. In: Proceedings of SPIE, vol. 5404 (2004)

108. Ou, Y., et al.: A real time race classification system. In: 2005 IEEE International Conference on Information Acquisition. IEEE (2005)
109. Manesh, F.S., Ghahramani, M., Tan, Y.P.: Facial part displacement effect on template-based gender and ethnicity classification. In: 2010 11th International Conference on Control Automation Robotics & Vision. IEEE (2010)
110. Salah, S.H., Du, H., Al-Jawad, N.: Fusing local binary patterns with wavelet features for ethnicity identification. In: Proceedings of World Academy of Science, Engineering and Technology, vol. 79. World Academy of Science, Engineering and Technology (WASET) (2013)
111. Han, H., Otto, C., Liu, X., Jain, A.K.: Demographic estimation from face images: human vs. machine performance. IEEE Trans. Pattern Anal. Mach. Intell. 37(6), 1148–1161 (2015). https://doi.org/10.1109/TPAMI.2014.2362759
112. Momin H, Tapamo J-R (2016) A comparative study of a face components based model of ethnic classification using gabor filters
113. Anwar, I., Ul Islam, N.: Learned features are better for ethnicity classification(2017). arXiv preprint arXiv:1709.07429
114. Masood, S., Gupta, S., Wajid, A., Gupta, S., Ahmed, M.: Prediction of human ethnicity from facial images using neural networks. In: Data (2018)
115. Khan, K., et al.: A Facial Feature Discovery Framework for Race Classification Using Deep Learning (2021). arXiv preprint arXiv:2104.02471
116. Vo, T., Nguyen, T., Le, C.T.: Race recognition using deep convolutional neural networks. Symmetry 10(11), 564 (2018)
117. Liu, W., et al.: Ssd: single shot multibox detector. In: Leibe, B., Matas, J., Sebe, N., Welling, M. (eds.) Computer Vision – ECCV 2016: 14th European Conference, Amsterdam, The Netherlands, October 11–14, 2016, Proceedings, Part I, pp. 21–37. Springer, Cham (2016). https://doi.org/10.1007/978-3-319-46448-0_2
118. Greco, A., et al.: Benchmarking deep network architectures for ethnicity recognition using a new large face dataset. Mach. Vision Appl. 31(7), 1–13 (2020)
119. Ahmed, M.A., Choudhury, R.D., Kashyap, K.: Race estimation with deep networks. J. King Saud Univ.-Comput. Inf. Sci. 34, 4579–4591 (2020)
120. Ahmed, J.A., AlBdairi, Z.X., Alghaili, M.: Identifying ethnics of people through face recognition: a deep CNN approach. Sci. Program. 2020, 1–7 (2020). https://doi.org/10.1155/2020/6385281
121. Pratama, I.S., Kurniadi, F.I.: Ethnicity classification based on facial features using viola-jones algorithm. IJNMT (Int. J. New Media Technol.) 7(1), 39–42 (2020)
122. Lu, X., Chen, H., Jain, A.K.: Multimodal facial gender and ethnicity identification. In: International Conference on Biometrics. Springer, Heidelberg (2006)
123. Zhong, C., Sun, Z., Tan, T.: Fuzzy 3D face ethnicity categorization. In: Tistarelli, M., Nixon, M.S. (eds.) Advances in Biometrics, pp. 386–393. Springer, Heidelberg (2009). https://doi.org/10.1007/978-3-642-01793-3_40
124. Ding, H., Huang, D., Wang, Y., Chen, L.: Facial ethnicity classification based on boosted local texture and shape descriptions. In: 2013 10th IEEE International Conference and Workshops on Automatic Face and Gesture Recognition (FG), pp. 1–6. IEEE (2013)
125. Berretti, S., Del Bimbo, A., Pala, P.: 3D face recognition using isogeodesic stripes. IEEE Trans. Pattern Anal. Mach. Intell. 32(12), 2162–2177 (2010)
126. Abate, A.F., et al.: 2D and 3D face recognition: a survey. Pattern Recogn. Lett. 28(14), 1885–1906 (2007)

Multi-agents as Data Mining Classifiers and Crawlers to Get Intelligent E-Advertisements

Hanan Q. Jaleel[1], Jane J. Stephan[2] , and Sinan A. Naji[3][(✉)]

[1] Baghdad College of Medical Sciences, Baghdad, Iraq
[2] Al-Esraa University College, Baghdad, Iraq
[3] University of Information Technology and Communications, Baghdad, Iraq
dr.sinannaji@uoitc.edu.iq

Abstract. E-advertisement, also called online advertisement, is an advertisement type that utilizes the internet to convey its marketing to customers. Multi-agent systems are considered a subdomain of Artificial Intelligence that has witnessed fast development due to their flexibility to resolve complicated problems . This paper suggests a technique that utilizes intelligent software multi-agents as data mining classifiers and crawlers inside them, in order to classify the user query products keywords to correct the class number of the dataset inside every agent. The scientific value of this work is to improve marketing in such a way that the agent whose dataset confirms the best keywords for a user's query will be chosen to retrieve ad URLs from their dataset using the crawler algorithm to satisfy the needs of customers . In addition, the agent crawler can crawl the web to get the advertisements that most match the user query. The proposed system classifies the dataset inside each agent with several machine-learning classifiers such as Decision Tree, KNN, Random Forest, and Naive Bayes, with evaluating performance metrics for them. The usage of several classifiers shows that the Random Forest is the best classifier with the highest evaluation metrics, and used to be an online real-time classifier inside each agent.

Keywords: Multi-Agents · Data Mining · Classification Algorithms · E-Advertisements · Web Crawlers

1 Introduction

E-advertisement is highly important as a type of advertising that utilizes the internet and web, for the intention of marketing messages delivery that engages the consumers to read and further create more interest for clicking the thread. E-advertisements aid in merchandise and selling the services and products via colorful and interacting catalogs, and supply the public with available information. In addition, it allows consumers to make regional or global purchases [1, 2]. Electronic or online advertisements are more interesting to consumers since advertisers concentrate on coinciding with the consumer's interests. Furthermore, e-advertisements can occur simultaneously in a number

A. M. Al-Bakry et al. (Eds.): NTICT 2022, CCIS 1764, pp. 107–124, 2023.
https://doi.org/10.1007/978-3-031-35442-7_6

of varieties involving sound, video, text, or a combination of all of them. Instances of e-advertisements involve ads that appear on search engine pages, media advertisements, banner advertisements, as well as e-mail marketing, involving spam e-mail [3, 4].

Multi-agent systems MAS are considered as systems involving a group of interactive elements called agents. These agents behave as entire autonomous elements that can collaborate with other agents and determine how and what to achieve various types of functions to accomplish their goals in the environment [5, 6]. MAS can be regarded as an agent network that participates in their knowledge and collaborates with each other [7, 8]. Moreover, several MAS paradigms are constructed such that the main problem is subdivided into numerous tractable sub-problems, which can be furthermore partitioned into various agents solving problems with their own objectives. MAS can be classified in the computer science subdomain, which relies in general on Artificial Intelligence (AI) principles and the idea of distributed systems.

Due to the exponential increase in the number of agents and their dissimilarity and diverse collections, a participating framework should exist to aid the proper data sharing and collaboration among agents. The message's semantics is important to ensure that the agent's communication has a similar meaning of interchanging information. The agent communication language ACL provides this shared framework. ACL should assure consistency which denotes that similar performatives should involve similar semantics. ACL also has to assure affection and closeness which means that the messages should utilize the same words to tell the same things [9, 10]. Moreover, ACL is required to simplify the collaboration and communication among agents such as to connect their goals and beliefs. ACL should allow agents to support other agents to accomplish objectives, notice their work, declare their advancement, reject performing tasks, and confirm accomplishing objectives for neighbor's agents [9, 11].

Text and document classification is an essential learning issue that is the main part of many information retrievals and management processes. Text classification is the process of automatically arranging a collection of documents or text records into classes from a pre-identified set. This process has numerous applications, particularly for arranging, categorizing, exploring as well as expressing a massive volume of information [12, 13]. The classification task is to design a classifier model that is appropriate for present data not only to supply structural coherence but also to simplify data retrieving. Document classification is the process of partitioning documents into some classes or groups. In each class, a higher similarity degree exists while the similarity of documents that are in various classes should be as small as possible. The classification task can be partitioned into two types: supervised and unsupervised. In the supervised classification type, labeled documents can be gathered into pre-identified categories. A classifier model can be built depending on the existing data samples that rely on assigning the unlabeled data samples to their particular categories [13–15].

Broadly, machine learning (ML) techniques are employed in achieving the text clarification issue. These methods can be partitioned primarily into supervised and unsupervised approaches [16]. For supervised algorithms, each dataset example consists of the input data object and the desired result. A supervised approach dissolves the training dataset and generates a classifier model that is utilized to map other examples. The supervised technique tries to learn a model that is utilized in anticipating the outcome of the tested example [16–18]. There are many supervised machine learning approaches that are employed in the classification problem, for example, Naive Bayes, Random Forest, Decision Tree, and K-Nearest Neighbors [19–21].

A web crawler is a software that browses the web in a methodical, regular and automated way. The World Wide Web has a graphical framework such that the web page's hyperlinks can be utilized to open other pages. Via following up the web-linked framework, the crawler can navigate numerous new pages beginning from the first webpage [22]. The web crawler can transfer from one page to another using the page's graphical structure. The crawlers may also be called web spiders and spider bots. These programs are designated to retrieve pages and add them to a local warehouse. Crawlers can be utilized mainly to make a copy of the visited web pages that are later handled via a search engine, which will perform an indexing process on the downloaded web pages, in order to aid the fast searching task. The function of the search engine is to save web page information, which is retrieved from the web using the crawler[23].

The web crawler works begin with a primary URLs collection called a URLs seed. The crawler downloads the pages to place them in the URLs seed and retrieves new links that exist in the downloaded web pages. The extracted pages are indexed and stored in the repository storage region, such that to retrieve them later when they are needed [23]. The retrieved URLs from the downloaded web pages are verified to see whether their relevant documents are downloaded or not. If there are not, the URLs are allocated to the crawler for additional downloading. This task is iterated until there are no URLs lost. Consequently, the crawler will repeatedly persist in adding new URLs to the search engine repository. The major function of the web crawler is to add new hyperlinks to the frontier and select a frontier URL for furthermore handling after each iterative step [24].

The main contribution of this paper is the development of intelligent software multi-agents as data mining classifiers while using crawlers inside them, in order to classify the user query products keywords to correct the class of the dataset inside every agent.

The main idea behind improving the results is that the agent whose dataset best matches the user's query keywords is selected to retrieve the URLs of the advertisements from its dataset via the crawler algorithm. Furthermore, the crawler of the best agent can crawl the World Wide Web to obtain the e-advertisements web pages that meet and match the user query keywords. The proposed technique classifies the products dataset, as well as the smaller sub-datasets inside each agent with numerous data mining classifiers, and calculates the evaluation metrics for each one of them. The proposed method selects the classifier with the higher measurement values to be the online real-time classifier inside all agents.

The paper arrangement is as follows: Sect. 2 illustrates the related work. Section 3 introduces the proposed system and its work and functions. Section 4 presents the proposed system stages and explains in detail each one of them. Section 5 explains the results and discussion. Finally, Sect. 5 supplies a conclusion to the paper.

2 Related Work

In the work of Roopa et al. [25], a proposed mobile agent technique for online advertisements has been presented. The proposed technique achieves the advertising task of posting ads on different advertisement publishing websites at the same time. The proposed framework permits the users to fast advertisements accessing that are closest to their concerns, as well as saving network bandwidth and time in the task of publishing advertisements instead of using the traditional method. Roopa et al. [26] suggested an approach for digital watermarking disclosing and uncovering the approach for e-advertising, that embraces synchronous and cooperative mobile agents to handle and protect the advertisements, that consist of text and images, from illegitimate use by providing a copyright protection platform with 2-levels before publishing at different advertisements publishing websites. Al-Asfoor et al. [27], suggested a multi-agent system framework for resource advertisements that raises interoperability, overcomes the heterogeneity of nodes and provides the framework scalability. The proposed system presents an updated approach to modify the resource information that is effective concerning network communications. In addition, the proposed system provides a new technique for building and thereafter distributing resource advertisements to the neighbor nodes in order to reduce the network overhead by handling the nodes' subsets instead of the entire network. The proposed model has been applied and examined using a simulation environment that is network simulator NS-2. The evaluation of the proposed system has presented good results concerning the system performance and the impact of the advertisements overhead on the performance of the network.

In the research of Hong et al. [28], an agent-based online advertisement technique using the pull mechanism has been suggested. In this mechanism, customers are capable of actively declaring demands. Thus, advertisers can find out and anatomize probable customers for designating suitable advertisements. The proposed system also handles an agent-based online advertisements system that involves multi-agents to achieve the pull mechanism. There exist personal agents for customers to free and dispense the demands and requirements actively promoted by advertisers. In addition, the proposed system provides advertisers with animated conversation agents for interaction with customers in an expressive manner.

In [29], Kazeinko proposed a customized advertisement system that provides the most appropriate advertisements for a given user who navigates the website. To perform this aim, several data resources are handled in one consistent vector space, such as the website contents of publishers and advertisers, premier user sessions, the banners and clicks history, the current behavior of the user, as well as the advertisement policy raising specific campaigns. The multi-agent system that executes on the publisher's website is presented to arrange customized advertising. Every collaborative agent is in charge of a distinct and certain task: click-through data investigation, web usage mining, web content mining, user observing, advertising recommendation, and handling.

Pourpanah et al. [30], presented a multi-agent system using the Q-learning approach to handle classification issues. A confidence measure by utilizing an integration of Bayesian form and Q-learning is devised. Particularly, several learning agents compose a combination of Q-learning with neural networks, which can be used to formulate the proposed Q-learning MAS for classification purposes. The proposed system time complexity is resolved by using the big O-notation technique. Furthermore, several benchmarks are utilized to estimate the proposed system performance, which involves large and small datasets that might have noise. To resolve the proposed system's effectiveness in a statistical way, the bootstrap technique with a 95% trusting interval is utilized. The proposed system outcomes refer to the system's efficiency in integrating the learning agents' predictions to enhance the entire performance of classification.

In [31], González-Briones et al. proposed a multi-agent system that combines various methods in gaining, preprocessing, and handling images for gender and age classification has been provided. The proposed system has been examined in the building of an office. The use of a multi-agent system permits various functions to be achieved concurrently, and the effectiveness of various methods can be compared together. The system results show that a preprocessing phase is required in order to make the various classification approaches, such as Fisherfaces, Local Binary patterns, Eigenfaces, and Multilayer perceptron to function well. Fisherfaces technique has been verified to be more efficient than Multiplayer perceptron, as well as the time of training was short. For age classification, Fisherfaces provide better results compared to other systems' classification methods. The usage of filters has been permitted to decrease dimensionality; consequently, the workload has decreased, which leads the proposed system to achieve the classification task in real-time.

Zhou et al. [32] developed a technique that performs the multi-agent Q-learning calculation manageable by dealing with Q-function with respect to joint-action and state as a high dimensional and high order tensor and thereafter, resembles it with factorized pair interacting. Moreover, the proposed technique utilizes a complex deep learning framework for calculating the factorized Q-function, shares the parameters of the model among all agents inside the same set, and evaluates the ideal agents' joint activities via a coordinate descent technique. Comprehensive experiments on two various problems of multi-agent explain the effectiveness gain of the proposed technique compared to strong baselines, specifically when there exists a large agent's number.

In the work of Drakaki et al. [33], a multi-agent system is presented for decision-making on the defect conditioning of three-stage squirrel cage induction motors. The combined agents describe various health situations of similar induction motors, with defects that may appear in the rotor bars. The agents are utilized for training the experiment data of the system. A superintendent agent primarily collaborates with agents that utilize the feed-forward ANN technique, which is trained using the back-propagation method, and achieves the final defect diagnosing via computing their replies. When the system cannot make a decision about the defect kind, the superintendent agent can use another agent that implements the k-nearest neighbor technique. The proposed approach fulfills higher defect diagnosing occurrence.

3   The Proposed System

The proposed system shows and displays the product's URLs advertisements (Ads) that match the user queries. The proposed system uses four agents which consist of a data mining classifier and crawler inside each one in order to get the most suitable Ads according to user query keywords. Each agent contains its own dataset records, a crawler, and a machine learning classifier inside it. The system uses a network of multi-agents systems to show the most proper Ads in accordance with user query keywords from the products dataset and the web. The crawler crawls the agent's dataset to search for the product, if it founds the product ads URL, the proposed system shows the product advertisement from the dataset, else if the product advertisement URL does not exist in the dataset of the agent, the proposed system crawls the web to get the most suitable advertisements that match the user query. So, four intelligent software agents are allocated in different servers along with products dataset inside each agent.

The proposed system uses a machine learning classifier inside each agent in order to classify the product's user query. The proposed system returns a different class number as a classification result of the classifier by the four agents for the same query, because of the variance of the used dataset in every agent. The proposed system makes the right decision about the most appropriate class of the user query after voting among intelligent agents and returns the most suitable class number by the best agent after the voting process. The determined class number can be utilized to mine and crawl the advertisements URLs in the identified class and retrieve the suitable e-advertisement that matches the user query.

The utilized dataset is called GrammarandProductsReviews.csv, which involves product categories with their relevant attributes such as manufacturers, cities, advertisement URLs of products, customer reviews, and many other attributes. The proposed system receives an input query of product keywords from the user on the client side and sends it over the network to four agents which reside in various virtual servers. The proposed technique classifies the user query keywords to its appropriate class according to the customized agent's products dataset. The agents classify the same products query to their predicted class and provide different classification results for the query depending on their customized different datasets of products. The proposed system performs a decision-making process depending on voting among agents to decide the best appropriate class number for the user query among them.

First of all, the proposed system preprocesses the original dataset by applying several preprocessing tasks such as tokenization, stop word removal, stemming, and text normalization. The proposed technique implements several machine learning algorithms such as K-Nearest Neighbors (KNN), Decision Tree, Random Forest, and Naive Bayes (NB) to classify the dataset into classes, and estimates the performance of the classifiers by computing the precision, recall, and F1- measure for each one of them. The proposed system finds out that Random Forest is the best and more accurate classifier in classifying the original dataset among others, with the highest precision, recall, and F1-measure values. Thereafter, the proposed system splits the original products dataset equally into four smaller datasets, such that these subsets have an equal number of records inside each one.The proposed system gets four equal sub-datasets with equal record numbers,, in order to place them in the four agents, by assigning one subset to each individual agent. Each agent will work on its own dataset inside it. In addition to a specialized sub-dataset, each agent will contain a classifier model in it, which is trained and tested on the agent dataset.

The classifier is used to classify the received user query keywords to their appropriate class number according to the agent dataset. Each agent also involves a web crawler inside it, which can be used to crawl the advertisement's URLs in the dataset and mine them, using the user query keywords, in order to retrieve the most suitable and matched advertisements URLs from the dataset. The web crawler can be used also to crawl the World Wide Web to get the most appropriate advertisement's URLs that match the user query.

The block diagram of the proposed system was presented in Fig. 1. As shown in this figure, the system is based on four agents, such that each agent can work on his own particular dataset. After classifying the user query by the four agents into different class numbers, the proposed system compares the classification results of the agents by calculating the similarity or matching rate of each query keyword that exists in the agent dataset. As shown in Fig. 1, decision-making is done by choosing the best agent with

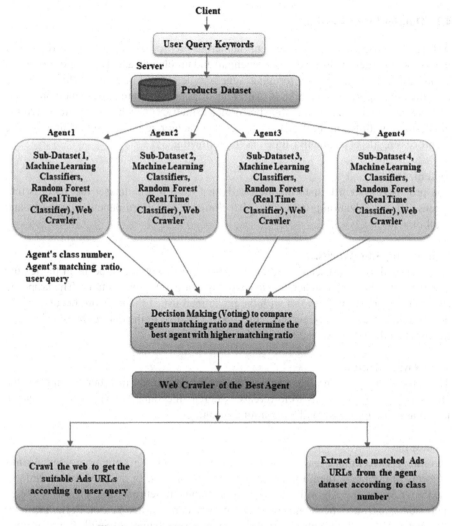

Fig. 1. General block diagram of the proposed system.

the highest matching rate of user query to its own dataset keywords. Then the crawler returns the URLs of ads that match the user's query and displays them to the user.

4 Proposed System Stages

E-advertisement is considered as a type of advancement or improvement that utilizes the internet and web, for the intention of marketing messages delivery, that engages the consumers to read and further create interest for clicking the thread. E-advertisements aid in merchandise and selling services and products via colorful and interacting catalogs, and supply the public with available information.

4.1 Dataset Preprocessing

At first, the proposed system implements numerous preprocessing tasks on the records of the dataset in order to eliminate non-beneficial and unrelated data. The proposed system cleans the dataset records and formulates them to be entered into the machine learning classification algorithms, in order to clarify the original dataset records to their predicted classes, and calculates the evaluation performance metrics of each classifier to determine the best one with the highest metrics values that categorize the dataset accurately. The preprocessing tasks can be illustrated as the following.

Tokenization.
The proposed system transforms the words that exist in the dataset text records into tokens. The tokenization process may also eliminate undesired punctuation marks and symbols.

Eliminating Stop Words.
The proposed system discards and eliminates the stop words that occur in the textual record keywords like (at, a, her, the, his, etc.) by using a stop words table. The proposed system compares each keyword with the predefined list, if the keyword occurs, then it will be eliminated from the record. This task is repeated in the dataset records in order to eliminate their stop words.

Text Normalization.
This process may be implemented on the record keywords in order to uniform the character case of keywords to lowercase, whereas the same keywords that appear in lowercase and uppercase will have similar meanings.

Stemming.
Stemming is a technique that is used to find out the different sorts of morphological kinds of terms to minimize them to one particular stem or root. In the proposed technique, the Porter Stemming Algorithm is applied to all the dataset records keywords to obtain their stems, and save the stemmed tokens in the records of the dataset. Porter stemmer eliminates the keywords suffixes, such that the keyword (suppliers) will be transformed to (supply) and the keyword (cleaners) will be converted to the root (clean), and so on.

4.2 Feature Extraction

After achieving the stemming process on the keywords of the dataset records, the proposed technique converts every text keyword into its corresponding Term Frequency-Inverse Document Frequency (TF-IDF) value by applying the TF-IDF formula. The TF-IDF values are numerical weights that represent the importance of keywords in the dataset records. Every text record is transformed to a feature vector using the bag of words method or vector space model. Every feature vector contains the TF-IDF weights that conform to the keywords in every record. Then, the proposed technique substitutes the keywords in the text record with a TF-IDF values feature vector that represents the weights of the keywords in every record. Thereafter, the proposed technique utilizes the preprocessed records which involve TF-IDF feature vectors as input vectors to the machine learning classifiers.

4.3 Dataset Classification

The original dataset records are classified using four machine learning classification algorithms: Naive Bayes, K-Nearest Neighbor (KNN), Random Forest, and Decision Tree classification algorithms in order to build their classifier's models. The proposed technique splits the dataset into two portions: the training set that comprises 70% of the dataset records, and the testing set that forms 30% of the records. The proposed system trains every classification algorithm by utilizing the training set feature vector instances in the training phase. For the testing phase, every classifier categorizes the testing set feature vector records to their appropriate classes. The proposed system computes the evaluation metrics of the precision, recall, and F1-measure for each classifier model to evaluate its performance. The system decides which classifier can classify better the dataset records with the highest evaluation metrics values.

Naive Bayes Classifier.
It is a simple probabilistic classifier that is based on the Bayesian rule with effective independence assumption. Naive Bayes algorithm presents considerable performance under conditions such that the occurring keywords are independent of each other. It includes training and testing phases, which are applied to the dataset records that contain feature keywords. The two phases of the Naive Bayes NB classifier can be explained as the following:-

Training Phase. The dataset training begins with calculating the records number in every class and the total dataset records, in order to obtain the class prior probability. This process is repeated for every class in the dataset. The NB classifier is trained with the features or keywords that occur in the classes:

a. Calculate the prior probabilities $P(\omega_i)$ of the classes using the following Eq. [34]:

$$P(\omega_i) = \frac{|\omega_i|}{N} \tag{1}$$

where ω_i represents the class type (or class number); $|\omega_i|$ represents the text records' number in every class, and N is the total number of records in the dataset.

b. Calculation of conditional likelihood or probability for each feature in the record that exists in each class using the following Eq. [34]:

$$p(x|\omega_i) = \prod_{i=1}^{n} p(x_i|\omega_j) \tag{2}$$

Testing Phase. In the testing phase, the NB classifier classifies text records in the testing dataset into their appropriate classes. This phase utilizes the computed features likelihoods of the training set records from the training stage, in order to categorize the new text testing records. The testing stage is achieved as follows:

a. Implement Naive Bayes NB classifier using the testing datasets.
b. Utilize the keyword's likelihoods of the existing testing record from the training stage.
c. If the feature or keyword likelihood does not occur in the training phase, then the NB performs the laplacian smoothing method to deal with the problem of zero-probability by increasing each counter of zero occurrence keywords.
d. Calculate the posterior probability of the tested record utilizing the Eq. [34, 35]:

$$P(\omega_i|x) = \frac{p(x|\omega_i) \times P(\omega_i)}{p(x)} \tag{3}$$

where $p(x)$ is the pdf of x and for which we have:

$$P(x) = \sum_{i=1}^{n} p(x|\omega_i) \times P(\omega_i) \tag{4}$$

By multiplying the keywords likelihoods of the existing tested record for every class with the class prior probabilities which are calculated previously in the training stage.

e. After computing the posterior probabilities of the testing record for every class, the Naive Bayes classifier contrasts the outcomes to find out the greatest probability among them, thereafter, allocates the tested record to the higher probability class.

K-Nearest Neighbor (KNN) Classifier

The first stage in achieving the KNN classification algorithm is to load the feature vectors of the training set that describes the weights of the keywords. The KNN training stage stores the feature vectors of the training set with their relevant labels of classes. In the testing stage, the KNN algorithm can determine the value of K that is estimated via trials and experiments several times in order to discover the ideal K value such as 2, 3, or 5 or it may be specified depending on the dataset via utilizing the following equation [18]:

$$K = sqrt(N)/2 \tag{5}$$

where N identifies the number of instances in the training set.

For the testing data set, the algorithm obtains each tested feature vector and calculates the distance between the tested feature vector and the trained feature vector weights based on the Euclidean Distance equation, which is depicted as the following [36]:

$$dist(x_i, x_j) = \sqrt{\sum_{r=1}^{n}(a_r(x_i) - a_r(x_j))^2} \tag{6}$$

Thereafter, the computed distances are sorted in descending arrangement, such that the top rows are obtained from the arranged list, which describes the K nearest neighbors to the test feature vector. The algorithm identifies the predicted class of the test feature vector via utilizing plurality voting of the nearest neighbor's class, such that obtaining the most repeated class in the nearest neighbors, and the most frequent class will be allocated to the test feature vector.

Decision Tree Classifier

Decision free builds the classification model in a tree framework format. it partitions the dataset into small subsets, while concurrently the relevant decision tree is enhanced and evolved. The decision tree categorizes textual training based on feature or attribute values. Every decision tree node represents a training record feature to be relegated, and each branch expresses a value of a node. A decision tree is built utilizing a top-down approach that partitions the training data recursively on the attribute that best relegates the training records. The decision tree conception begins by dividing the data based on the attribute value that is useful in data relegation. The attribute that best partitions the trained records will express the tree root node. The decision tree classifier is repeated on each divided data part, generating subtrees until the training data records are divided into subsets of the same class. At every step of a dividing process, a statistical criterion called Information Gain (IG) is utilized to specify what attributes or features better partition the training textual records. The Decision Tree classification algorithm can be expressed in two stages:

The Training Stage. The training stage involves constructing the tree, since the main goal is to find out at every one of the tree decision nodes, the optimal testing attribute which reduces the mixing of classes, with each subset produced by the test.

The Testing Stage. The testing stage begins at the root node of the tree, then, the attribute specified by the root node is examined. The test result permits moving down the decision tree branch that is relevant to the checked record attribute. This task is iterated till the algorithm encounters a leaf node. This is the cause that the testing instance record is categorized by tracing a path from the root of the tree to the leaf nodes. The algorithm enhances the greedy search that implements a heuristic search function by utilizing probability for comparison purposes.

Information Gain and Entropy Measurement

The measure that is utilized from the information theory domain in building the decision tree is known as Entropy. It is confirmed that the entropy is relevant and close to the information, which means that the higher the value of entropy, the more required information to completely describe the data. In building decision trees, the aim is to reduce the entropy of the dataset until it arrives at the leaf nodes so that the subset has zero entropy and expresses all the instances of a single class, i.e., all instances of data have the same target attribute or class value. To calculate the entropy of the training set dataset D, the following equation was used [36]:

$$Entropy(D) = \sum_{i=1}^{n} -p_i log_2 p_i \qquad (7)$$

where p_i is the proportion of D belonging to class i, which involves different values. To compute the information gain which represents the reduction of entropy that outcomes from partitioning the data on an attribute, the following equation is applied:

$$Gain(f, D) = Entropy(D) - \sum_{v=1}^{n} \left(\frac{|D_v|}{|D|} \times Entropy(D_v) \right) \qquad (8)$$

where $|D|$ represents the elements number in the dataset, $|D_v|$ represents number of instances with v value of an attribute f, and v represents the set of distinct values of an attribute f.

Random Forest Classifier
It represents an ensemble classifier that involves several decision trees and finds out the class outcome of each tree. It is usually rapid and can extend to several input attributes and select instances without pruning. In the phase of training, the trees can be evolved to maximum depth and each tree is classified independently. In the testing stage, the attribute is assigned to each tree, and the forest chooses the maximal voting class across all the trees, by utilizing the majority vote on average.

4.4 Splitting the Dataset

The product dataset records are divided and splitted into four distinct smaller datasets, with an equal number of records in each one of them. Every dataset is placed inside one of the four agents, such that each agent can use its own smaller sub-dataset, and classify its records using data mining classification algorithms in order to build the classifier's models. In addition, each agent may use the crawler algorithm inside it to crawl and mine its own dataset to get the advertisement URLs of the products that match the user search query.

4.5 Agents as Data Mining Classifiers

After placing the four smaller sub-datasets in their corresponding agents, the agents utilize several classifiers inside them in order to classify their dataset records. Every agent uses KNN, Decision Tree, Random Forest, and Naive Bayes classification algorithms to train and test on its own dataset, in order to produce its own classifiers models. The classification algorithms classify the dataset records, and the performance metrics in terms of precision, recall, and F1-measure of each classifier are calculated. The classifier metrics are computed in order to get the most accurate classifier with the highest metrics values. After comparison, the proposed system finds out that the Random forest classifier is more accurate and precise than others with the highest precision, recall, and F1-measure values. Consequently, the Random Forest is selected to be applied inside all agents, which is worked in real-time.

4.6   Preprocessing the User Query at Clients

When the user enters a product query on the client side, several preprocessing tasks are achieved to preprocess the query keywords, before sending them to the agents. First of all, the query is tokenized, in order to get distinct and individual tokens, removing any unwanted symbols or punctuation marks. The stop words such as (a, the, her, his, are, is... etc.) are eliminated from the query tokens. The keywords or tokens are normalized to get all of them in lowercase letters. The tokens are stemmed to get their stems or roots by removing the suffixes using Porter Stemmer. After preprocessing the query tokens, the preprocessed tokens or keywords are sent simultaneously to the four agents who represent servers on the network.

4.7   Classifying the Query Inside Each Agent

When the query tokens are received by the agents, they classify the keywords or tokens using the Random Forest classifier which represents the real-time classifier model inside each agent. Each agent may classify the query keywords to a different class number according to the dataset inside every agent. Thus, the four agents may return different class numbers for the same query according to their own dataset. The agents perform a similarity or matching process to compute the similarity of the query keywords to the dataset keywords of every agent, in order to find out the most similar and matching agent with the more similar keywords to the keywords of the query. The matching process can be achieved by calculating the Euclidean Distance between the query keywords and the keywords of each agent's dataset, with calculating a matching or similarity ratio that represents the matching or similarity rate of the query to the dataset keywords of every agent.

4.8   Agent's Decision-Making

In order to decide and specify the agent that has the largest similarity ratio of matching its dataset keywords with the user query, the agents should communicate with each other and send their similarity ratios for comparison. The agents can communicate with each other over the network, using TCP/IP protocol suite to send their data packets using the Knowledge Query Manipulation Language (KQML) with its message formats and performatives to connect with other agents and in order to send their similarity ratios to each other for comparison. In this way, each agent can have its own similarity ratio with all similarity ratios of other agents and can sort all the agents' similarity ratio values in descending order. Every agent finds the highest similarity ratio among all other ratios from other agents. The agents decide the best agent which has the highest similarity ratio and adopts its classification result (class number) to be the best classification outcome for the query tokens. For example, if the similarity ratios are 20%, 50%, 70%, and 10% for agents 1, 2, 3, and 4 respectively, then after a comparison of these values, the agents decide that agent 3 is the best agent with higher similarity ratio of 70%, and the proposed system adopts its class number.

4.9　Crawling the Dataset URLs and the Web Pages

After determining the best agent with the highest similarity ratio to the user query and adopting its class number as the classification result, the proposed system uses the crawler algorithm inside the best agent to crawl the advertisements URLs inside the determined class number in the agent dataset, in order to get a copy of the advertisements URLs that match the user query keywords. The crawler algorithm replicates, downloads, and indexes URLs in order to search within those URLs for the user's query keywords. The crawler returns the URLs of ads that match the user's query and displays them to the user. In other words, the crawler explores the World Wide Web in order to discover web pages that match the user query, make a copy of these web pages, download, and index them. The web crawler returns a list of web pages that confirms the keywords of the user query, in order to display them to the end user. If the product doesn't exist in the agents' datasets at all, the web crawler only crawls the web to get the web pages URLs that match and confirms the user query of products keywords.

5　Results and Discussion

This part illustrates the obtained results from classifying the products dataset using machine learning classifiers, which involves the calculated evaluation metrics of each classifier in terms of precision, recall, and F1-measure values. Also, the performance evaluation metrics of the classifiers inside each agent are explained. The results showed that the Random Forest algorithm was the best classifier with the best metrics values of precision, recall, and F1-measures. In addition, the similarity or matching ratios of the four agents with random different search queries is also illustrated.

The proposed system computes the confusion matrix that uses TP, TN, FP, and FN of the classifier classes, thereafter, it finds out the evaluation metrics to estimate the performance and efficiency of every classifier model. The performance metrics in terms of precision, recall, and F1-measure of the used classifiers to classify the products dataset can be depicted in Table 1.

As shown in Table 1, the Random forest classifier is the best and more accurate classifier in categorizing the dataset, with highest metrics values of 0.86981677, 0.58328191, 0.61830625 which represents precision, recall, and F1-measure respectively.

The proposed system splits the dataset equally into four smaller sub-datasets, with equal records number, in order to assign them to the four agents, such that each agent will have its own smaller dataset. The datasets inside agents are classified using classification algorithms, evaluating the performance measures of each classifier, in order to determine the classifier with the highest metrics values to be the real-time classifier that works

Table 1. The outcomes of evaluation metrics for all classifiers in classifying the products dataset

Classification Algorithm	Precision	Recall	F1-Measure
Naive Bayes	0.86571357	0.57282178	0.61025739
Random Forest	0.86981677	0.58328191	0.61830625
Decision Tree	0.86391428	0.57662222	0.61017257
KNN	0.86599614	0.57953791	0.61126639

inside every agent. Tables 2, 3, 4, and 5 show the evaluation performance metrics of all classifiers inside agents 1, 2, 3, and 4 respectively.

Table 2. The evaluation performance metrics of the classifiers in agent 1.

Classification Algorithm	Precision	Recall	F1-Measure
Naive Bayes	0.86571357	0.57282178	0.61025739
Random Forest	0.87767755	0.58170877	0.61437154
Decision Tree	0.86597659	0.57826025	0.61179441
KNN	0.84271052	0.50197058	0.53996474

Table 3. The evaluation performance metrics of the classifiers in agent 2.

Classification Algorithm	Precision	Recall	F1-Measure
Naive Bayes	0.86858420	0.57899921	0.61444899
Random Forest	0.86985470	0.58216623	0.62519241
Decision Tree	0.86669786	0.57885846	0.61338321
KNN	0.86420790	0.57153283	0.61457437

Table 4. The evaluation performance metrics of the classifiers in agent 3.

Classification Algorithm	Precision	Recall	F1-Measure
Naive Bayes	0.82657301	0.46389271	0.51263766
Random Forest	0.89985461	0.59368728	0.65592518
Decision Tree	0.85324012	0.47293187	0.62312741
KNN	0.87325410	0.54254231	0.51446327

From the above tables, it is observed that the Random Forest clarifier is the best classifier model with highest values of precision, recall and F1-measure metrics. Thus,

Table 5. The evaluation performance metrics of the classifiers in agent 4.

Classification Algorithm	Precision	Recall	F1-Measure
Naive Bayes	0.85654301	0.56786824	0.51332890
Random Forest	0.89435062	0.59816533	0.59532498
Decision Tree	0.82135479	0.57115524	0.52528235
KNN	0.80135742	0.56243672	0.52743567

Table 6. The similarity or matching ratios of the agents with different user query keywords.

User Query	Agent 1 Similarity Ratio with Class No	Agent 2 Similarity Ratio with Class No	Agent 3 Similarity Ratio with Class No	Agent 4 Similarity Ratio with Class No	Best Agent
Red Bag Chanel	40.68672 Class No. 1	24.61291 Class No.1	36.65417 Class no.1	28.70299 Class no.22	Agent 1
Baby Lotion	36.61805 Class No.3	20.5107601 Class No.2	32.58149 Class no.20	61.50641 Class no.4	Agent 4
Canon Digital Camera	24.41203 Class No. 12	36.91936 Class No. 1	32.58149 Class No. 14	69.70726 Class No. 21	Agent 4
Samsung Mobile A12	0.41224 Class No. 5	32.80341 Class No. 16	0.14769 Class No. 8	0.49083 Class No. 4	Agent 2
Dior Personal Care	40.68675 Class No. 3	42.91936 Class No. 7	28.50880 Class No. 14	90.20940 Class No. 20	Agent 4
Duru Shampoo	16.27469 Class No. 12	28.71506 Class No. 8	41.10427 Class No. 0	30.58149 Class No. 10	Agent 3

the Random Forest is used as a real-time classifier inside each agent, in order to classify the user query keywords. Table 6 illustrates the similarity or matching ratios of the four agents with various user products query keywords, identifying the best agent which has the highest similarity ratio to the query keywords and its classification class number. The proposed system uses the class number obtained from the best agent as a classification result, and it is used by the web crawler inside the best agent to crawl the advertisements URLs inside this class that matches the user query keywords, in order to get the most matched and suitable advertisements URLs from the agent dataset.

6   Conclusions

E-advertisement is the most significant and attractive marketing approach concerning the internet customers. Multi-Agent Systems consist of a collection of interacting computing elements known as agents where these agents act as complete autonomous entities that can interact with each other and decide what and how to perform different kinds of tasks.

This paper presents a technique that is based on a Multi-agents system augmented with data mining classifiers and crawlers. The idea behind that is to analyze and categorize the user's query product keywords to their appropriate class, according to the customized dataset that resides in each agent. Four machine-learning techniques are used to classify the user query; these are: Naive Bayer, Random Forest, KNN, and Decision Tree. Thereafter, the best-selected agent whose dataset most matches the user query can use its own crawler to retrieve the most confirmed ads URLs from its own dataset. The proposed technique classifies the product's original dataset with the agent's sub-datasets using the above-mentioned classifiers and calculates three metrics for each one of them. The performance metrics show that the Random Forest classifier is the most optimal algorithm with higher metrics values inside each agent. Consequently, it is proposed to be used in the real-time model for all the agents. The results show that Multi-agents architecture is highly dynamic and scalable to be applied for E-advertisement with high flexibility to be extended in the future for new functions with knowledge derived from purchase history, rating products, gathering information, etc. where each agent is in charge for a separate task. Furthermore, as the classification can be done in real-time, the load of classification was highly minimized. For future work, more machine learning techniques such as linear regression, logistic regression, boosting algorithm, etc. can be studied and applied to enhance the system's performance.

References

1. Horbal, N., Naychuk-Khrushch, M., Orlykova, B.: Internet advertising: the specifics, tendencies of development and impact on sales. ECONTECHMOD: An Int. Quart. J. Econ. Technol. Modell. Process. **6**, (2017)
2. Marzan, D.C., Gonzales, V.C.: The implication of online advertising as a source of website development. CVCITC Res. J. **1**, 41–42 (2014)
3. Tavor, T.: Online advertising development and their economic effectiveness. Austr. J. Bus. Manage. Res. **1**(6), 121 (2011)
4. Ratliff, J.D., Rubinfeld, D.L.: Online advertising: Defining relevant markets. vol. 7 (2019)
5. Balaji, P.G., Srinivasan, D.: An introduction to multi-agent systems. In: Innovations in multi-agent systems and applications-1, pp. 1–27: Springer, (2010) https://doi.org/10.1007/978-3-642-14435-6_1
6. Dorri, A., Kanhere, S.S., Jurdak, R.: Multi-agent systems: a survey. Ieee Access **6**, 28573–28593 (2018)
7. Mostafa, S.A., Ahmad, M.S., Mustapha, A., et al.: A concise overview of software agent research, modeling, and development. Softw. Eng. **5**(1), 8–25 (2017)
8. Al-Karkhi, A.: Task Recovery in Self-Organized Multi-Agent Systems for Distributed Domains. University of Essex (2018)
9. Ahmed, M., Ahmad, M.S., Yusoff, M.Z.Z.: A review and development of agent communication language. Electron. J. Comput. Sci. Inform. Technol. **1**(1), (2009)
10. Kaur, A., Jain, S.: Kqml-from scenario to technology. Int. J. Adv. Stud. Comput. Sci. Eng. **7**(3), 30–34 (2018)
11. Mian, N.A., Ahmad, F.: Agent based architecture for modeling and analysis of self adaptive systems using formal methods. Int. J. Adv. Comput. Sci. Appl. **9**(1), 563–567 (2018)
12. Thangaraj, M., Sivakami, M.: Text classification techniques: a literature review. Interdis0. J. Inf. Knowl. Manag. **13**, 117 (2018)

13. Kalita, D.: Supervised and unsupervised document classification: a survey. Int. J. Comput. Sci. Inform. Technol. **6**(2), 1971–1974 (2015)
14. Jindal, R., Malhotra, R., Jain, A.: Techniques for text classification: literature review and current trends. webology, **12**(2), (2015)
15. Patra, A., Singh, D.: Neural network approach for text classification using relevance factor as term weighting method. In: Int. J. Comput. Appl., **68**(17), (2013)
16. Soofi, A.A., Awan, A.: Classification techniques in machine learning: applications and issues. Journal of Basic and Applied Sciences **13**, 459–465 (2017)
17. Osisanwo, F., Akinsola, J., Awodele, O., et al.: Supervised machine learning algorithms: classification and comparison. Int. J. Comput. Trends Technol. (IJCTT) **48**(3), 128–138 (2017)
18. Trstenjak, B., Mikac, S., Donko, D.: KNN with TF-IDF based framework for text categorization. Proc. Eng. **69**, 1356–1364 (2014)
19. Singh, D., Malhotra, S.: Intra News Category Classification using N-gram TF-IDF Features and Decision Tree Classifier.
20. Sjarif, N.N.A., Azmi, N.F.M., Chuprat, S., et al.: SMS spam message detection using term frequency-inverse document frequency and random forest algorithm. Proc. Comput. Sci. **161**, 509–515 (2019)
21. Le, C.-C., Prasad, P., Alsadoon, A., et al.: Text classification: Naïve bayes classifier with sentiment Lexicon. IAENG Int. J. Comput. Sci **46**(2), 141–148 (2019)
22. Yu, L., Li, Y.,Zeng, Q. et al.: Summary of web crawler technology research, p. 012036
23. Chatterjee, S., Nath, A.: Auto-explore the web–web crawler. In: Int. J. Innov. Res. Comput. Commun. Eng. **5**(4), 6607–6618 (2017)
24. Kausar, M.A., Dhaka, V., Singh, S.K.: Web crawler: a review. In: International Journal of Computer Applications, **63**(2), 31–36 (2013)
25. Roopa, G., Nirmala, C.: Mobile Agent Framework for Web-Advertising.
26. Roopa, G., Nirmala, C.: Security for e-Advertisements using Digital Watermarking and Mobile Agents.
27. Al-Asfoor, M., Fasli, M., Al-Majeed, S.: A Multi-Agent System-Based Resource Advertisement Model for Grid Environments. In: Özcan, A., Zizka, J., Nagamalai, D. (eds.) CoNeCo/WiMo -2011. CCIS, vol. 162, pp. 337–347. Springer, Heidelberg (2011). https://doi.org/10.1007/978-3-642-21937-5_32
28. . Hong, Z.-W., Chin, K.-Y., Liou, Y. P. et al.: An agent-based Internet advertising system by using PULL mechanism, pp. 1–6
29. Kazienko, P.: Multi-agent system for web advertising, pp. 507–513
30. Pourpanah, F., Tan, C.J., Lim, C.P., et al.: A Q-learning-based multi-agent system for data classification. Appl. Soft Comput. **52**, 519–531 (2017)
31. González-Briones, A., Villarrubia, G., De Paz, J.F., et al.: A multi-agent system for the classification of gender and age from images. Comput. Vis. Image Underst. **172**, 98–106 (2018)
32. Zhou, M., Chen, Y., Wen, Y.: et al.: Factorized q-learning for large-scale multi-agent systems, pp. 1–7
33. Drakaki, M., Karnavas, Y.L., Karlis, A.D., et al.: Study on fault diagnosis of broken rotor bars in squirrel cage induction motors: a multi-agent system approach using intelligent classifiers. Power Appl **14**(2), 245–255 (2020)
34. Hart, P.E., Stork, D.G., Duda, R.O.: Pattern Classification: Wiley Hoboken (2000)
35. Theodoridis, S., Koutroumbas, K.: Pattern Recognition: Elsevier, (2006)
36. Mitchell, T.M.: Machine learning, McGraw-hill New York (1997)

Automated Multi-style Iraqi Cars License Recognition Based on Convolutional Neural Network Technology

Shaimaa K. Ahmed(✉) ⓘ, Zobeda H. Naji ⓘ, and Maather Alshaibi ⓘ

Department of Computer Engineering, College of Engineering, University of Diyala, Baqubah, Diyala, Iraq
shaimaa_khamees@uodiyala.edu.iq

Abstract. Automated identification is one of the modern trends in computer vision researches. Recognizing car plate license is a highly requested technology for security and commercial purposes. Many challenges face the accuracy and performance of such systems due to the local limitations like none unified plate style and nonstandard camera views or environment. This study proposes a system to recognize car plate license based on CNN trained model. The dataset used in the training process have been gathered by extracting and segmenting three local car plates. A number of image processes and blob detecting methods have been used to enhance plate detection in different camera views and angles. The study results show that the proposed system can achieve accuracy at 95% level in noticeably short time. Other Neural network multilayer perceptron-based models have been used to compare the performance of the CNN Model.

Keywords: CNN · Neural network · Car plate recognition · computer vision · Automated identification

1 Introduction

Car transportation is nowadays considered as the backbone of any country including Iraq. Due to its significance, an increasing priority has been given to automation in the administration of this field. Depending on surveillance in monitoring cars made it easier to adopt and extend its potentials from just monitoring and video recording, automated analyzing, recognizing and alerting [1]. Numbering cars can result in achieving security, managing, parking, and monitoring issues [2]. Automated Car License Plate Recognition (ACLP) has been used as a solution for those issues. ACLP has its own limitations such as broken plates, cars with multi style plate license numbers. In addition, other restrictions face ACLP applications. ACLP is considered as a significant system of road enforcement, hometown security management, parking ticketing, and police traffic control [3].

In particular, the automated license plate detection system is a key factor in intelligent transportation systems. It has already been commercialized as a toll payment system. Many researchers have proposed solutions against environmental changes. They have also suggested techniques for improving the performance of detection via continuous conduction. Generally, the systems of license plate detection depend on steps such as the extraction of features, searching, classification, and estimation of location [4].

To identify the license number, ACLP includes five essential models: Data Preprocessing, Extraction of Edges, Localization, segmentation of character and the recognition of character [5].

In this study, Extraction of Edges and Localization are merged together to determine and extract the plate region in the frame. Morphology operation is used to enhance Vehicle License Plate (VLP) detection.

The technique of Dilation is used for the gray image to fill holes, join lines and sharping edges by adding pixels to boundaries. On the other hand, Erosion is basically used for thinning the shape edges of binary image by removing pixels from the object's boundaries [6].

Blob analysis method involves eliminating noise blob, assembling the blob fragmentation and splitting to shape the Segmentation model. Mostly, Segmentation model includes three steps. First, adjusting and generating the binary image. Second, blob analyzing and illuminating the noisy blob. Finally, selecting the characters and numbers blobs. [7].

The final model is responsible for training. It involves using a dataset to recognize plate characters and numbers printed with different Iraqi styles. This model is based on a well-known model named CNN which enables officials to work with scale, rotate with minimal preprocessing [8].

Our local traffic system contains multiple styles to register cars. Also, the surveillance system setup is random and not base on organized coordination make car licenses recognition a challenge to any proposed digital system.

This study proposes a system for recognizing local Iraqi car plate licenses using CNN model. It includes all Iraqi official styles. The proposed model takes into consideration the number of digits in each plate style by supporting flexibility digit detecting during preprocessing stage. The system has shown an excellent level of accuracy in acceptable time with uncontrolled environment.

2 Literature Survey

Wang et al. (2019) declared that many of the methods used in Car license recognition are not reliable in real world implementation. They proposed more accurate and low-cost method using multi-task convolutional neural (MTLPR). The authors trained the Multi-task Convolutional Neural Networks (MTCNN) to create license detection and invent a speed excellent accuracy system [9].

Nazri et al. proposed using a camera to capture the car rear side in order to recognize the car license number and save it into database. Using this method, the car will be verified at the attached gate. This proposed system used to eliminate the need for extra verification card to open the gate [2].

The authors invented a License Plate detection and recognition (LPDR) using two-dimensional wavelet transform to extract the edges of the image vertically and CNN classifier. The experience gives a high accuracy using a Morocco car plate license [10].

Chowdhury used Night License Plate Images (NLPI) dataset and UCSD benchmark dataset in order to test the distortion effective of multi factors. The authors proposed Fractal Series Expansion (FSE) model to improve the quality of plate license extracted image. The proposed model gives high probability to distinguish the plate pixels from the background [11].

Alghyaline focused on local plate licenses using two phases of CNN based on You only look once (YOLO) framework to enhance the detection of plate with a big size image frame. The authors applied the system in Real time You tube video and achieved particularly good results [12].

Hendry used CNN based on YOLO's 7 to analyze Taiwan local car license plates. The author proposed using slide window to detect plate 6 digit. The invented system achieved excellent results with consideration to environment conditions such as darkness, dimness and raining [13].

Hui Li proposed segmentation free method using trained CNN Model to investigate characters in plate image and distinguish text-none text areas.

The author empowered the invented system by trained Recurrent neural networks (RNNs) with long short-term memory to extract features from the CNN extracted images [14].

In this paper, we create an Iraqi plate license number recognition framework based on CNN algorithm. The Car licenses local database created by the authors using Different plate styles and angles and different times of the day and night. The framework created based on the CNN model is capable of detection and recognition multi style with a different view. The framework achieved excellent accuracy with 91%.

3 Dataset

In this paper, dataset gathered by the authors using fifty random private license car plates including three styles; old style, modern style, and north region style. 422 images were produced to create dataset for the purpose of training a machine learning model to recognize Iraqi different - style car plate licenses. Images captured by a mobile camera with 64mp were chosen randomly, at different times and from different Baghdad streets. Each image plate is divided into small pieces; each piece includes one letter or number from the plate number license. The images dataset are separated into categories; each category represents a letter or number in Arabic. The number of images in each category is not fixed since different numbers of images have been used in each category. The dataset images are formulated in different sizes depending on the letter or number shape. In first stage the Preprocessing for image dataset was include various operation performed where segmentation image, blob detection method and crop tool was using as shown in Fig. 1. In Car Plate Recognition, localizing and extracting the plate was done from the car photo shoot. Several techniques used to localize and extract the plate such as Edge Detection," an image process tool used to find the boundaries in the pictures" as shown in Fig. 2. Dataset images include only the required shape; all unrequired background are removed.

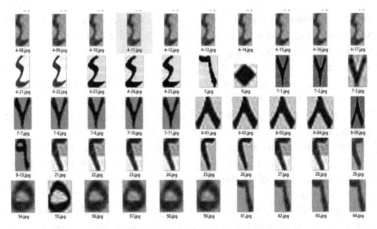

Fig. 1. Shows extracted dataset samples.

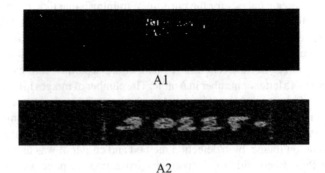

Fig. 2. Describes the steps of edge detection.

Erosion and dilation are fundamental morphological operations used to enhance recognition and plate localization. Another preprocessing operation was applied which is removing the small objects smaller than 2000 pixels. Fig. 3 A1 represents the removal of small objects and A2 represents the erosion process.

A1

A2

Fig. 3. A1 shows the result of Erosion and A2 shows dilation implementation.

The preprocessing for the image data set also includes histograms to improve contrast in the image, as shown in Fig. 4. After that the image was converted into binary. By treating the image as an array, it was possible to calculate the general location of the car plate. Along with the array's number of columns, the number of rows is also determined. The maximum row and column with pixel values of 1 are counted and taken into account as the approximate location of the plate. The captured image was resized to 72 × 72 columns and rows to be prepared for the next learning.

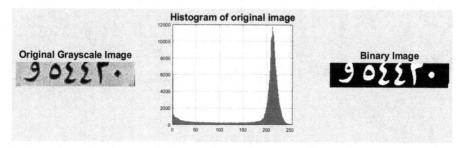

Fig. 4. Represents converting image into binary image before blob measuring process.

4   Build and Train CNN Model

After plate extraction, it was saved as a jpg image and the datasets letters were used to train the model to ensure its ability to predicate the Iraqi style plate letters. The process consists of several stages through which the model passes before the model can achieve the predication of car license number.

4.1   Dataset Preparing

At this stage, in our case, the dataset is extracted from the collected car plates. Measure and Color Blobs method used to divide the plate into parts, each part includes a letter or a number of the plate license number. In other meaning Bolo detects the bright feature in histogram image based on Laplacian of Gaussian (LOG). First we extract the image dimension, convert image to histogram, check image pixel color and apply the binary threshold and remove the small dotes. Once the image ready, bright areas collected, measured, and saved as a new image. Figure 5 represents how to extract the letter and characters from the plate images.

The blob measuring operation results in unequal number of letters and characters groups. In order to build a trained model, the dataset should be equal for all groups. Table 1 shows each group number of images. Images selected randomly from the original dataset. CNN Model required trained images with fixed sizes as shown in the Fig. 5. The images size unified by 70 × 80 pixels. The 100-threshold chosen after certain number of trailers to get best result (Fig. 6).

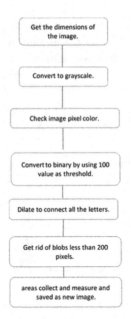

Fig. 5. Represents the extraction of image dataset.

Table 1. Shows the dataset labels

Original number of labels in dataset	Count	labels in dataset after reducing	Count
0	99	0	29
1	78	1	29
2	57	2	29
3	91	3	29
4	44	4	29
5	44	5	29
6	41	6	29
7	44	7	29
8	33	8	29
9	29	9	29
ا	26	ا	29
م	31	م	29
ر	30	ر	29
و	45	و	29
ي	58	ي	29

Fig. 6. Represents the extracted blobs.

4.2 CNN Model

The model was built by using 2-dimension layer Convolutional neural network. Each layer contains number of filters where the input layer connects to the hidden layer and hidden layer connect to the output layer respectively. Slide convolutional filter applied to the dataset input image [15]. A filter is applied to the image in all vertical and horizontal directions. In this model, number of filters is 20 and each filter sized 5 × 5. The region in the dataset input image that contains the connected neurons is defined as the filter size. Number of filters refers to how many neurons in the region of the connected neurons. Batch normalization applied in order to accelerate the training process of the CNN, and eliminated the need for being much carefully about the initializing [16]. In this model, the ReLue Layer was used as an activation function which is work as threshold convert any value less than zero to zero, Eq. 1 describe the work of ReLue Layer [17].

$$f(x) = \{x, x \geq 00, x < 0 \tag{1}$$

Fully connected layer was used in this model, all inputs are connected across layers to every active unit to perform training process. Softmax function is used as active function also for extra normalization. Finally, the classification layer works with the previous layers including the size of the output, the fully connected layer and the softmax function layer was used to identify the number of classes. Model was trained to recognize three styles of Iraq car plate licenses. The average time for the model to predicate a license is 2 ms. The time could be reduced based on the computer processing power.

5   The Result and Measuring Accuracy

The train model achieved excellent accuracy in plate character number recognition. Number of Epoch used to increase accuracy. Every Epoch represents a one iteration of whole training process including all the samples. On 13 epochs the accuracy performance stabled. Figure 7 shows the accuracy performance of the training model.

We observe improved model correctness and performance by increasing the number of epochs. Table 2 shows the difference with each epochs number.

The model shows excellent predication for the car plate license number. Table 3 shows predication of the car plate license over number of tested times until getting the correct license number. The trained model shows excellent result in acceptable time.

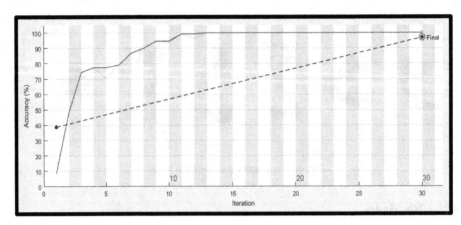

Fig. 7. Shows the change in accuracy over epochs number.

Table 2. Describes the differences among the experiment numbers of epochs

Epochs number	accuracy	Time by second
2	76.97	2 s
5	78.5	5 s
10	90.1	10 s
13	95.15	14 s

Figure 8 represented the MLP model with 100 intermediate layer and 5 outputs represented the licenses predication numbers and character. The model used to compare the performance of CNN invented model as shown in Table 4. The same configuration used to test all the car licenses images presented in the test. Same captures angels, times and conditions used for both models. Number of hidden layers in MLP model determine Optimizely using try and error to get best result using through this model. The result of the MLP predication shows less performance than CNN based model. MLP model required more than two tries to get the correct result.

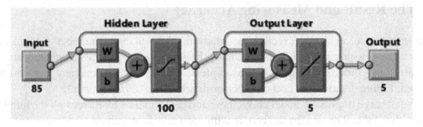

Fig. 8. MLP model structure

Table 3. Shows the result of the system predication using the MLP trained model compared to the result of CNN model, all sample plate extracted using the Plate Extraction model.

Car image			
Car plate extracted by the system			
Number of tests to get the correct plate license	2	1	1
Accuracy	99.1 for the last test	97.5	98.7
Time	11 sec	11 sec	11 sec
Car image			
Car plate extracted by the system			
Number of tests to get the correct plate license	1	1	1
Accuracy	99.3	95.1	98.7
Time	12 sec	15 sec	13 sec

Table 4. Described the comparison between model performance

Sample Plate	CNN model Tested Times until get the correct number	MLP model Tested Times until get the correct number
١ ٥٥٨١٠	2	5
١١١٢٣٨	1	8
٥٧٢١٣	1	7
٥٠٠٨٤١	1	5
٩٥١٧٢	1	3
١ ٧٢٧٦٣	1	7

6 Conclusion

Most of the car plate license number recognition systems require standard environment and equipped camera. In addition to that, Iraq has multiple car plate styles which add more challenges to any system for car plate license recognition. In this work, we proposed a conventional neural network-based system to detect and recognize Car plates in multiple styles and none-standard view. The proposed system includes multiple models in order to achieve recognition and localization. CNN model trained using automated extracted dataset calculated from 50 cars images captured randomly from real world environment. The extracted dataset used to train CNN model to predicate the care plate. The recognition model shows excellent accuracy with acceptable time for the tested cars samples. The model gives correct predication with 90% of the cars. In comparison with Neural network multiple layer perceptron model, CNN model gives better results and performance than MLP model in addition to saving time.

References

1. Wady, S.H., Ahmad, F.H., Ahmed, H.O.: Iraqi Kurdistan vehicle license plate recognition system based on client-server network. J. Zankoi Sulaimani (2017)
2. Nazri, M.S.B.M., Tengku, T.L.A.F.B., Gaafar, L., Sofian, H., Sajak, A.A.B.: IoT parking apps with car plate recognition for smart city using node red. In: 2020 11th International Conference on Information and Communication Systems (ICICS), pp. 324–330. IEEE (2020)
3. Abd Halim, S., Zulkifli, M.S.: Detection and recognition of broken character in car plate image. UITM J. 124–127 (2020)
4. Lee, D., Yoon, S., Lee, J., Park, D.S.: Real-time license plate detection based on faster R-CNN. IEEE (2020)

5. Chunyu, C., Fucheng, W.,: Application of image processing to the vehicle license plate recognition. In: Proceedings of the 2nd International Conference on Computer Science and Electronics Engineering (ICCSEE 2013) (2013)

6. Chowdhury, W.S., Khan, A.R., Uddin, Jia: Vehicle license plate detection using image segmentation and morphological image processing. In: Thampi, S.M., Krishnan, Sri, Corchado Rodriguez, J.M., Das, Swagatam, Wozniak, Michal, Al-Jumeily, Dhiya (eds.) SIRS 2017. AISC, vol. 678, pp. 142–154. Springer, Cham (2018). https://doi.org/10.1007/978-3-319-67934-1_13

7. Yoon, Y., Ban, K., Yoon, H., Kim, J.: Blob extraction based character segmentation method for automatic license plate recognition system. In: IEEE International Conference on Systems, Man, and Cybernetics, Anchorage, AK, USA, pp. 2192–2196 (2011)

8. Radzi, E., Wong, Y.C., Hamid, N.A., Ali, N., Ibrahim, MM.: A design of license plate recognition system using convolutional neural network. Int. J. Electr. Comput. Eng. (2019)

9. Wang, W., Yang, J., Chen, M., Wang, P.: A light CNN for end-to-end car license plates detection and recognition. IEEE Access 7, 173875–173883 (2019)

10. Slimani, I., Zaarane, A., Al Okaishi, W., Atouf, I., Hamdoun, A.: An automated license plate detection and recognition system based on wavelet decomposition and CNN. Array 8, 100040 (2020)

11. Chowdhury, P.N., Shivakumara, P., Jalab, H.A., Ibrahim, R.W., Pal, U., Lu, T.: A new fractal series expansion based enhancement model for license plate recognition. Sig. Process. Image Commun. 89, 115958 (2020)

12. Alghyaline, S.: Real-time Jordanian license plate recognition using deep learning. J. King Saud Univ. Comput. Inf. Sci. 34(6), 2601–2609 (2020)

13. Chen, R.C.: Automatic license plate recognition via sliding-window darknet-YOLO deep learning. Image Vis. Comput. 87, 47–56 (2019)

14. Li, H., Wang, P., You, M., Shen, C.: Reading car license plates using deep neural networks. Image Vis. Comput. 72, 14–23 (2018)

15. Borra, S.P.R., Pradeep, N.V.S.S., Raju, N.T.S., Vineel, S., Karteek, V.: Face recognition based on convolutional neural network. Int. J. Eng. Adv. Technol. (IJEAT) 9(4), 156–162 (2020)

16. Ioffe, S., Szegedy, C.: Batch normalization: accelerating deep network training by reducing internal covariate shift. In: International Conference on Machine Learning. PMLR (2015)

17. Oostwal, E., Straat, M., Biehl, M.: Hidden unit specialization in layered neural networks: ReLU vs. sigmoidal activation. Phys. A Stat. Mech. Appl. 564, 125517 (2021)

18. Kempf, C., Tian, J., Kurz, F., D'Angelo, P., Schneider, T., Reinartz, P.: Oblique view individual tree crown delineation. Int. J. Appl. Earth Obs. Geoinformation 99, 102314 (2021)

Information Systems

Food Recommendation System Based on Data Clustering Techniques and User Nutrition Records

Hayder Hussein Al-Chalabi[1,2] and Mahdi Nsaif Jasim[3(✉)]

[1] Informatics Institute for Postgraduate Studies (IIPS), Baghdad, Iraq
ms202010601@iips.icci.edu.iq
[2] Al-Farahidi University, Baghdad, Iraq
[3] University of Information Technology and Communications, Baghdad, Iraq
mahdinsaif@uoitc.edu.iq

Abstract. Food plays a vital role in the daily life; everybody needs a balanced diet to maintain a healthy body. Nowadays, the list of foods is continue growing. Some are natural, others are artificial, and they are reengineered and emerging every day, so choosing healthy food is becoming a more complex task. The food recommendation system (FRS) is a response to this need. It is used to give a recommended list of appropriate meal content that suits every client, and a website is built to solve part of this problem. RS helps users to find the right food groups. This paper gives an overview of RS types and defines FRS. In order to obtain a reasonable impression of the power and challenges of the RS field, a powerful model has been chosen, called the Gaussian Mixture Model GMM. The model clusters the dataset into 20 clusters. Some of them are more coherent and highly similar, while others have less similarity value. The use of Euclidean Distance and Manhattan Distance produced a similar recommended list according to user preferences depending on food nutrition. Also, using Cosine Similarity and Correlation will obtain a slight difference between its results and the first two algorithms. It's clear that the Euclidean distance outperforms the other methods.

The current research presents three extra parameters certainty, exceeded, and outlier detection, not dealt by the previous related works which are representing data confidence, overweight, outliers consequently.

Keywords: Recommender Systems · Food Recommendation System · FRS · Clustering · K-means · Gaussian Mixture Model · GMM · Nutrition · Content-Based Filtering. Euclidean Distance · Manhattan Distance · Cosine Similarity · Correlation

1 Introduction

Due to the growth in diseases and patients, healthy FRS becomes more urgent to implement to reduce these numbers. The nutritional value of a meal might be estimated for chronic diseases patients using a FRS. A RS is necessary for the selection of a product among of thousands of options. The RS assists customers or users in locating the

© The Author(s), under exclusive license to Springer Nature Switzerland AG 2023
A. M. Al-Bakry et al. (Eds.): NTICT 2022, CCIS 1764, pp. 139–161, 2023.
https://doi.org/10.1007/978-3-031-35442-7_8

appropriate food groups. There are many different chronic diseases like diabetes, hyperlipidemia, and blood pressure turbulence [1] that can be controlled well and kept under human control when using the correct food group or nutrition by following specific types of diet. Most of them can cause death; chronic diseases may vary according to a patient's age, height, weight, or even both. For example, obesity disease can be healed using nutritional therapy [2]. Not all chronic diseases can be cured, such as blood pressure disease or diabetes disease, which have more than five known types [3], but the most known types are diabetes type 1 or (DT1), and diabetes type 2 or known as (DT2). Gestational diabetes affects pregnant women [4]. Make the suggested FRS web-accessible to help patients, clients, and users find correct food group. Using the Python programming language to make preprocessing to the collected dataset. The proposed method doesn't diagnose diseases, but rather suggests and recommends the appropriate nutritions for each client based on their preferences.

2 Machine Learning

Machine learning (ML) is a technique for teaching machines to handle data better. The goal of machine learning is to gain knowledge from data. To tackle data challenges, machine learning employs a variety of algorithms [5]. ML algorithms have infiltrated all aspects of our existence. Algorithms propose foods, movies, books, things to consume or purchase, and places to visit. ML algorithms are employed in recommender systems (RS) to deliver better user recommendations. However, the ML area lacks a defined classification system for its algorithms, owing to the many techniques and variants in that sector [6]. As a result, selecting an ML method that meets one's needs when constructing a RS becomes complex and perplexing. Furthermore, researchers may find it difficult to track the use and trends of ML algorithms in RSs. The clustering algorithm will be used to make food groups.

3 The Recommender Systems

Recommender systems (RSs) are defined as "decision support systems that assist users in identifying one or more items (solutions) that meet their requirements."[7]. The fundamental objective of RS is to recommend relevant items to clients/users. Because the information is too large for humans to handle, this is why the (RS) was established [8]. Many application fields use a recommender system approach, such as recommending food, music, books, TV shows, tourist spots, learning materials, websites, and e-government, e-learning, e-commerce, and e-business services [9]. Therefore, it is highly crucial in our daily lives. It has received extensive attention, is applied in academia and industry, and has achieved many research results [10]. Most (RS's) are either content-based, collaborative filtering [11] which includes a model-based [11] and memory-based filtering[12], or hybrid-based [10]. Also, there are other techniques such as knowledge-base and Demographic-based [10, 13]. As shown in Fig. (1) [14].

For most (RS's) research, the goal is to improve rating prediction or ranking metrics (learning to rank for a recommendation) [15]. There are three phases in recommender systems: (i) initial phases, which contain the informational data that the system has

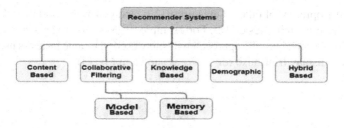

Fig. 1. The recommender system approaches

before the recommendation process begins (ii) the input data phase, which contains the information that the user must communicate to the system for the system to generate a recommendation, and (iii) a final phase in which an algorithm integrates background and input data to provide recommendations [16].

3.1 Content-Based Filtering (CBF)

Content-based techniques have been used to personalize suggestions depending on users' preferences [17]. They are dependent on the user's prior input, which will subsequently be used to filter all of the elements of the system. Users will be suggested articles with the greatest similarity score, and it will make predictions based on the item's attributes from their prior history [18]. For example, recommending a type of food that has been categorized as "salty" to a user who likes salty food, see Fig. (2).

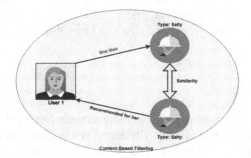

Fig. 2. The content-based filtering

3.2 Collaborative Filtering (CF)

Collaborative Filtering (CF) is a common recommendation algorithm that relies on its forecasts and suggestions on other users' ratings or behavior in the system [19]. CF is a classic recommendation model widely used in web applications and Internet of Things (IoT) services [18]. Traditional CF suggests products to users who have similar tastes (e.g., comparable preferences), filters out information based on similar interests with other users. The approach of (CF) recommends products/items, to a target clients based on the similar opinions of other clients/users [20], and generally recommends things to users who have a similar taste [18]. For example, if user1 likes vegetables and fruits, and user2 likes vegetables, the approach will show user2 the same tastes as user1, which means it will display fruits also for user2, as shown in Fig. (3).

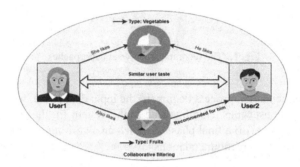

Fig. 3. The collaborative filtering

3.3 Hybrid

There is no RS that can be applied to all the cases that have been suggested. As a result, individuals attempt to solve the problem by combining several RSs. A Hybrid recommendation, which combines various RS's, should mitigate or compensate for the inadequacies of the individual algorithms [21]. Moreover, the combination is useful. A hybrid recommendation system combines several different recommendation approaches or techniques. It may take the use of various suggested technologies, to overcome the drawbacks of each and achieve better recommendation outcomes than a single recommendation technology [22].

4 The Clustering

Clustering is an unsupervised machine learning technique that puts related items into a single cluster based on their quality. Clustering is a crucial activity in data analysis and data mining applications. It's a technique for grouping things based on the maximization of intraclass similarity while reducing interclass similarity. In other words, the better the clustering, the higher the similarity inside a group and the bigger the disparity across groups [23]. Clustering can also be define as the process of assigning a group of items to a combination so that objects in the same group are more related than those in other groups. An ordered group of data objects with common attributes is a cluster. Cluster analysis is the process of discovering data similarities based on the properties of the data and grouping similar data items into clusters. There are various conditions for clustering data in data mining [24]. These criteria are scalability, the capacity to cope with many properties, and flexibility. The ability to handle dynamic data and the detection of clusters of any shape, minimal domain expertise is required to identify input parameters. Capable of dealing with noise and outliers, the sequence of the input records is unimportant. High three-dimensionality and user-specified limitations are included. Usability and interpretability. The types of data sets that are processed for analysis of clustering are interval scaled variables, binary variables, and ordinal, nominal, and ratio variables [25]. There are also a variety of clustering algorithms that may be divided into the following categories: partitioning methods, hierarchical methods, density-based methods, grid-based methods and model-based methods [26, 27, 28]. There are several methods available for clustering: K-Means Clustering, Hierarchical Clustering, and Gaussian Mixture Model.

4.1 The K-means Clustering

The K-Means algorithm is a very commonly used clustering method in machine learning and data mining. Macqueen proposed it for the first time in 1967 [29, 30]. It has high scalability and other advantages due to its simple and efficient properties, especially for massive data sets. The primary principle behind the K-means method is to split a data set into several clusters through iteration, with data inside each cluster having a high similarity and data between clusters having a low similarity, and the number of clusters must be established ahead of clustering time [29]. K-Means clustering is an iterative strategy for grouping data points that requires identifying local maxima over all rounds. It begins by forming groups of randomly picked centroids to analyze the data points. The optimization is then carried out using an iterative process. The groups are generated by utilizing Euclidian distance to calculate the closest distance to the centroid [31]. The data points may be grouped into k groups that meet the following conditions: each cluster must include at least one item, and each object must belong to precisely one cluster. The procedure starts by picking k items from the dataset to serve as the initial cluster centers. Then, depending on the mean value of the items in the cluster, each object is allocated to the group to which it is most comparable. The new mean value of the items for each group is then updated or recalculated. This method is repeated until the criterion function is satisfied [27].

4.2 K-means Algorithm

The K-means clustering algorithm works as follows [32]:

```
Input: Data points D, Numbers of clusters K.
Output: Data points with cluster membership.
Begin
        1: Initialize K centroids randomly.
        2: Associate each point in D with nearest centroids. It will divide the
        data points into K cluster
        3: Recalculate the position of centroids.
        4: Repeat 2 and 3 until there are no more changes in the membership of
data point.
End
```

Fig. 4. The K-means algorithm

4.3 The Pros and Cons of the K-means Clustering

The Pros of the algorithm are: relatively simple to implement (simple), scales to large data sets (flexible), guarantees convergence (tight), can warm-start the positions of centroids, easily adapts to new examples, generalizes to clusters of different shapes and sizes, such as elliptical clusters, and K-Means analysis improves clustering accuracy (accuracy) [29]. On the other hand, the cons of the algorithm are: the number of clusters is a parameter of the algorithm, initialization of cluster centers significantly affects the result of clustering, sensitivity to emissions (outliers) and noise, and an iterative approach does not guarantee convergence to an optimal solution [27].

5   Related Work

In the article [33] on Apache Spark1, this study provides a feature-based meal recommendation system. First, they computed user similarity using user evaluation, which is augmented by food characteristics. Then they use the food that similar users like to estimate what meals the target user might like. Finally, it may propose Top-N foods to users based on their preferences. The characteristics of food might be the original substance of the dish or the essential procedure when it is cooked. Experiments revealed that this algorithm could address the problem of many customers and meals, and the parallel algorithm can effectively regulate the algorithm's running time. We also, demonstrate that when the data is sparse, the accuracy is higher, and we may increase the compute node to reduce processing time. While in [23], the proposed method by the authors will recommend diet and therapy for autistic youngsters depending on their symptoms. The system uses the k-means algorithm to categorize symptoms and association rule mining to propose foods and remedies.

The dataset utilized in this study was obtained from the VAERS government website, which is controlled by the Centre for Disease Control. The accuracy and ease of use of the system received the highest scores of 4.1 and 4, respectively, for result acceptance. It implies that the system received a quick reaction from consumers. The articulacy and execution speed all receive more than three points, and the score is pretty good. The diet and therapy suggestion system has been successfully implemented, and it is beneficial to parents of autistic children. In research [34], the authors have made the first effort to add health and nutrition into the meal recommendation problem by first assessing the user's nutritional needs based on their unique profiles (age, gender, height, etc.). They then take the top choices, as determined by a cutting-edge recipe recommendation system, and seek to combine them algorithmically. Each plan adheres to worldwide health agency requirements. They proved that it is possible to integrate recommended dishes into balanced meal plans in accordance with nutritional agency requirements. They learned how to create better planning algorithms in the future by evaluating circumstances where it was difficult or impossible to generate plans. The authors in [35] suggested a Food Recommendation System (FRS) for diabetes patients based on food clustering analysis. In terms of nutrition and dietary characteristics, the system will recommend the appropriate replacement foods. For food clustering analysis, they employed a Self-Organizing Map (SOM) and K-mean clustering, which is based on the similarity of eight key nutrients for diabetes patients. Finally, nutritionists assessed the FRS, finding it highly effective and valuable in the nutrition field. The average quantization error and topographic error are 0.126 and 0.0103, respectively. A new approach for recommending a healthy diet using a predictive data mining algorithm was proposed by [19]. The researchers created a data mining algorithm that recommends healthy eating habits and patterns for users who want to know how many calories they burned, how many macronutrients they consumed, etc. Based on individual eating habits and body information, the patient diet advice system simulates users' unique diets and nutritional preferences. Although this study helps forecast healthy meals for patients and nutritionists/doctors, it has the disadvantage of lacking a flexible model and only achieving essential design solutions per patient's requirements. In this paper, A. Banerjee and N. Nigar [36] proposed a Nourishment Recommendation Framework (NRF) where they collect data from youngsters, evaluate it, and then provide an output that includes a better food plan. Its goal is to give healthy meals to children aged 8 to 13 years old based on their age, growth, gender, and health data. The proposed approach will assist youngsters in obtaining the necessary nutrients for growth, development, and other bodily processes. This study employs the Logistic Regression and Naïve Bayes methods. And, although logistic regression has an accuracy of 85%, Naïve Bayes has an accuracy of 84%. Eventually, Ribeiro et al. [37] developed a content-based RS and mobile app that maintains a personalized weekly meal plan by calculating nutritional needs while following static parameters like meat and fish separation, food repetition restriction, and other similar ones.

Older adults were used in tests of the recommender system and mobile app to determine the appropriateness and quality of the meal plans advised on the one hand, and the usability of the mobile app for this specific population on the other. The user testing results were quite positive, over 70% of participants considered following the meal plan recommendations and using an app like the one offered.

6 The Proposed Methodology

Our proposed methodology for a food recommendation system based on data clustering techniques and user nutrition records is shown in Fig. (5). There are three phases. We will discuss this in detail later in this section. The first phase will be dataset collection and preprocessing. The second phase is dataset clustering and analysis. The third phase is the recommended list filtering and output.

6.1 Phase One: Dataset Collection and Preprocessing

Phase One -Stage One: In this part of the methodology, the target dataset.

"OpenFoodFacts" is selected to work on, which is collected from openfoodfacts and Kaggle; it's a very well-known dataset, a free, open, collaborative dataset of food products from around the world, with ingredients and nutrition facts. It contains over 600 000 + products from 150 countries, with a 1.01 GB file size, supplied by the openfoodfacts.org website. Everyone who has already used the OpenFoodFacts app knows that there is no check or test for the user's inputs. For example, you can even type in negative amounts of fat if you want to. Because of these circumstances, we can assume that there are a lot

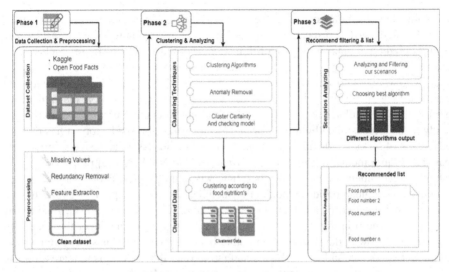

Fig. 5. The proposed methodology

last_modified datetime	product_name	generic_name	quantity	packaging	packaging tags	brands	brands_ta gs	categories	categories tags	categories_en	origins	origins_ta gs	manufact uring_plac es	countries_en	ingredients_text	allergens
2016-09-17T09:18:13Z	Farine de blé noir	NaN	1kg	NaN	NaN	Ferme r'y R'nao	ferme-r-y-r-nao	NaN	NaN	NaN	NaN	en:FR	en:france	France	NaN	NaN
2017-03-09T14:22:37Z	Bananas Chips Sweetened (Whole)	NaN	NaN	NaN	NaN	NaN	NaN	NaN	NaN	NaN	NaN	US	en:united-states	United States	Bananas, vegetable oil (coconut oil, corn oil ...	NaN
2017-03-09T14:32:37Z	Peanuts	NaN	NaN	NaN	NaN	Torn & Glasser	torn-glasser	NaN	NaN	NaN	NaN	US	en:united-states	United States	Peanuts, wheat flour, sugar, rice flour, tapio...	NaN
2017-03-09T10:35:31Z	Organic Salted Nut Mix	NaN	NaN	NaN	NaN	Grizzlies	grizzlies	NaN	NaN	NaN	NaN	US	en:united-states	United States	Organic hazelnuts, organic cashews, organic wa...	NaN
2017-03-09T10:34:13Z	Organic Polenta	NaN	NaN	NaN	NaN	Bob's Red Mill	bob-s-red-mill	NaN	NaN	NaN	NaN	US	en:united-states	United States	Organic polenta	NaN

Fig. 6. Sample of OpenFoodFacts dataset

of mistakes in the OpenFoodFacts dataset. We now want to look closer at Fig. (6) the given data and analyze possible false data.

Phase One - Stage Two: Besides the obvious mistakes like negative or too high values entries, the GMM is used to find anomalies depending on the natural structure of the given data. In addition to that, it's also used to see if there are any natural structures in the data. This would be helpful to cluster the products. But before clustering, we want to clean up the missing values because these are hard to fill up, the proposed model can't deal with "NaN-data". To drop features with a high percentage of missing values (unwanted features) while maintaining and keeping the importance and quality of the dataset, the proposed model creates a scatterplot to preview the distribution of missing values features over all the dataset, which contains features with almost no entries at all. In ML, a dataset with missing attribute values is challenging to analyze in data mining models. Only from the rich complete data can accurate information be extracted [38]. As Fig. (6) shows, there is a little peak at about 20–30% of "nan_values"; these features should be excluded because they're missing too many values, and as mentioned [38], the model should drop these features because they're missing too many values.

Dropping these features to clean and optimize the dataset and enhance the results. The data with low missing values can be found at about 10% of "nan_values" or less. For that, the threshold for removing affected features is 10% as a limit for deleting unwanted features. Therefore, see Fig. (7).

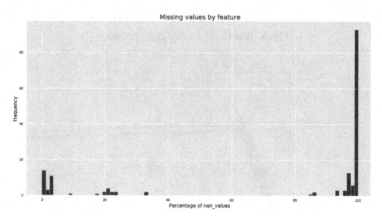

Fig. 7. The distribution of missing features

Only 29 features with less than 10% of missing values are left. This is much better than the 163 features before. We can see that there are still a good number of important features. But there are also some features we probably don't need for our further analysis. So now let's only take the following features: fat_100g, carbohydrates_100 g, sugars_100 g, proteins_100 g, salt_100g, energy_100 g, which are related to nutrition.

After that, we dropped products with incomplete nutrition tables, and we came up with a percentage of incomplete tables of 9.944, which means there are about 10% of products without completed product information. Let's delete these products now, so our data is complete and ready for analysis and clustering.

Phase One - Stage Three: Now the data is cleaned and ready for processing. But before we start, we want to take a closer look at the individual features. The energy a product contains can mainly be calculated through its amount of carbs, fat, and proteins. According to [39], Food and Agriculture Organization (FAO) is a specialized agency of the United Nations. Each 1g of fat contains about 37 kJ of energy; 1g of carbohydrates and proteins contains about 17 kJ of energy. Because of the complicated input process in the OpenFoodFacts app, some users start to type in the wrong values. Energy is also often given in kJ and kcal so that the users can get even more confused. By calculating energy based on the features of fat, carbohydrates, and proteins and comparing it to the given value of energy, we can detect if some entries might be wrong and could probably even correct them in some cases. Figure (8).

It seems like the reconstructed energy almost matches the given amount of energy. But let's look at a plot of both amounts of energy for a better conclusion. Figure (9).

In Fig. (9), we can see that both amounts of energy are mostly close to each other or identical, but some information still doesn't fit that well because they differ from the

	fat_100g	carbohydrates_100g	sugars_100g	proteins_100g	salt_100g	energy_100g	reconstructed_energy
1	28.57	64.29	14.29	3.57	0.00000	2243.0	2267.85
2	17.86	60.71	17.86	17.86	0.63500	1941.0	2032.23
3	57.14	17.86	3.57	17.86	1.22428	2540.0	2835.70
7	18.75	57.81	15.62	14.06	0.13970	1833.0	1953.04
12	36.67	36.67	3.33	16.67	1.60782	2230.0	2336.91

Fig. 8. The reconstructed energy column

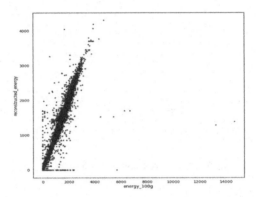

Fig. 9. The given energy VS The reconstructed energy

linear interrelation we can see. Everything that differs greatly from the straight line we can see seems to be an outlier.

Some products have a given amount of energy of 0 kJ while the reconstructed energy is higher. This means that there are values of fat, carbohydrates, and proteins higher than the 0 g given, so the given amount of energy is probably wrong. On the other hand, there are also amounts of reconstructed energy equal to 0 kJ, while the given amount of energy is higher. In these cases, the values of fat, carbohydrates, and proteins in our data have to be 0 g, but they are probably higher in reality. Because of these findings, it would be good if we also considered the reconstructed energy for our clustering. There is another obvious mistake: fat, carbohydrates, and proteins are given based on (100 g). So, if the sum of these features is higher than (100), the model would also knows that there is something wrong with the given dataset. These are represented as exceeded feature/column as showing in Fig. (10).

carbohydrates_100g	sugars_100g	proteins_100g	salt_100g	energy_100g	reconstructed_energy	g_sum	exceeded	product
80.36	46.43	5.36	0.63500	2912.0	2989.55	125.01	1	Chocolate Scone
100.00	60.00	5.00	0.25400	1255.0	1785.00	105.00	1	Fruit Ninja, Fruit Snacks, Original
66.67	26.67	6.67	0.84582	2230.0	2286.91	100.01	1	Hello Panda, Choco Biscuits With Choco Cream, …
66.67	26.67	6.67	0.93218	2230.0	2286.91	100.01	1	Biscuits With Strawberry Cream
66.70	33.30	6.67	0.93100	2230.0	2288.59	100.07	1	Hello Panda

Fig. 10. The exceeded column

As we can see, some products were registered with this mistake. As a result, there are 394 products with this mistake in our data alone. In Fig. (11), we can see the distribution of our features; g_sum is the summation of fat, carbs, and proteins.

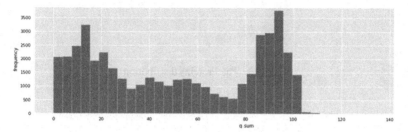

Fig. 11. The g_sum distribution

All distributions have their highest peak at about 0g (or a bit higher) per 100 g, which seems to be a bit odd at first sight. This comes from the fact that not all products include all of the nutrients above. For example, products with a high amount of carbohydrates (e.g. pasta or rice) often don't contain much fat, and products with a high amount of fat (e.g. nuts) often don't contain many carbohydrates. Carbohydrates seem to have the widest distribution: every amount of carbohydrates between 0g and 100g can be found in products, while most products contain up to 15–20 g of carbohydrates per 100 g. This wide distribution makes sense because so many products contain at least a little bit of sugar (carbohydrates). Take a look at the carbohydrate distribution in Fig. (12).

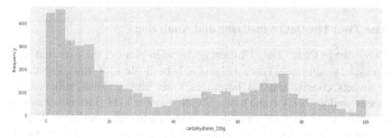

Fig. 12. The carbohydrates distribution

The protein distribution in Fig. (13) shows that the occurrence of protein in the product is also relatively low. The highest amount is about 5g per 100g, and most products contain an amount of protein lower than 30 g per 100 g.

A bit different is the energy distribution in Fig. (14). Though we measure the amount of energy per 100 g, energy is not measured in grams but in kJ. Because of that, we can't compare it to the other distributions. We can see that the distribution includes two peaks, one at 0 cal and one at about 1500 kJ. Between these two pikes, the distribution describes something similar to a parable. The maximum amount seems to be about 4500 kJ. But most products only contain up to 2500 kJ. The distribution of our reconstructed energy is

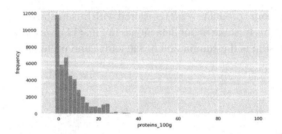

Fig. 13. The Proteins distribution

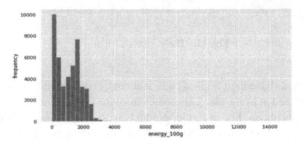

Fig. 14. The Energy distribution

similar. Still, by comparing both distributions, we can see some small differences (like the height of some individual bars), just like in the scatterplot of Fig. (14). We only want to use features that we have already chosen in this phase for our analysis.

6.2 Phase Two: The Data Clustering and Analyzing

Phase Two – Stage One: Data Clustering. Now, in phase-2 the expected number of clusters must be determined. There will probably be clusters for fruits, vegetables, grain products, sweets, cookies & cakes, beverages, meat, sausages, fish, milk products, oils, nuts & seeds, and probably some more. So, the number (15) clusters is recommended because that seems to be a good amount for the data in this experiment. The proposed model clustered the products in the column certainty. Also, we can see in Fig. (15) how certain our model is by predicting the affiliation of a product to one cluster.

fat_100g	carbohydrates_100g	sugars_100g	proteins_100g	salt_100g	energy_100g	reconstructed_energy	g_sum	cluster	product_name	certainty
50.00	23.33	6.67	6.67	1.27000	2372.0	2460.00	80.00	2	Fire Roasted Hatch Green Chile Almonds	0.84
22.22	57.41	5.56	12.96	0.28194	1548.0	2062.87	92.59	2	Organic Unswt Berry Coconut Granola	0.94
12.00	23.00	0.00	22.00	2.16000	1210.0	1233.00	57.00	2	Salade Cesar	0.89
39.29	80.36	46.43	5.36	0.63500	2912.0	2989.55	125.01	2	Chocolate Scone	0.94
1.00	24.00	1.00	39.00	9.80000	1046.0	1110.00	64.00	2	Marmite Original Pate A Tartiner 125G	0.79

Fig. 15. The certainty of items in clusters

Phase Two – Stage Two: Before asking the model to find outliers in our dataset, we have to tell how much the affected data differ from the normal data. We want to do this by choosing a suitable epsilon. Therefore, we want to visualize the log probabilities of the data to decide how we want to select this epsilon. We have determined the 12% percentile because it divides the data where the log probability falls sharply. As shown in Fig. (16).

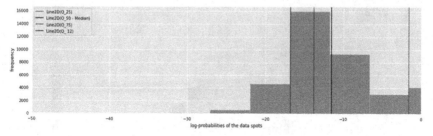

Fig. 16. The right percentiles selection

Now we can finally detect the outliers in the data. In the column anomaly, if the value is "0" the product is not an outlier and vice versa. See Fig. (17).

fat_100g	carbohydrates_100g	sugars_100g	proteins_100g	salt_100g	energy_100g	computed_energy	g_sum	product_name	certainty	anomaly
28.57	64.29	14.29	3.57	0.00000	2243.0	2210.71	96.43	Banana Chips Sweetened (Whole)	0.99	0
17.86	60.71	17.86	17.86	0.63500	1941.0	1996.51	96.43	Peanuts	0.46	1
57.14	17.86	3.57	17.86	1.22428	2540.0	2721.42	92.86	Organic Salted Nut Mix	1.00	0
18.75	57.81	15.62	14.06	0.13970	1833.0	1915.54	90.62	Organic Muesli	0.89	0
36.67	36.67	3.33	16.67	1.60782	2230.0	2263.57	90.01	Zen Party Mix	0.49	1

Fig. 17. The outlier's detection

Phase Two – Stage Three: Similarities between clusters. Using Python to calculate how similar and dissimilar our different clusters are, as shown in Fig. (18), we found that there are clusters with much higher similarity than others. Many clusters show anti-correlation or do not correlate. The dissimilarity in the feature space is what the model looks for. This can guarantee that the cluster can provide different types of products. Unfortunately, the proposed method also discovers certain highly correlated clusters with nearby cluster centers, such as the pasta (cluster 8) and the grains (cluster 16). It appears to make sense in this case. Despite the fact that both products are nearly dentical, pasta appears to be distinct from the grains. That's good, but we should try to understand in the feature space what makes this difference.

Comparing the clusters (cluster 8 and cluster 16) can give a better understanding of why similar clusters remain distinct. They are generally very similar in all features in feature space, and the feature distributions rarely overlap. Even if they are quite close together, small, and slight adjustments in some features make the distinction.

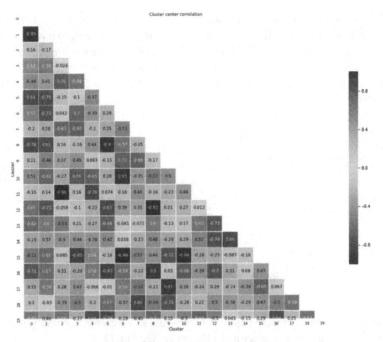

Fig. 18. The similarities between clusters

6.3 Phase-3: Recommended List Filtering and Output

The last phase shows the selection of the outperformed algorithm that gives users much more accurate results. Outcome clusters are compared with user preferences array. It will be discussed in detail in Sect. (7). After that, the user will get the recommended food list according to food nutrition. Figure (19).

Fig. 19. The recommended food lists

7 Results and Evaluation

The results are shown in four scenarios with four different algorithms. Each algorithm will be presented with one scenario intended to produce the most recommended k-list close to user preferences, and the results will be compared. We've used similarity matrix and distance similarity algorithms between user preferences for the dataset and selected food: Euclidean Distance, Manhattan Distance, Cosine Similarity, and Correlation. The first matrix is our result dataset after the preprocessing and clustering processes that we've already seen in section six, phase two, which refered to as dataset_matrix. The second matrix, user_matrix, is a selected food item for the user (user input). Both matrices will be converted into a dataframes with six features which represent food nutrition (fat, carbohydrates, sugars, proteins, salt, and energy). Euclidean Distance will be used in First scenario to extract and calculate the similarity distance between "dataset_matrix" and "user_matrix" after applying a descending sort function and excluding the first row, which will be user input, to ensure that it will return the top-recommended list to the user. While Manhattan Distance used in the Second scenario, the Cosine Similarity is what is used in the Third scenario, and lastly, the Correlation, which is used in the Fourth scenario. User input can be seen in Fig. (20).

	fat_100g	carbohydrates_100g	sugars_100g	proteins_100g	salt_100g	energy_100g	product_name	cluster
This is your food choice								
0	28.57	64.29	14.29	3.57	0.0	2243.0	Banana Chips Sweetened (Whole)	4

Fig. 20. The user input

The First scenario: using the Euclidean distance algorithm, in the Python language, one can calculate the distances between user preferences and the dataset. Table (1) shows a recommended list based on Euclidean distance. In order to compute the distance between user preferences and the optimized nutrition dataset, the Euclidean Distance Eq. (1) [40] is used to calculate the results shown in Table (1).

$$d(p, q) = \sqrt{\sum_{i=1}^{n}(q_i - p_i)^2} \tag{1}$$

where p, q = two points in Euclidean n-space, q_i, p_i = Euclidean vectors, starting from the origin of the space (initial point) and n = n-space.

Table (1) shows how tight similarity within the same cluster and less similar values in the inter-cluster and that behavior is coincident with the theoretical foundation and considered excellent results.[40].

In the second scenario, by selecting the same user input in Fig. (20), to make the wise comparison. The results shown in Table (2) exploit the required results with a high degree of confidence. To compute the distance between user preferences "user_matrix" and the optimized nutrition dataset "dataset_matrix" for the second scenario, the Manhattan Distance Eq. (2) [41] is used to calculate the results in Table (2).

$$md(p, q) = \sum_{i=1}^{n}|p_i - q_i| \tag{2}$$

where p, q = two points in Manhattan n-space, q_i, p_i = Manhattan vectors, starting from the origin of the space (initial point) and n = n-space.

Table 1. Recommended list - using Euclidean distance

Euclidean Distance	product_name	fat_100 g	Carbohydrates _100 g	sugars_ 100 g	proteins _100 g	salt_100 g	Eergy_100 g	g_sum	cluster
0.00000	Banana Chips Sweetened	28.57	64.29	14.29	3.57	0.0000	2243.0	96.43	4
5.12114	Root Vegetable Chips with Sea Salt	28.57	60.71	17.86	3.57	0.8153	2243.0	92.85	4
5.371248	Premium Air- Popped Whole Grain Popcorn, Sweet…	32.14	60.71	14.29	3.57	1.8135	2243.0	96.42	4
6.032412	Original Sweet Potato Chips	28.6	60.7	10.7	3.57	1.2700	2243.0	92.87	4
6.221690	Sweet Potato Chips with Sea Salt	32.14	60.71	17.86	3.57	0.6350	2243.0	96.42	4
6.323812	Mini Cheese Sandwich Crackers	28.57	60.71	10.71	7.14	1.2700	2243.0	96.42	4

Table 2. Recommended list - using Manhattan distance

Manhattan Distance	product_name	fat_100g	Carbohdrates _100g	sugars_100g	proteins_100g	salt_100g	Eergy_100g	g_sum	cluster
0.0000	Banana Chips Sweetened	28.57	64.29	14.29	3.57	0.0000	2243.0	96.43	4
7.1500	Ripe Plantain Chips, Maduros	28.57	64.29	7.14	3.57	0.0000	2243.0	96.43	4
7.9653	Root Vegetable Chips with Sea Salt	28.57	60.71	17.86	3.57	0.81534	2243.0	92.85	4
8.9636	Premium Air- Popped Whole Grain Popcorn, Sweet & Salt	32.14	60.71	14.29	3.57	1.81356	2243.0	96.42	4
9.0550	Baked Corn Snacks	28.57	64.29	7.14	3.57	1.90500	2243.0	96.43	4
11.355	Sweet Potato Chips with Sea Salt	32.14	60.71	17.86	3.57	0.63500	2243.0	96.42	4

Table 3. The Recommended list - using Cosine similarity

Cosine Similarity	product_name	fat_100g	Carbohdrates _100 g	sugars_100 g	proteins_100 g	salt_100 g	Eergy_100 g	g_sum	cluster
1.000000	Banana Chips Sweetened	28.57	64.29	14.29	3.57	0.00000	2243.0	96.43	4
1.000000	Real Fruit Filling	21.24	46.9	10.62	2.65	0.83058	1628.0	70.79	2
0.999999	Apple Pie	12.8	29.6	7.2	2.4	0.58928	1004.0	44.8	2
0.999999	Banana Chips	33.33	66.67	16.67	3.33	0.00000	2372.0	103.33	4
0.999998	Fresh Plantain Chips, Spicy	29.41	64.71	10.59	2.35	1.13538	2230.0	96.47	4
0.999998	Pre-Baked Pie	13.24	29.41	7.35	2.21	0.57912	983.00	44.86	2

Table 4. Recommended list - using Correlation

Correlation	product_name	fat_100 g	Carbohydrates _100g	Sugars _100 g	Proteins _100 g	salt_ 100 g	Energy_100 g	g_sum	Cluster
1.000000	Banana Chips Sweetened	28.57	64.29	14.29	3.57	0.0000	2243.0	96.43	4
1.000000	Real Fruit Filling	21.24	46.90	10.62	2.65	0.83058	1628.0	70.79	2
1.000000	Old Fashioned Apple Pie	13.24	29.41	7.35	2.21	0.57912	983.0	44.86	2
0.999998	Shortbread Cookies	30.00	63.33	10.00	6.67	0.80518	2230.0	100.00	4
0.999998	Sliced Cream Cake	17.78	28.89	20.00	4.44	1.07188	1209.0	51.11	2
0.999998	Salted Caramel Popcorn	25.00	57.14	14.29	7.14	1.81356	1795.0	89.28	4

It obvious that the difference between the second and fifth rows of "Ripe Plantain Chips, Maduros" and "Baked Corn Snacks" consecutively in Manhattan results. It is because sugars_100 has values less than the ones in the Euclidean results, and because the overall "Manhattan Distance" for these products is the closest to user preferences.

In the third scenario: in this scenario it can be noticed that there is a difference from the two algorithms, Euclidean and Manhattan, as showing in Table (3).

The Cosine Similarity score gives us another set of recommended lists with a mixture of clusters (cluster 4 and cluster 2). And as we mentioned early in *Phase two*, the similarity between clusters can be noticed. The similarity of clusters 4 and 2 is 0.76.

In the Fourth scenario: the Correlation between dataset_matrix and user_matrix after converting the dataset_matrix into a pivot table is used. Then finding the Correlation between the pivot and user input matrices. Table (4) shows the similarity between Cosine Similarity results and Correlation results. Also, in this scenario, our recommended list shows 2 mixture clusters, 4 and 2, correlated clusters with 0.76 similarities recommended list shows 2 mixture clusters, 4 and 2, correlated clusters with 0.76 similarities.

8   The Performance of the Proposed FRS

As a result, comparing with other related works that discuss in section five, the evaluation comparison is showing in Table (5).

Table 5. Comparison with related works

Ref. id	Recommendation approach	Dataset	resolved problem		
			exceeded calculation	certainty of items in clusters	Outlier detection
23	Collaborative	from Centre for Disease Control managed VAERS government website	x	x	✓
34	Demographic based	their own datasets	x	x	✓
35	Content-based	"Nutritive values for Thai food" provided by Nutrition Division, Department of Health, Ministry of Public Health	x	x	✓
Proposed System	Content-based	Openfoodfacts	✓	✓	✓

9 Conclusions

The model clusters the dataset into 20 cluster, some of them are more coherent and higher similar, while others are less similarity value, as it mentioned in Phase two, stage three. In this study, it concludes that the results of using the proposed methodology, and as it early discussed, the use of Euclidean Distance and Manhattan Distance produced a similar recommended list according to user preferences depending on food nutrition's. Also using Cosine Similarity will obtain a slight difference between its results and the first two algorithms. It's clear that the Euclidean Distance outperforms the other methods. The Euclidean Distance and Manhattan Distance algorithms will be used to recommend food lists to the user according to food nutrition's to give the user more options and food lists with same range of nutrition's. Also, the web application will work according to these two algorithms. In spite of the comparison of the current research with the related works results is not fair, because each one of them applied to different datasets. But it's clear that the results of the proposed system outperform their results and deals criteria not handled by the others.

References

1. Baek, J., Kim, J., Chun, J., Chung, K.: Hybrid clustering based health decision-making for improving dietary habits, vol. 1, pp. 1–14 (January 2019). https://doi.org/10.3233/THC-191730
2. Martinon, P., Fraticelli, L., Giboreau, A., Dussart, C., Bourgeois, D., Carrouel, F.: Nutrition as a key modifiable factor for periodontitis and main chronic diseases. J. Clin. Med. **10**(2), 1–26 (2021). https://doi.org/10.3390/jcm10020197
3. Egan, A.M., Dinneen, S.F.: What is diabetes? Med. (United Kingdom) **47**(1), 1–4 (2019). https://doi.org/10.1016/j.mpmed.2018.10.002
4. Heba Abdelgader Mohammed, H.H.: Towards Developing Type 2 Fuzzy Logic Diet Recommendation System for Diabetes. In: 2018 10th Computer Science and Electronic Engineering , pp. 56–59 (2018). https://doi.org/10.1109/CEEC.2018.8674186
5. Batta, M.: Machine learning algorithms - a review. Int. J. Sci. Res. (IJ, **9**(1), 381–386 (2020). https://doi.org/10.21275/ART20203995
6. Portugal, I., Alencar, P., Cowan, D.: The use of machine learning algorithms in recommender systems: A systematic review. Expert Syst. Appl. **97**, 205–227 (2018). https://doi.org/10.1016/j.eswa.2017.12.020
7. Kumar, B.: Approaches, issues and challenges in recommender systems: a systematic review. Indian J. Sci. Technol. **9**(1), 1–12 (2016). https://doi.org/10.17485/ijst/2016/v9i47/94892
8. Liu, J., Duan, L.: A Survey on knowledge graph-based recommender systems. In: IEEE Advanced Information Technology, Electronic and Automation Control Conference, pp. 2450–2453 (2021). https://doi.org/10.1109/IAEAC50856.2021.9390863
9. Malik, S., Rana, A., Bansal, M.: A survey of recommendation systems: recommendation models, techniques, and application fields. Inf. Resour. Manag. J. **33**(4), 53–73 (2020). https://doi.org/10.4018/IRMJ.2020100104
10. Wang, N., Zhao, H., Zhu, X., Li, N.: The review of recommendation system. In: Xie, Y., Zhang, A., Liu, H., Feng, L. (eds.) GSES 2018. CCIS, vol. 980, pp. 332–342. Springer, Singapore (2019). https://doi.org/10.1007/978-981-13-7025-0_34
11. Ali, S.I.M., Majeed, S.S.: A review of collaborative filtering recommendation system. Muthanna J. Pure Sci. **8**(1), 120–131 (2021). https://doi.org/10.52113/2/08.01.2021/120-131

12. Bobadilla, J., Bojorque, R., Esteban, A.H., Hurtado, R.: Recommender systems clustering using Bayesian non negative matrix factorization. IEEE Access **6**, 3549–3564 (2017). https://doi.org/10.1109/ACCESS.2017.2788138

13. Jain, H., Anika, M.: Applying Data Mining Techniques in MOOC Recommender System for Generating Course Recommendations (2017)

14. Priyanka, P.: A survey paper on various algorithm's based recommender system. IOSR J. Comput. Eng. **19**(3), 27–32 (2017). https://doi.org/10.9790/0661-1903042732

15. Sun, Y., Zhang, Y.: Conversational recommender system. In: 41st Int. ACM SIGIR Conference on Research and Development in Information Retrieval, SIGIR 2018, pp. 235–244 (2018). https://doi.org/10.1145/3209978.3210002

16. Kumar, M.V., Kumar, P.N.V.S.P.: A study on different phases and various recommendation system techniques. Int. J. Recent Technol. Eng. **7**(5), 38–41 (2019)

17. Trattner, C., Elsweiler, D.: Food Recommender Systems: Important Contributions, Challenges and Future Research Directions (November 2017). http://arxiv.org/abs/1711.02760

18. Phorasim, P., Yu, L.: Movies recommendation system using collaborative filtering and k-means. Int. J. Adv. Comput. Res. **7**(29), 52–59 (2017). https://doi.org/10.19101/IJACR.2017.729004

19. Jaiswal, V.: A new approach for recommending healthy diet using predictive data mining algorithm. Int. J. Res. Anal. Rev. **6**(1), 58–66 (2019). www.ijrar.org

20. Fkih, F.: Similarity measures for collaborative filtering-based recommender systems: review and experimental comparison. J. King Saud Univ. - Comput. Inf. Sci. (2021). https://doi.org/10.1016/j.jksuci.2021.09.014

21. Thorat, P.B., Goudar, R.M., Barve, S.: Survey on collaborative filtering, content-based filtering and hybrid recommendation system. International Journal of Computer Applications **110**(4), 31–36 (2015). https://doi.org/10.5120/19308-0760

22. Shah, K., Salunke, A., Dongare, S., Antala, K.: Recommender systems: An overview of differ K. ent approaches to recommendations. In: Proceedings of 2017 International Conference on Innovations in Information, Embedded and Communication Systems, ICIIECS 2017, vol. 2018, pp. 1–4 (2018). https://doi.org/10.1109/ICIIECS.2017.8276172

23. Premasundari, M., Yamini, C.: Food and therapy recommendation system for autistic syndrome using machine learning techniques. In: Proceedings of 2019 3rd IEEE International Conference on Electrical, Computer and Communication Technologies, ICECCT 2019, pp. 1–6 (2019). https://doi.org/10.1109/ICECCT.2019.8868979

24. Shah, H., Napanda, K., Lynette, D.: Density based clustering algorithms. Int. J. Comput. Sci. Eng. **3**(11), 54–57 (2015)

25. Lopez-Arevalo, I., Aldana-Bobadilla, E., Molina-Villegas, A., Galeana-Zapién, H., Muñiz-Sanchez, V., Gausin-Valle, S.: A memory-efficient encoding method for processing mixed-type data on machine learning. Entropy **22**(12), 1–21 (2020). https://doi.org/10.3390/e22121391

26. Wang, T., Ren, C., Luo, Y., Tian, J.: NS-DBSCAN: A density-based clustering algorithm in network space. ISPRS Int. J. Geo-Information **8**(5) (2019). https://doi.org/10.3390/ijgi8050218

27. Doroshenko, A.: Analysis of the distribution of COVID-19 in Italy using clustering algorithms. In: Proceedings of 2020 IEEE 3rd International Conference on Data Stream Mining & Processing, DSMP 2020, pp. 325–328 (2020). https://doi.org/10.1109/DSMP47368.2020.9204202

28. Zhu, X., Li, Y., Wang, J., Zheng, T., Fu, J.: Automatic recommendation of a distance measure for clustering algorithms. ACM Trans. Knowl. Discov. Data **15**(1), 1–22 (2021). https://doi.org/10.1145/3418228

29. Cai, X., Hu, Z., Zhao, P., Zhang, W.S., Chen, J.: A hybrid recommendation system with many-objective evolutionary algorithm. Expert Syst. Appl. **159**, 113648 (2020). https://doi.org/10.1016/j.eswa.2020.113648

30. Koosha, H., Ghorbani, Z., Nikfetrat, R.: A Clustering-Classification Recommender System based on Firefly Algorithm (2021). https://doi.org/10.22044/JADM.2021.10782.2216

31. Patil, P., Karthikeyan, A.: A survey on k-means clustering for analyzing variation in data. In: Ranganathan, G., Chen, J., Rocha, Á. (eds.) Inventive Communication and Computational Technologies. LNNS, vol. 89, pp. 317–323. Springer, Singapore (2020). https://doi.org/10.1007/978-981-15-0146-3_29

32. Borlea, I., Precup, R., Borlea, A.: improvement of k-means cluster quality by post processing resulted clusters. Procedia Comput. Sci. **199**, 63–70 (2022). https://doi.org/10.1016/j.procs.2022.01.009

33. Xu, W., Li, Y., Wei, L., Wu, Z.: A feature-based food recommendation on apache spark. In: Proceedings of 5th International Conference on Advanced Cloud Big Data, CBD 2017, pp. 123–128 (2017). https://doi.org/10.1109/CBD.2017.29

34. Elsweiler, D., Harvey, M.: Towards automatic meal plan recommendations for balanced nutrition. In: RecSys 2015 - Proceedings 9th ACM Conference on Recommender Systems, pp. 313–316 (2015). https://doi.org/10.1145/2792838.2799665

35. Min, W., Jiang, S., Liu, L., Rui, Y., Jain, R.: A survey on food computing. ACM Comput. Surv., **52**(5) (2019). https://doi.org/10.1145/3329168

36. Banerjee, A., Nigar, N.: Nourishment recommendation framework for children using machine learning and matching algorithm. In: 2019 International Conference on Computer Communication and Informatics, ICCCI 2019, pp. 1–6 (2019). https://doi.org/10.1109/ICCCI.2019.8822102

37. Ribeiro, D., Machado, J., Ribeiro, J., Vasconcelos, M.J.M., Vieira, E.F., De Barros, A.C.: SousChef: Mobile meal recommender system for older adults. In: ICT4AWE 2017 - Proceedings of 3rd International Conference on Information and Communication Technologies for Ageing Well and e-Health, Ict4awe, pp. 36–45 (2017). https://doi.org/10.5220/0006281900360045

38. Raja, P.S., Thangavel, K.: Missing value imputation using unsupervised machine learning techniques, vol. 24(6). Springer, Berlin Heidelberg (2020)

39. FAO, The State of Food and Agriculture: Agricultural Trade and Poverty, FAO Agric. Ser., vol. 36(0081–4539), p. 211 (2005)

40. Raju, V.N.G., Lakshmi, K.P., Jain, V.M., Kalidindi, A., Padma, V.: Study the influence of normalization/transformation process on the accuracy of supervised Classification," Proc. 3rd International Conference on Smart Systems and Inventive Technology, ICSSIT 2020, Icssit, pp. 729–735 (2020). https://doi.org/10.1109/ICSSIT48917.2020.9214160

41. Dina, N., Kashef, R.: Deploying Different Clustering Techniques on a Collaborative-based Movie Recommender. p. 6 (2021)

EEG Data Compression Using Tap9/7 Wavelet Transform and Double Shift-Coding

Hend A. Hadi[1(✉)] and Loay E. George[2]

[1] Ministry of Education\General Education Director of Baghdad Karkh-3, Baghdad, Iraq
hend_amir2007@yahoo.com

[2] University of Information Technology and Communication (UoITC), Baghdad, Iraq

Abstract. The main challenge of transmitting or storing Electroencephalogram (EEG) signals is the size of EEG data recordings. In this paper, an efficient and fast EEG compression system based on bi-orthogonal wavelet transform (Tap9/7) is proposed. It consists of three primary steps: (1) Tap (9/7) wavelet transform, which decomposes the EEG signal into low and multi-high subbands; (2) Progressive hierarchical quantizer, which quantizes wavelet subbands; and (3) double-shift coding, which encodes the input stream with three code-words while using the fewest total bits possible. When evaluating the efficiency of the EEG compression system, the compression ratio (CR) and mean square error (MSE) were the metrics that were utilised. The complexity of the compression system was reduced when using the Tap (9/7) wavelet transform, which also produced superior results in terms of CR and MSE compared to those obtained using the Discrete Wavelet Transform (DCT). The experimental tests are carried out with the CHB-MIT dataset, and the best compression ratio (CR = 7) is accomplished with an error level that is close to zero (MSE = 0.044).

Keywords: EEG Compression · Tap9/7 · Delta Modulation · Double-shift encoder · Histogram · Compression-Ratio · Mean Square Error

1 Introduction

Data compression techniques were applied in many fields, to efficiently transmit or store sounds, texts, images, and signals [1]. EEG signal is the recordings of the electrical activity of the brain, it is a non-surgical technique in which the electrodes are attached, in a pairwise manner, to the scalp to get the difference in voltage between specific spatial locations [2, 3]. Additionally, EEG is frequently used in a variety of disciplines, including the diagnosis of brain diseases and in brain-computer interfaces (BCI) [4]. The medical data is sensitive and required to be error-free [5]. The data can be transmitted remotely from one device to any device, such as a hospital terminal. Continuous care monitoring in the intensive care unit increases the amount of data transmitted through communication channels. This data must be transmitted quickly and without loss, so lossless compression is essential [6]. Although lossy compression provides a suitable compression rate with near-zero error, data without distortion is required for intelligent systems to accurately

© The Author(s), under exclusive license to Springer Nature Switzerland AG 2023
A. M. Al-Bakry et al. (Eds.): NTICT 2022, CCIS 1764, pp. 162–170, 2023.
https://doi.org/10.1007/978-3-031-35442-7_9

detect diseases or abnormal events [7]. As a result of the importance and sensitivity of EEG data for medical professionals and researchers, a great number of studies have been carried out in this field in an effort to achieve the best possible compression results with zero or nearly zero error [2, 8].

In a lossless compression system, (Hejrat, 2017) employ inter- and intra-channel correlations. First, a differential pulse-code modulation technique is used as a preprocessing step to extract intra-channel correlation. Next, channels are grouped into distinct clusters, and arithmetic coding is utilised to determine the clusters' centroid. In the second stage, the distance between each cluster's data and its centroid is computed and then compressed using arithmetic coding. The proposed method demonstrated a higher compression rate than the presented ones [7].

(Srinivasan, 2013) proposed lossless/near-lossless compression systems using volumetric coding and image for multichannel EEG compression systems. Appropriate representations are used to utilize EEG channel correlations. Volumetric data (tensor) or image (matrix) are used to represent multichannel EEG, and then a wavelet transform is applied to those representations. The proposed compression systems are designed based on the principle of "lossy plus residual coding", consisting of a wavelet-based lossy coding layer followed by arithmetic coding on the residual. The proposed systems are applied to three EEG datasets. The proposed multichannel compression systems attained a good compression ratio compared to systems based on single-channel compression [8].

A proposal to build a lossless EEG compression system was made by Sriraam (2012), and it suggested using neural network predictions in conjunction with the correlation dimension (CD). The coefficient of determination (CD) is a measure of the correlation between EEG samples that is used to characterise irregular EEG signals. The CD value of each segment is then calculated after the input EEG signals have been segmented into one-second chunks using the segmentation tool. After that, the segments that had CD values that were the most similar were grouped together to form blocks. Because of this configuration's increased accuracy, the predictor needed fewer bits to be transmitted [9], which was a benefit to the transmission process.

(Wongsawatt, 2006) proposed a lossless multi-channel compression system by making use of the inter-correlation between EEG channels and the Karhunen-Loeve transform. In addition to this, they reduced the amount of unnecessary temporal repetition by utilising an integer time-frequency transform [10].

An effective and speedy EEG compression system that is based on the bi-orthogonal wavelet transform (Tap9/7) and double shift coding has been proposed in this body of work. An earlier study [11] suggests using DCT in conjunction with double shift coding in order to compress EEG signals. As can be seen in the section devoted to the experimental results, Tap9/7 demonstrates superior performance to DCT in terms of CR and MSE when it comes to efficiently compressing EEG data with near-zero error.

The contents of this paper are outlined below. In Sect. 2, the EEG data compression system will be presented and described. Section 3 contains a presentation of the experimental findings as well as a comparison with other relevant works. The conclusions are presented in the fourth section.

2 The Proposed Compression System

In our earlier research, we developed and validated a lossless EEG compression system using the Motor Movement Imagery dataset [12]. In another work, an EEG compression system based on DCT and Delta modulation was produced [11]. In this work, a new study on EEG data compression using biorthogonal (Tap9/7) wavelet transform is presented. The EEG compression scheme is applied through three stages; these stages are (A) Transformation, (B) Quantization, and (C) Encoding. Firstly, biorthogonal (Tap9/7) wavelet transform is applied. Secondly, the outputs are passed through a progressive hierarchical quantizer to eliminate the existing psycho-visual redundancy. Finally, the quantized values are encoded by the double-shift coding. The structure of the compression system is shown in Fig. 1.

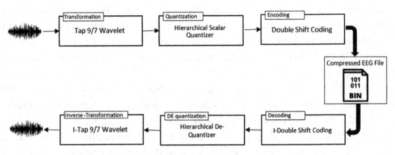

Fig. 1. (2): The proposed EEG compression system

2.1 Transformation (Bi-orthogonal Tap9/7)

The Bi-orthogonal Transform (Tap9/7) is one type of Cohen_Daubechies_Feauveau (CDF) orthogonal bi-orthogonal wavelet [13]. The Tap9/7 transform decomposes the original signal into multi-high (detailed) and low (approximation) sub-bands. For the high sub-band, no analysis is done any further, while the output low sub-band is then divided into new low and high signals [14]. Seven coefficients are included for the high pass filter, while nine coefficients are included for the low pass filter [14]. Applying the lifting and scaling steps, respectively, will result in the completion of this transformation. The lifting step is achieved using a series of phases: Split phase, Predict phase, and Update phase [15]. Tap9/7 has more complexity and accurate results than other transforms [14].

2.2 Hierarchical Quantization

Hierarchical Quantization maps the values of outcomes sub-bands from real numbers to integers [16]. Quantization is a process that involves the removal of irrelevant data as well as a decrease in the number of bits needed to accurately represent and store the values of the Tap9/7 coefficients. This reduction in the number of bits is accomplished through the elimination of redundant information [17, 18]. Hierarchical quantization divides each sub-band coefficient by an Eq. (1)-generated quantization value (Qstp):

$$Q_{stp}(level_i) = Q_{stp}(level_{i-1}) * alpha \qquad (1)$$

where i is the ith wavelet level, and alpha <1.

2.3 Encoding (Double Shift Coding)

The double shift coder, an improved shift coder, is recommended for encoding quantized values (that uses three code words, the short code word to encode the most frequent small values, and the two long code words, to encode other less frequent large values). Double shift coding requires partitioning values into three sets. The first set encodes the most common symbols with a short code-word. The other two sets, which occur less often, are encoded with a long code and then separated into two sets using one shift bit that is either 0 or 1. These steps make up the double-shift coder [19].

Delta Modulation. In order to reduce the signal values, (DM) is computed to determine the difference between each pair of values that are adjacent to one another. (DM) is a simplified and specialised form of differential pulse code modulation (DPCM), and it is accomplished by utilising the Eqs. (2) and (3) [20]:

$$DM(i) = S(i) - S(i-1) \quad if\ i > 0 \qquad (2)$$

where DM (i) is the ith item of delta modulation array, S is the transformed signal:

$$DM(0) = S(0) \qquad (3)$$

In order to reduce the amount of complexity in the coding process, the "mapping to positive" step is applied to the results of the "DM" step. In order to accomplish this, the positive values are mapped to even numbers, and the negative values are mapped to odd numbers. This is done so that the values can be recognised during the decompression stage [22]. The negative results of applying delta modulation can be turned into positive results using Eq. (4) [21]:

$$X_i = \begin{cases} 2X_i & if\ X_i > 0 \\ -2X_i - 1 & if\ X_i < 0 \end{cases} \qquad (4)$$

where Xi refers to the ith component of the array that is being utilised for delta modulation.

After the mapping from negative to positive has been finished, the histogram of the newly created positive array, which is referred to as the His array, is computed in order to determine the value that is the highest that is possible. In order to find two short code words in addition to the two long code words, it is essential to use the maximum value on the code optimizer.

A Coding Optimizer. Is utilised in order to establish the optimal bit length of the code words (a short code word and two longs) that will be used to encode the entire stream. The optimizer works with the histogram array and makes use of the histogram array's maximum value in order to search for the optimal bits required to encode the entire input stream with the fewest possible total bits.

Shift Encoder. Using the three code words provided by the optimizer, the input stream is finally given the opportunity to be encoded before being saved away as a binary file.

3   Experimental Results and Comparison with Related Works

The CHB-MIT dataset is utilised in the experimental tests that are carried out to assess the efficiency of the presented EEG compression system. This dataset is comprised of 23 EEG channels that were recorded from pediatric patients with epilepsy who were being treated at the "Children's Hospital in Boston, Massachusetts. [7, 22]. A total of 256 Hz were used to sample each individual channel that was included in this dataset. In this research, the utilisation of delta modulation on Tap9/7 was investigated. The results of the tests demonstrated that the performance of the system with Tap9/7 is significantly higher than that of the method that based on DCT [10].

The compression ratio (CR) is a metric for compression, and it is necessary to know how much information can be removed from the input data while data compression is taking place in order to keep only the information that is the most important and crucial to the original data. In this particular piece of research, the compression ratio, abbreviated as CR, is utilised in order to evaluate the effectiveness of the system. Compression is quantified using the CR scale. The expression that defines CR is as follows: (6) [23, 24]:

$$CR = \frac{UnCompressed\ Size}{Compressed\ Size} \tag{5}$$

Table 1 shows a selection of the results that are tested for the proposed compression system's performance in terms of CR and MSE, as well as the effect of wavelet levels and some quantization values. In accordance with Eq. (1). Figure 2 shows a curve that can be interpreted as an indicator of the overall performance of the system. When the wavelet level is set to 5, $Q0 = 1$, and $Q1 = 5$, Table 2 presents the CR and MSE values for each of the four distinct files.

On the CHB-MIT dataset, the outcomes of the proposed method were compared to the outcomes of a number of other works that are related; the outcomes of this comparison are shown in Table 3. The proposed system maintained an MSE that was very close to zero while demonstrating a higher CR than other works that are comparable (See Fig. 3).

Table 1. The impact of using wavelet levels and some tested quantization coefficients.

Wavelet-level	Q_1	Q_0	MSE	CR
5	1	1	0.006	4.54
4	1	1	0.005	4.55
3	1	1	0.005	4.57
2	1	1	0.004	4.58
1	1	1	0.004	4.71
2	2	2	0.017	5.23
5	3	1	0.018	5.40
4	3	1	0.018	5.43
3	3	1	0.017	5.45
6	5	3	0.061	6.08
6	5	4	0.073	6.08
5	5	3	0.063	6.11
5	5	4	0.077	6.12
7	7	6	0.143	6.59
7	7	7	0.163	6.59
8	8	7	0.179	6.79
8	8	8	0.199	6.79

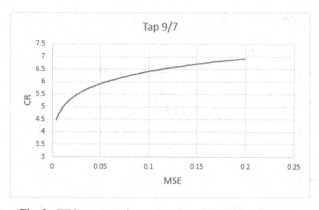

Fig. 2. EEG compression system based Tap9/7 performance

Table 2. The outcomes in terms of CR and MSE of some tested files, the wavelet level = 5, Q1 = 5, and Q0 = 1.

EEG-file	CR	MSE
Chb1	6.54	0.048
Chb2	6.04	0.048
Chb3	7.00	0.044
Chb5	6.05	0.048

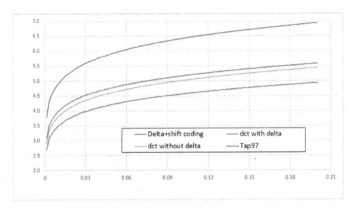

Fig. 3. The comparison of the results obtained using Tap9/7 and previously proposed methods.

Table 3. The comparison with recent studies in terms of CR.

EEG-file	Proposed-method	[7]	[8]	[9]	[10]
Chb1	6.54	2.04	1.93	1.7	1.63
Chb2	6.04	1.61	1.68	1.67	1.38
Chb3	7.00	1.87	1.86	1.83	1.55
Chb5	6.05	1.9	1.77	1.61	1.45

4 Conclusions

A new investigation into an EEG compression method that uses Tap9/7, delta modulation and double shift coding is presented in this research. The DCT transform was outperformed by the utilisation of Tap9/7, which resulted in improved compression performance (i.e., an increase in CR and a decrease in MSE) while maintaining the quality of the EEG data. The wavelet levels as well as the quantization parameters (i.e., increasing the wavelet levels and quantization parameters increases the CR and MSE) can affect the effectiveness of the compression system. The number of total bits that should be used for encoding an entire input sequence can be calculated with the help of double shift coding. The Chb3 file is compressed with the best possible CR = 7, achieved with an MSE of 0.044. The findings are evaluated in light of a prior study that made use of DCT and delta modulation, in addition to a few related works in terms of CR, and they are found to have a satisfactory level of performance.

An improvement can be done in the future by combining the DCT and Tap9/7 Wavelet transforms into a single compression system in order to increase the compression ratio. This would allow the system to take advantage of the benefits offered by both transforms in order to achieve a higher compression ratio. In addition, another method of coding can be utilised in order to test the functionality of the system that has been presented.

References

1. Antoniol, G., Tonella, P.: EEG data compression techniques. IEEE Trans. Biomed. Eng. **44**(2), 105–114 (1973)
2. Hadi, H.A., George, L.E.: EEG based user identification and verification using the energy of sliced dft spectra. Int. J. Sci. Res. (IJSR) **6**(9), 46–51 (2017)
3. Shaw, L., Rahman, D., Routray, A.: Highly efficient compression algorithms for multichannel EEG. IEEE Trans. Neural Syst. Rehabil. Eng. **26**(5), 957–967 (2018)
4. Dao, P.T., Li X.J., Do, H.N.: Lossy Compression Techniques for EEG Signals. In: International Conference on Advanced Technologies for Communications (ATC) (2015)
5. Higgins, G., et al.: The effects of lossy compression on diagnostically relevant seizure information in EEG signals. IEEE J. Biomed. Health Inform. **17**(1), 121–127 (2012)
6. Zhang, Z., Jung, T.-P., Makeig, S., Rao, B.D.: Compressed sensing of eeg for wireless tele-monitoring with low energy consumption and inexpensive hardware. IEEE Trans. Biomed. Eng. **60**(1), 221–224 (2012)
7. Hejrati, B., Fathi, A., Mohammadi, F.A.: Efficient lossless multi-channel eeg compression based on channel clustering. Biomed. Signal Process. Control **31**, 295–300 (2017)
8. Srinivasan, K., Dauwels, J., Reddy, M.R.: Multichannel EEG compression: wavelet-based image and volumetric coding approach. IEEE J. Biomed. Health Inform. **17**(1), 113–120 (2013)
9. Sriraam, N.: Correlation dimension based lossless compression of EEG signals. Biomed. Signal Process. Control **7**(4), 379–388 (2012)
10. Wongsawat, Y., Oraintara, S., Tanaka, T., Rao, K.R.: Lossless Multi-channel EEG Compression. ISCAS IEEE, pp. 1611–1614 (2006)
11. Hadi, H.A., George, L.E.: Comparative Study Using DCT, Delta Modulation and Double Shift coding for Compressing Electroencephalogram Data. Accepted Manuscript Iraqi J. Sci.(IJS), **63**(7) 2022
12. Hadi, H.A., George, L.E.: Lossless EEG Data Compression Using Delta Modulation and Two Types of Enhanced Adaptive Shift Coders. In: New Trends in Information and Communications Technology Applications. NTICT 2021. Communications in Computer and Information Science (2021)
13. Hadi, H.A., George, L.E.: Brainwaves for user verification using two separate sets of features based on DCT and wavelet. Int. J. Adv. Comput. Sci. Appl. **9**(1), 240–246 (2018)
14. Ahmed, Z.J., George, L.E., Hadi, R.A.: Audio compression using transforms and high order entropy encoding. Int. J. Electr. Comput. Eng. **11**(4), 3459–3469 (2021)
15. Beladgham, M., Bessaid, A., Lakhdar, A.M., Taleb-Ahmed, A.: Improving quality of medical image compression using biorthogonal CDF wavelet based on lifting scheme and SPIHT coding. Serbian J. Electr. Eng. **8**(2), 163–179 (2011)

16. Gray, R.M., Neuhoff, D.L.: Quantization. IEEE Trans. Inf. Theory **44**(6), 2325–2383 (1998)
17. Ahmed, Z.J., George, L.E.: A Comparative Study Using LZW with Wavelet or DCT for Compressing Color Images. In: 2020 International Conference on Advanced Science and Engineering (ICOASE) (2020)
18. Sagheer, A.M., Farhan, A.S., George, L.E.: Fast Intra-frame compression for video conferencing using adaptive shift coding. Int. J. Comput. Appl. **81**(18), 29–33 (2013)
19. Ahmed, Z.J., George, L.E.: Audio Compression Using Transform Coding with LZW and Double Shift Coding. In: International Conference on New Trends in Information and Communications Technology Applications(NTICT 2021) (2021)
20. George, L.E., Hassan, E.K., Mohammed, S.G., Mohammed, F.G.: Selective image encryption based on DCT, hybrid shift coding and randomly generated secret key. Iraqi J. Sci. **61**(4), 920–935 (2020)
21. Ahmed, A.H., George, L.E.: Color image compression based on wavelet, differential pulse code modulation and quadtree coding. Res. J. Appl. Sci. Eng. Technol. **14**(2), 73–79 (2017)
22. Shoeb, A.H.: Application of Machine Learning to Epileptic Seizure Onset Detection and Treatment, (Doctoral dissertation, Massachusetts Institute of Technology) (2009)
23. Hung, N.Q.V., Jeung, H., Aberer, K.: An evaluation of model-based approaches to sensor data compression. IEEE Trans. Knowl. Data Eng. **25**(11), 2434–2447 (2012)
24. Sayood, K.: Introduction to Data Compression, Waltham, MA 02451. Elsevier, USA (2012)

Network

Implementation of Network Slicing for Multi-controller Environment Based on FlowVisor

Suadad S. Mahdi[1,2] and Alharith A. Abdullah[1(✉)]

[1] College of Information Technology, University of Babylon, Babil, Iraq
suadad.safaa@uomus.edu.iq, alharith@itnet.uobabylon.edu.iq
[2] Al-Mustaqbal University College, Babil, Iraq

Abstract. As a result of the development of new generation networks, which include many heterogeneous services and devices, it was necessary to find a technology capable of covering the diversity that occurred. Virtual Software Defined Network (vSDN) is one of the most important technologies in the field of networking. It is concerned with optimizing the use of network infrastructure by creating virtual networks (network slicing) within the same physical network, considering the isolation of each network from the other. This paper uses mininet network emulation to configure network infrastructure and FlowVisor hypervisor to virtualize infrastructure and enable multiple SDN controllers. It also presents the implementation of three scenarios for implementing network slicing and comparing them. The results show that the greater the number of tenants and dividing the network into more than two slices, the performance approaches and may be equal to the network performance without using FlowVisor, and this leads to controlling the delay rate and the data transfer rate.

Keywords: vSDN · Network Slicing · SDN · Network Virtualization · FlowVisor

1 Introduction

Network Slicing (NS) is one of the most significant technologies for enabling 5G networks since it was developed to address an issue for the growing network services. With NS, the 5G network infrastructure has been separated into many logical networks called network slices, and each network slice has its size and structure and is dedicated to providing specific network services [1].

Network slicing will allow network operators to create different services for slices and customize their operations through the advantages of two core technologies, virtualization and Software Defined Networking (SDN) [2]. Virtualization summarizes the entire network resources to satisfy the flexibility of providing various resources for heterogeneous services, while software-defined networks separate the control plane and the data plane to provide greater flexibility and efficiency in managing virtual networks [3].

Software Defined Network (SDN) architecture has changed the limitations of the current network infrastructure by separating the control plane from the forwarding plane

A. M. Al-Bakry et al. (Eds.): NTICT 2022, CCIS 1764, pp. 173–188, 2023.
https://doi.org/10.1007/978-3-031-35442-7_10

[4]. As a result of the separation between control logic and data levels, network devices (such as switches) have become uncomplicated forwarding devices. This means the SDN switch gets routes to pass instead of using its resources to handle network packets. Thus, the network control has become centralized and programmable and connects to Application Programming Interfaces (APIs) with the data plane. At the same time, virtualization works to pool network resources virtually through network monitoring software (such as FlowVisor) and creates separate virtual networks (slices) [2].

Many researchers have addressed the concept of network slicing and its implementation in several scenarios. Where AL-Badrany, Z., & Al-Somaidai, M. B. [5] presented a method for implementing network slicing using FlowVisor as a slicing tool and focused their work on calculating the network latency for each slice using two heterogeneous controllers, POX and Ryu. But, Scano et al. [6] implemented the concept of network slicing in a way that relies on software-defined networking and a single controller. Their work is focused on creating configuration on SDN controller to share network resources over several slices, but each network slice behaves as a traditional network, not an SDN. Kurniawan et al. [7] presented a scenario for implementing SDN-based network slicing and using FlowVisor. The researchers found that FlowVisor provides complete isolation between network slices because traffic within one slice is not affected by traffic at other slices.

The present research applied network slicing in a single owner, multiple controller scenario by utilizing a mininet network emulator to provide the infrastructure. While FlowVisor is used to virtualize infrastructure resources and manage the division of a physical network into several logical slices. Each network slice is handled by its SDN controller to achieve perfect isolation between the slices. This study explains the practical steps for implementing infrastructure slicing using FlowVisor in three scenarios. In addition, it compares the scenarios in terms of delay and throughput.

The rest of the paper is formatted as follows: Sect. 2 reviews the concept of network slicing, Sect. 3 explains the scenarios for implementing network slicing based on SDN, Sect. 4 explains our mechanism used to implement slicing, Sect. 5 summarizes the results and performance evaluation, and the conclusion, Sect. 6, sums up the study.

2   Concept of Network Slicing

The concept of network slicing was first introduced with the concept of network overlay, which groups various network resources to construct virtual networks from the same core resources [8]. This idea gave rise to Virtual Local Area Networks (VLANs) [9], but they lack the benefit of programmability.

Today, the concept of network slicing is ready to create programmable network slices isolated from each other and release them to the real world due to the integration of two core technologies, namely network virtualization, software-defined networking and the ability to abstract resources [10].

Network slicing is the process of dividing a physical network into many logical networks (slices) and allocating resources to each slice and associated services [2, 11]. As a result, the network operator may offer optimum solutions for a wide range of market scenarios requiring services with varied functionality, performance and isolation [10].

The concept of network slicing is depicted in Fig. 1, which shows the establishment of logical networks for various services.

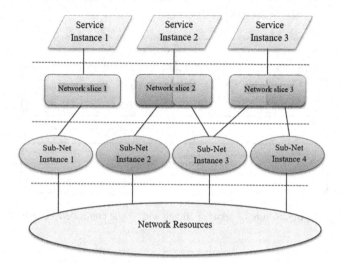

Fig. 1. Network slicing concept

3 Scenarios of Network Slicing Based-SDN

There are two scenarios for implementing network slicing based on software-defined networks. The first scenario is that a single SDN controller is responsible for managing network slices, and a northbound API is used to perform management and coordination tasks on the SDN controller.

This scenario is for a limited extent of the network because a single controller controls all the different network slices, leading to performance problems. It also represents a single point of failure and affects the reliability and availability of network tasks. In addition, each slice operates as a "traditional" network (Not SDN) [6]. Figure 2 shows the network slicing architecture using a single controller/coordinator.

Whereas the second scenario consists of a multi-controller and a single owner, supporting an SDN proxy (Network Hypervisor) in which the network infrastructure is divided into many virtual networks, and the infrastructure owner is usually the person who controls the SDN proxy [12].

Multiple virtual tenants can use this scenario to deploy their SDN controllers on the network slices management infrastructure and maintain isolation between them. Figure 3 shows the structure of the SDN proxy in the slicing environment.

As indicated in Fig. 4, one of the most important hypervisors used to achieve this scenario is FlowVisor, which works as an SDN proxy intercepting messages between the data layer and the control layer [13].

FlowVisor is an infrastructure resource virtualization layer that enables the creation of multiple network slices, and each slice includes a dedicated SDN controller. With

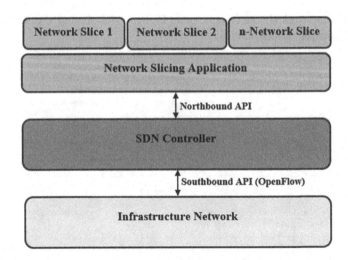

Fig. 2. Architecture of network slicing with single controller/orchestrator

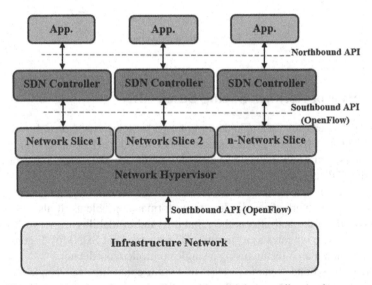

Fig. 3. Architecture of network slicing with multiple controllers/orchestrators

FlowVisor, network slices are conceptually separated from each other, and communication between the infrastructure and FlowVisor takes place through the OpenFlow protocol, as well as between FlowVisor and SDN controllers. It has been noted that FlowVisor does not exercise any controls over the activities that each network slice controller may describe in its flows, even though it provides isolation across various virtual networks (network slices) [14]. As a result, it makes it possible for malevolent controllers to plan a denial-of-service attack that prevents FlowVisor from responding to valid requests and disrupts network functionality.

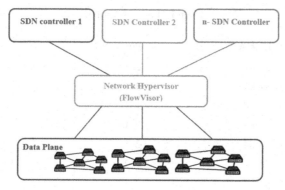

Fig. 4. Network slicing with SDN proxy

4 Methodology

Since our goal is to generate network slices on SDN, a simple and uncomplicated topology was used, as shown in Fig. 5.

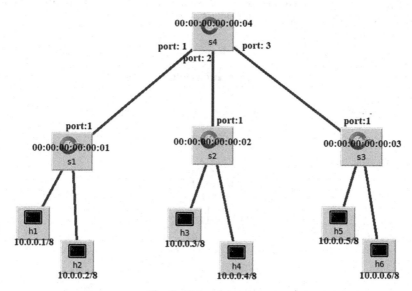

Fig. 5. Network topology

To fully understand the implementation of this structure, the numbering was fixed on the switch port, as shown in Table 1.

Based on this topology, three different architectures were applied:

- **Architecture 1:** Consists of one network slice with one SDN controller.
- **Architecture 2:** Consists of two network slices with two SDN controllers.

Table 1. Port numbering

Link A-B	Port A-B
S1-h1	2–1
S1-h2	3–1
S1-S4	1–1
S2-h3	2–1
S2-h4	2–1
S2-S4	1–2
S3-h5	2–1
S3-h6	3–1
S3-S4	1–3

• **Architecture 3:** Consists of three network slices with three SDN controllers.

Architecture 1 consists of a single network slice consisting of four Openflow switches connected to the SDN controller (pox controller). This architecture is implemented without a FlowVisor controller, as shown in Fig. 6.

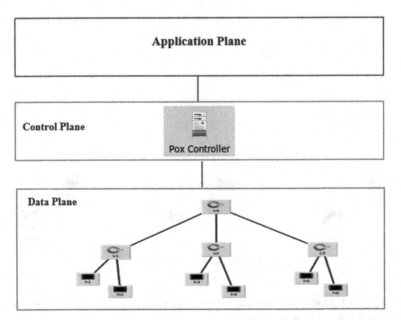

Fig. 6. SDN architecture without FlowVisor

FlowVisor is used in architecture 2 to divide the infrastructure network into two network slices, slice 1 and slice 2.

Slice 1 includes Ports 1, 2 and 3 from OpenFlow switch (S1), Ports 1, 2 from OpenFlow switch (S2), and Ports 1 and 2 from OpenFlow switch (S4).

While Slice 2 includes ports 1 and 3 from OpenFlow switch (S2), port 1,2 and 3 from OpenFlow switch (S3), and ports 2 and 3 from OpenFlow switch (S4). Each network slice is controlled by a separate SDN pox controller to preserve isolation between network slices, as shown in Fig. 7.

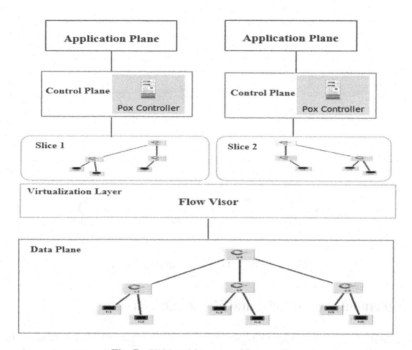

Fig. 7. SDN architecture with two slices

The infrastructure of architecture 3 is separated into three network slices: slice 1, slice 2 and slice 3, as shown in Fig. 8. FlowVisor divides the network according to the ports, where, Slice1 is represented by ports 1, 2 and 3 from an OpenFlow switch (S1) and port 1 from an OpenFlow switch (S2). While Slice 2 includes OpenFlow switch (S2) ports 1, 2 and 3, as well as OpenFlow switch (S4) port 2. Slice 3 includes OpenFlow switch (S3) ports 1, 2 and 3, and OpenFlow switch (S4) port 3. Each of the three slices in this architecture is connected to its SDN controller through the OpenFlow protocol.

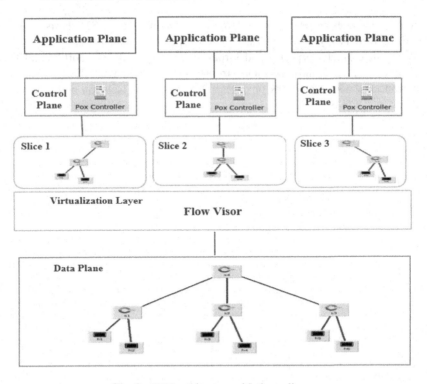

Fig. 8. SDN architecture with three slices

5 Implementation Details and Evaluation Results

This section reviews the practical implementation of the network slicing concept based on software-defined networks. In addition, the section presents methods for validating and evaluating network slicing.

5.1 Implementation Details of Network Slicing

The proposed methodology was implemented on a personal laptop with an Intel core (TM) i7-8750H CPU running at 2.20 GHz and 32 GB of RAM and Windows 10 Pro x64 as the operating system.

Four virtual machines were created using VMware-workstation-15.5.7 with Ubuntu 14.04 Lts as the operating system. The first virtual machine (with the name vSDN) contains both a mininet emulator (version 2.3.0) with Open vSwitch and FlowVisor (version 1.4) [15]. In the second, third, and fourth virtual machine, the POX controller is installed as an SDN controller plane that supports the OpenFlow protocol (version 1.0) [16].

A simple Python script was created to configure the topology consisting of 4 Open-Flow switches and 6 hosts, and implemented using a mininet network emulator as shown in Fig. 9.

```
mininet@ubuntu:~/mininet/custom$ sudo python SDNTop.py
*** Creating network
*** Adding hosts:
h1 h2 h3 h4 h5 h6
*** Adding switches:
s1 s2 s3 s4
*** Adding links:
(h1, s1) (h2, s1) (h3, s2) (h4, s2) (h5, s3) (h6, s3) (s1, s4)
(s2, s4) (s3, s4)
*** Configuring hosts
h1 (cfs -1/100000us) h2 (cfs -1/100000us) h3 (cfs -1/100000us)
h4 (cfs -1/100000us) h5 (cfs -1/100000us) h6 (cfs -1/100000us)
*** Starting controller
c
*** Starting 4 switches
s1 s2 s3 s4 ...
*** Starting CLI:
```

Fig. 9. Topology generation using mininet

The following architectures will be implemented using the same topology:

In architecture 1, all Openflow switches are connected to a remote controller by IP 192.168.23.140 and port 2008, as shown in Fig. 10.

```
poxcontroller1@ubuntu:~/pox$ ./pox.py openflow.of_01 --port=2008 forwarding.l2_learning
POX 0.5.0 (eel) / Copyright 2011-2014 James McCauley, et al.
INFO:core:POX 0.5.0 (eel) is up.
INFO:openflow.of_01:[00-00-00-00-00-01 2] connected
INFO:openflow.of_01:[00-00-00-00-00-02 5] connected        The controller has global view
INFO:openflow.of_01:[00-00-00-00-00-04 3] connected        of all OpenFlow Switches
INFO:openflow.of_01:[00-00-00-00-00-03 4] connected
```

Fig. 10. Connected OpenFlow switch to remote controller of architecture 1

Besides, a simple application was run in the pox controller in order to build a flow table into OpenFlow switches and allow the packets to pass depending on the flow entry in its flow table.

In architecture 2, a network virtualization layer has been added on top of the data plane by installing FlowVisor. Through the virtualization layer, two slices (slice1 and slice2) were created to divide the network topology, as shown in Fig. 11. IP and port of SDN controller are also responsible for this slice setting.

After creating slices, the flowspace is added to each slice by setting the switch port to the flowspace and defining each flowspace in its slice by adding the slice name. Figure 12 shows the mechanism for adding flowspace.

```
vsdn@ubuntu:~$ fvctl add-slice slice1 tcp:192.168.23.140:10001 admin@slice1
Password:
Slice password:
Slice slice1 was successfully created    IP and port of poxcontroller1
vsdn@ubuntu:~$ fvctl add-slice slice2 tcp:192.168.23.143:10002 admin@slice2
Password:
Slice password:
Slice slice2 was successfully created    IP and port of poxcontroller2
vsdn@ubuntu:~$ fvctl list-slices
Password:
Configured slices:
fvadmin          --> enabled
slice1           --> enabled
slice2           --> enabled          List the add slices
vsdn@ubuntu:~$ █
```

Fig. 11. Creating two slices based on FlowVisor

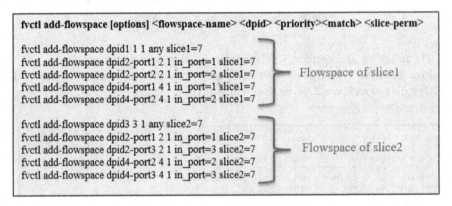

Fig. 12. Creating flowspace partitions

Finally, the two SDN controllers of each slice are run with an application that builds the flow-table on its network domain (that is, each controller has only a look at its part of the network topology). Figure 13 shows the operation of poxcontroller 1 and poxcontroller 2 on different ports.

Also, in Architecture 3, FlowVisor is used to create three network slices of the basic infrastructure, as shown in Fig. 14.

```
poxcontroller1@ubuntu:~/pox$ ./pox.py openflow.of_01 --port=10001 forwarding.l2_
learning
POX 0.5.0 (eel) / Copyright 2011-2014 James McCauley, et al.
INFO:core:POX 0.5.0 (eel) is up.
INFO:openflow.of_01:[00-00-00-00-00-02 2] connected      The controller can only see
INFO:openflow.of_01:[00-00-00-00-00-04 1] connected      OpenFlow Switch 1, 2, and 4
INFO:openflow.of_01:[00-00-00-00-00-01 3] connected
```

```
poxcontroller2@ubuntu:~/pox$ ./pox.py openflow.of_01 --port=10002 forwarding.l2_
learning
POX 0.7.0 (gar) / Copyright 2011-2020 James McCauley, et al.
WARNING:version:Support for Python 3 is experimental.
INFO:core:POX 0.7.0 (gar) is up.                         The controller can
INFO:openflow.of_01:[00-00-00-00-00-03 1] connected      only see OpenFlow
INFO:openflow.of_01:[00-00-00-00-00-04 2] connected      Switch 2, 3, and 4
INFO:openflow.of_01:[00-00-00-00-00-02 3] connected
```

Fig. 13. Controller of each slice in architecture 2

```
vsdn@ubuntu:~$ fvctl add-slice slice1 tcp:192.168.23.140:10001 admin@slice1
Password:
Slice password:
Slice slice1 was successfully created
vsdn@ubuntu:~$ fvctl add-slice slice2 tcp:192.168.23.143:10002 admin@slice2
Password:
Slice password:
Slice slice2 was successfully created
vsdn@ubuntu:~$ fvctl add-slice slice3 tcp:192.168.23.140:10003 admin@slice3
Password:
Slice password:
Slice slice3 was successfully created
vsdn@ubuntu:~$ fvctl list-slices
Password:
Configured slices:
fvadmin          --> enabled
slice1           --> enabled
slice2           --> enabled
slice3           --> enabled
vsdn@ubuntu:~$
```

Fig. 14. Creating three network slices

While Fig. 15 shows the flowspace of all the network slices, switch 1 is allocated to slice 1, switch 2 to slice 2, and switch 3 to slice 3. Switch 4 is divided among three slices, so each slice has one port from switch 4.

This architecture needs three SDN controllers on different ports to run the slices with a simple application to forward the packets, as shown in Fig. 16.

5.2 Validation and Evaluation of Network Slice

In order to validate the slicing, the ping test was relied upon to verify the accessibility of the hosts. In architecture 1, there are no network slices, so the ping test depends on the connection between the switches and the pox controller. Table 2 shows the results of the tests performed on each host that represent the success of the connection test in architecture 1.

```
vsdn@ubuntu:~$ fvctl list-flowspace
Password:
Configured Flow entries:
{"force-enqueue": -1, "name": "dpid1", "slice-action": [{"slice-name": "slice1", "permission": 7}], "queues": [], "priori
ty": 1, "dpid": "00:00:00:00:00:00:00:01", "id": 74, "match": {"wildcards": 4194303}}
{"force-enqueue": -1, "name": "dpid2", "slice-action": [{"slice-name": "slice2", "permission": 7}], "queues": [], "priori
ty": 1, "dpid": "00:00:00:00:00:00:00:02", "id": 75, "match": {"wildcards": 4194303}}
{"force-enqueue": -1, "name": "dpid3", "slice-action": [{"slice-name": "slice3", "permission": 7}], "queues": [], "priori
ty": 1, "dpid": "00:00:00:00:00:00:00:03", "id": 76, "match": {"wildcards": 4194303}}
{"force-enqueue": -1, "name": "dpid4-port1", "slice-action": [{"slice-name": "slice1", "permission": 7}], "queues": [], "
priority": 1, "dpid": "00:00:00:00:00:00:00:04", "id": 77, "match": {"wildcards": 4194302, "in_port": 1}}
{"force-enqueue": -1, "name": "dpid4-port2", "slice-action": [{"slice-name": "slice2", "permission": 7}], "queues": [], "
priority": 1, "dpid": "00:00:00:00:00:00:00:04", "id": 78, "match": {"wildcards": 4194302, "in_port": 2}}
{"force-enqueue": -1, "name": "dpid4-port3", "slice-action": [{"slice-name": "slice3", "permission": 7}], "queues": [], "
priority": 1, "dpid": "00:00:00:00:00:00:00:04", "id": 79, "match": {"wildcards": 4194302, "in_port": 3}}
vsdn@ubuntu:~$
```

Fig. 15. Flowspace of Architecture 3

```
poxcontroller1@ubuntu:~/pox$ ./pox.py openflow.of_01 --port=10001 forwarding.l2_learning
POX 0.5.0 (eel) / Copyright 2011-2014 James McCauley, et al.
INFO:core:POX 0.5.0 (eel) is up.
INFO:openflow.of_01:[00-00-00-00-00-04 1] connected
INFO:openflow.of_01:[00-00-00-00-00-01 2] connected
```
```
poxcontroller1@ubuntu:~/pox$ ./pox.py openflow.of_01 --port=10002 forwarding.l2_learning
POX 0.5.0 (eel) / Copyright 2011-2014 James McCauley, et al.
INFO:core:POX 0.5.0 (eel) is up.
INFO:openflow.of_01:[00-00-00-00-00-04 1] connected
INFO:openflow.of_01:[00-00-00-00-00-02 2] connected
```
```
poxcontroller1@ubuntu:~/pox$ ./pox.py openflow.of_01 --port=10003 forwarding.l2_learnin
POX 0.5.0 (eel) / Copyright 2011-2014 James McCauley, et al.
INFO:core:POX 0.5.0 (eel) is up.
INFO:openflow.of_01:[00-00-00-00-00-03 1] connected
INFO:openflow.of_01:[00-00-00-00-00-04 2] connected
```

Fig. 16. Three controllers of architecture 3

Table 2. Connectivity Test of architecture 1

Host	h1	h2	h3	h4	h5	h6
h1	✔	✔	✔	✔	✔	✔
h2	✔	✔	✔	✔	✔	✔
h3	✔	✔	✔	✔	✔	✔
h4	✔	✔	✔	✔	✔	✔
h5	✔	✔	✔	✔	✔	✔
h6	✔	✔	✔	✔	✔	✔

The connectivity test for architectures 2 and 3 is affected by the FlowVisor function that isolates each slice through a multi-tenant SDN system. The test is done using the pingall command, and the results are shown in Tables 3 and 4 for architectures 2 and 3, respectively.

The reason behind the successful connection test was that only hosts on the same tenant (same SDN controller) were successfully connected.

Table 3. Connectivity Test of Architecture 2

Host	h1	h2	h3	h4	h5	h6
h1	✔	✔	✔	✘	✘	✘
h2	✔	✔	✔	✘	✘	✘
h3	✔	✔	✔	✘	✘	✘
h4	✘	✘	✘	✔	✔	✔
h5	✘	✘	✘	✔	✔	✔
h6	✘	✘	✘	✔	✔	✔

Table 4. Connectivity Test of Architecture 3

Host	h1	h2	h3	h4	h5	h6
h1	✔	✔	✘	✘	✘	✘
h2	✔	✔	✘	✘	✘	✘
h3	✘	✘	✔	✔	✘	✘
h4	✘	✘	✔	✔	✘	✘
h5	✘	✘	✘	✘	✔	✔
h6	✘	✘	✘	✘	✔	✔

After validating the network slice, the performance of each of the three architectures is evaluated using the iperf tool [17]. Figure 17 shows the throughput value of TCP packets sent within 15 s in architectures 1, 2 and 3.

The discrepancy between the values of the throughput is not large, and the resulting value is higher than the value specified in the TIPHON standard [18]. The disparity is due to the presence of a virtualization layer between data and control layers, which decreased the value of the throughput in architectures 2 and 3 (without using FlowVisor).

It was also noted that with the increase in the number of tenants, the value of the throughput approaches that of Architectural 1 and produces almost the same value. This is due to the infrastructure being divided into more chips than in architecture 2 and the increased number of SDN controllers.

On the other hand, Fig. 18 shows the delay difference in each reviewed architecture. The observed delay values ranging from 0–10 ms are within the acceptable limits. The reason for the value discrepancy is that the FlowVisor performs some simple operations that lead to this delay.

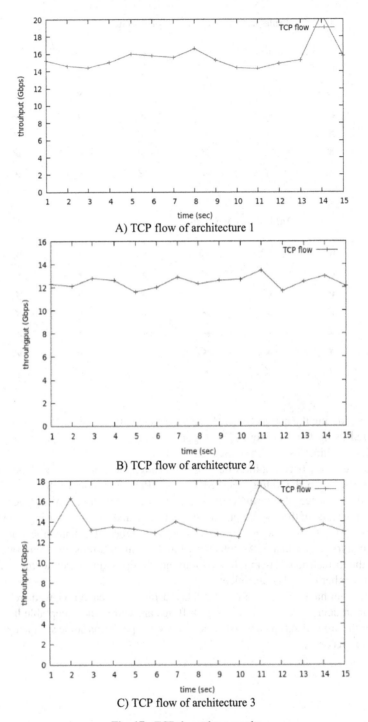

A) TCP flow of architecture 1

B) TCP flow of architecture 2

C) TCP flow of architecture 3

Fig. 17. TCP throughput results

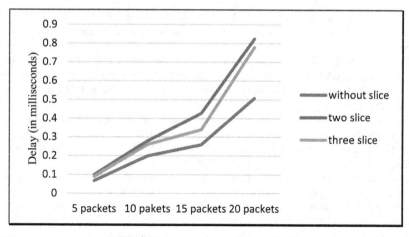

Fig. 18. Average transmission delay

6   Conclusion

Software-defined networking and network virtualization are among the most important technologies to keep pace with the development of the new generation of business networks, and network slicing is an example of this. In practice, the infrastructure is cut off through the use of a special controller that splits the network and can also isolate the slices from each other. The present research has conducted practical experiments to implement slicing using FlowVisor for different scenarios. It was found that as the number of tenants increases and the network is divided into more than two slices, the performance approaches and may be equal to the performance of the network without using FlowVisor, where the delay time decreased by 4% in the three slices scenario. Compared with the two-slice scenario, throughput increases due to distributing the load on more than two SDN controllers. Thus, relative and throughput delays caused by the processes within the virtualization layer can be controlled.

References

1. Chen, Q., Wang, X., Lv, Y.: An overview of 5G network slicing architecture. In: AIP Conference Proceedings. vol. 1967, no. 1, p. 020004. AIP Publishing LLC (2018, May)
2. Afolabi, I., Taleb, T., Samdanis, K., Ksentini, A., Flinck, H.: Network slicing and softwarization: a survey on principles, enabling technologies, and solutions. IEEE Commun. Surv. Tutorials **20**(3), 2429–2453 (2018)
3. Ordonez-Lucena, J., Ameigeiras, P., Lopez, D., Ramos-Munoz, J.J., Lorca, J., Folgueira, J.: Network slicing for 5G with SDN/NFV: concepts, architectures, and challenges. IEEE Commun. Mag. **55**(5), 80–87 (2017)
4. Schaller, S., Hood, D.: Software defined networking architecture standardization. Comput. Stand. Interfaces **54**, 197–202 (2017)
5. AL-Badrany, Z., Al-Somaidai, M.B.: Latency evaluation of an SDN controlled by flowvisor and two heterogeneous controllers. In: Al-Bakry, A.M., Al-Mamory, S.O., Sahib, M.A., Hasan, H.S., Oreku, G.S., Nayl, T.M., Al-Dhaibani, J.A. (eds.) NTICT 2020. CCIS, vol. 1183, pp. 3–16. Springer, Cham (2020). https://doi.org/10.1007/978-3-030-55340-1_1

6. Scano, D., Valcarenghi, L., Kondepu, K., Castoldi, P., Giorgetti, A.: Network slicing in SDN networks. In: 2020 22nd International Conference on Transparent Optical Networks (ICTON), pp. 1–4. IEEE (2020, July)

7. Kurniawan, M.T., Fathinuddin, M., Widiyanti, H.A., Simanjuntak, G.R.: Network slicing on SDN using FlowVisor and POX controller to traffic isolation enforcement. In: 2021 International Conference on Engineering and Emerging Technologies (ICEET), pp. 1–6. IEEE (2021, October)

8. Al-Asfoor, M., Abed, M.H.: The effect of the topology adaptation on search performance in overlay Network. In: Jeena Jacob, I., Gonzalez-Longatt, F.M., Kolandapalayam Shanmugam, S., Izonin, I. (eds.) Expert Clouds and Applications. LNNS, vol. 209, pp. 65–73. Springer, Singapore (2022). https://doi.org/10.1007/978-981-16-2126-0_7

9. Vakharkar, S., Sakhare, N.: Critical analysis of virtual lan and its advantages for the campus networks. In: Shakya, S., Bestak, R., Palanisamy, R., Kamel, K.A. (eds.) Mobile Computing and Sustainable Informatics. LNDECT, vol. 68, pp. 733–748. Springer, Singapore (2022). https://doi.org/10.1007/978-981-16-1866-6_56

10. Alotaibi, D.: Survey on network slice isolation in 5g networks: fundamental challenges. Procedia Comput. Sci. **182**, 38–45 (2021)

11. Napolitano, A., Giorgetti, A., Kondepu, K., Valcarenghi, L., Castoldi, P.: Network slicing: an overview. In: 2018 IEEE 4th International Forum on Research and Technology for Society and Industry (RTSI), pp. 1–4. IEEE (2018, September)

12. Blenk, A., Basta, A., Reisslein, M., Kellerer, W.: Survey on network virtualization hypervisors for software defined networking. IEEE Commun. Surv. Tutorials **18**(1), 655–685 (2015)

13. Sherwood, R., et al.: A network virtualization layer. OpenFlow Switch Consortium, Tech. Rep, 1, 132 (2009)

14. Costa, V.T., MK Costa, L.H.: Vulnerabilities and solutions for isolation in FlowVisor-based virtual network environments. J. Internet Serv. Appl. **6**(1), 1–9 (2015)

15. Flowvisor controller. https://github.com/OPENNETWORKINGLAB/flowvisor/wiki

16. POX controller. http://www.noxrepo.org/pox/about-pox/

17. Rajabzadeh, P.: Monitoring Network Performance with iPerf (2018)

18. NN, T.: Telecommunications and Internet Protocol Harmonization Over Networks (TIPHON General Aspects of Quality of Service (QoS)) (2002)

Security and Privacy

A Novel Ensemble Method for Network-Based Anomaly Intrusion Detection System

Ali H. Al-Shakarchi[1]([⊠]), Nabeel H. Al-A'araji[2], and Safaa O. Al-mamory[3]

[1] Collage of Information Technology, Ninevah University, Mosul, Iraq
`ali.al-shakarchi@uoninevah.edu.iq`
[2] University of Babylon, Hillah, Iraq
[3] Collage of Business Informatics, University of Information Technology and Communications, Baghdad, Iraq
`salmamory@uoitc.edu.iq`

Abstract. Anomaly intrusion detection technologies are essential for network and computer security as the threat gets more serious yearly. Ensemble learning techniques are promising machine learning methods in anomaly detection that aim to produce multiple models and combine their output in a specific manner to obtain a perfect attack detection. However, it's still difficult to choose an appropriate ensemble method for a particular dataset. This research is conducted on entry-disciplinary concept in which the knowledge is transferred between network security and machine learning. Thus, the problematic of anomaly detection in network traffic is considered, and two novel ensemble methods for anomaly detection is presented. In both methods, the decision rule (henceforth, Rule-set) which is extracted from two different families of classifiers Naïve Bayes and decision tree J48 will be used as an ensemble constitute classifiers. In the first method, a set of Rule Evaluation Metrics (henceforth, REMs) extracted from Rule-sets will be used for combining classifiers and solving rules conflict whenever occurred. While in the second method the paper presents a novel stacking approach as follows: a cover property of Rule-sets will be utilized to re-encode training instances and produce metadata set that is used for training a meta-level classifier which produces the ultimate result. The evaluation of the proposed methods will be conducted on CICIDS2017 dataset in a term of detection rate, execution time, false alarm rate, accuracy, and other interesting measures. The experimental results show attests their superiority of accuracy that reaches 99.8630% and 99.8642% for first and second methods respectively and lower execution time for both methods especially for the second proposed method, which is (0.25 s).

Keywords: Ensemble · Anomaly Detection · Decision Rule · Rule Evaluation Metrics · Rules Conflict · Stacking

1 Introduction

The rapid advanced in computer networks and communication technologies led to increasing the number of people that connected to the internet as a part of their daily life. These networks have been used to transfer sensitive information among may types of devices ranged from large computers, servers, to mobile devises and minicomputers. However, because of the large number of connections to these networks, a security concern has arisen [1, 2]. Despite that there is a large spectrum of network protection methods are available in the literature such as firewall, authentication, encryption, access control, etc., Advanced Intrusion Detection Systems (IDS) with the ability to detect new assaults are still required [3]. The main objective of such intelligent systems is to sniff and recognize the malicious behavior (abnormality) in the networks or devices and launch a warning to the manager [4]. Table 1 shows the IDSs categories.

The main concertation of all IDSs is to identify the arrived packet to decide if it is benign or not with an acceptable degree of confidence and as low false alarm as possible. To accomplish this task, several classification models available in the literature that could be employed. Each of these models has its strengths, weaknesses, and has a sophisticated method about how to take the decision. These models could be organized based on two main gauges: First regarding the model building mechanism For example, if a model is obtained and expressed as a tree, it is referred to as a Decision Tree (DT) model; if the model is represented by a set of IF-THEN rules (henceforth, Rule-set), it is referred to as a Rule-Based Classifier (RBC); and if the model is expressed as a set of equations, it is referred to as a Bayesian Classifier (BC). Second, regarding the model complexity. For instance, SVM and NN are considered as black-box models since they do not provide any explanation about the decision-making process, while DT and RBC are considered as white-box models because the mechanism of the decision-making process is easy and clear [5]. It will be beneficial if we enlarge models strengthens and reduce their weaknesses in one major system and this is done via choosing appropriate ensemble techniques.

Ensemble learning, which sometimes called committee-based-learning, or Multiple Classifier System (MCS) [6] allow one to combine multiple (homogeneous or heterogeneous) classifiers to classify new unknown pattern and achieve two important features of classifiers combination that is efficiency and accuracy [7].

Practically, after the number of classification models is trained and built utilizing part of the original dataset for training, the results of prediction from different classifiers are combined and the final decision is made up which is often tend to be more accurate than component classifiers [14, 15].

This paper will present two novel ensemble methods for anomaly detection in network traffic. In both methods, Rule-sets which are extracted from two heterogeneous classifiers named NB&J48 will be used as an ensemble constitute classifiers. For completing this goal, we extract set of decision rules from J48 and present a hot method of NB rule extraction. Two reasons behind choosing and converting NB&J48 into Rule-sets. First is due to the fact that these heterogeneous models will provide diversity property which is essential for any ensemble system to increase its accuracy. Second, Rule-sets are more comprehensible (less complexity) for human (white-box model) and simple for performing and checking with the help of specialized is a particular domain. In the first presented ensemble method, which called (Ensemble Based Rule Evaluation Metrics EBREMs), a set of Rule Evaluation Metrics (henceforth REMs) are extracted from Rule-sets and be used for combining classifiers and solving rules conflict whenever

Table 1. IDSs Categories [8–12]

IDS characteristics	Style	Characterization	Note
According to information source	Host-Based	Concentrate on data related to the system call and identifiers	While it protects a host, the network still vulnerable to an intruder
	Network-Based	Deals with network traffic data like source-destination IP address, port No, Protocol, etc.	The network as a whole has protected
According to the procedure of detection	Misuse like SNORT [13]	The detection mechanism based on matched the instance to be previously known attacks (signature-based) and launch an alarm	Although it has a high detection rate and a low false-positive rate, this technique fails to detect a newer attack and requires engagement with an expert to establish new signatures
	Anomaly	Discover unknown behaviour by identifying deviations from normal activities	Discover zero-day attack but suffer from high false-positive rate
According to detection methods	Statistical-Based	Utilize statistic techniques to reveal an attack by monitoring the traffic in a period and gave alarm if there is an unpredicted change occurred	Need less previous knowledge of benign behaviour, supply a precise alarm that takes place over a long time. Nevertheless, it could apt to being trained by the intruder
	Data mining and ML –Based	intending for discovering records from a dataset and construct a model to reveal intrusion	Capable of revealing a known and unknown intrusion. In addition to deal with huge data and discover unobserved info in the data

(*continued*)

Table 1. (*continued*)

IDS characteristics	Style	Characterization	Note
According to learning method	Supervised	This is referred to as direct classification. After a set of training patterns has been provided, one of the supervised methods is used to categorize examples	Despite the fact that it is a basic strategy that merely saves the decision boundary in memory after training, it required additional calculation time and prior knowledge of the dataset's classes
	Unsupervised	Called indirect classification. These techniques eliminated the need for training dataset (data without an actual output (class label))	Need less prior knowledge of target label. It does the classification via clustering the dataset into clusters based on instance's features hence, it is considered as more complicated than supervised
	Sime-supervised	Crossbred method that seek a small part of labelled instances for training task	Successes when sample of labelled instances are available

occurred. While in the second method, the paper presents a novel stacking ensemble approach which called (Stacking Based Rules Cover SBRC), as follows: a cover property of Rule-sets will be utilized to re-encode training instances and produce metadata set that is used for training a meta-level classifier which is responsible for the final decision. The most current CICIDS2017 dataset, which is a large dataset, will be utilized to evaluate our suggested approaches in terms of accuracy, detection rate, false alarm rate, and other interesting parameters. The experimental findings demonstrate that the proposed works are superior in terms of accuracy, which is 99.8630% for EBREMs and 99.8642% for SBRC methods, respectively, and execution time, which is (0.25 s) for SBRC.

The remainder of the paper is organized as follows: the next section will provide a quick summary of ensemble methods, ensemble combinations, and related research. Section 3 describes rule extraction from J48 and introduces a new approach to rule extraction from NB. Following the extraction of rule sets, Sect. 4 delves into two types of REMs: (Statistical and Empirical Metrics). Section 5 begins with an illustration of the EBREMs approach and how REMs have been used on it, followed by a detailed explanation of the SBRC method. Section 6 demonstrates the experiments, data set, and findings. Finally, we wrap up this article by laying out a vision for the future.

2 Ensemble Based System

For the classification tasks, an ensemble system is a composite model, consisting of a set of classifiers. The individual classifiers gave their own vote, and final prediction is returned via the ensemble based on the collection of votes [15]. This section will give an overview of ensemble techniques, combination methods, and related works in the field of Intrusion Detection Systems IDSs.

2.1 Ensemble Systems: A Quick Overview

In 1979, Dasarathy et al. [16] presented their first article on the ensemble concept, recommending that the feature space be divided using at least two classifiers. Hansen et al. [17] went even farther in 1990, discovering that predictions produced with a combination of classifiers are frequently more exact than predictions made with a single classifier. Other intriguing ensemble theories proposed by Schapire [18] in 1990 confirmed that weak classifiers might be improved to become powerful classifiers. All of the recently cited publications go in the direction of using and advocating new troupe tactics under a variety of labels and concepts.

2.2 Ensemble Methods

Robi Polikar [19] mentioned two key questions to think about when putting up any ensemble structure. Firstly, how the base classifier will be constructed? Second, how they contrast from one another? The rejoinder to these inquiries in the end will decide the diversity degree which is vital standards for further developing ensemble framework. As a general, the portrayal of ensemble methods could be summed up in Table 2.

Table 2. Ensemble Techniques Summarization

Characteristics	Methods	Descriptions
Based on ensemble structure [20]	Homogenous ensemble	Made up from two or more learner of the same types
	Heterogeneous ensemble	Made up from two or more learner of the different types
Based on applications used ensemble [7, 20]	Bagging	Using a different subset of training data with replacement from the whole dataset, and train classifiers of the same type, the output combined via voting
	Boosting (AdaBoost)	Enhancing the performance of weak classifier to be strong one, using a different subset of training data with replacement from the whole dataset, often train classifiers of the same type, the output combined via voting. There exist two versions of the AdaBoost(AdaBoostM1, AdaBoostM2)

(continued)

Table 2. (*continued*)

Characteristics	Methods	Descriptions		
	Stacking	An ensemble of heterogeneous classifiers is first created, whose outputs are used as inputs to a second level meta-classifier to learn the mapping between the ensemble outputs and the real accurate classes		
Based on ensemble construction [21]	Manipulating the training set	Resampling original dataset to create multiple training sets according to some sampling distribution		
	Manipulating the input features	A subset of attributes is picked to shape each training set either arbitrarily or in light of the suggestion of specialists		
	Manipulating target class (ECOC method)	The training set is changed into a twin class issue by haphazardly parceling the class names into two disjoint subsets, utilized a voting scheme as a mixed strategy		
	Manipulating the learning algorithm	Learning algorithm could be manipulated in such a way that allow to apply the same algorithm several times and produce different outputs. For example, NN, could produce a different model by changing network topology or initial weights		
Based on combination methods [19, 21–25]	Class labels Combination	Majority vote	unanimous voting	All classifiers agree to class output
			simple majority	More than half classifiers agree to class output
			plurality voting	Choices the class output of the classier that receive higher vote
		Weighted majority vote	Weighting the decisions of heavily trusted classifiers to improve overall performance	

(*continued*)

Table 2. (*continued*)

Characteristics	Methods	Descriptions		
		Behavior Knowledge Space (BKS)	In the training phase, use a search table that contains a combination formed by classifiers concerning the correct class. The genuine class for which a given labeling combination is observed most frequently during training is then determined, and it is decided whether it will appear in the testing phase	
		Borda Count	If and when the classifiers can rank order the classes, Borda count is utilized. Each class receives a vote, which is tallied across all classifiers, and the ensemble decision is made by the class with the most votes	
Continuous Outputs Combination	Algebraic Combination on	Mean Rule	The final decision is made up by averaging all classifiers ensemble	
		Weighted Average	It hybrid of mean and weighted majority vote	
		Trimmed Mean	Some classifiers my affect the final decision via giving unusual low or high support for particular class, to fix this problem, the inhibitor classifier will be removed	
		Minimum Rule	Take specific statistical metrics of the classifiers' outputs	
		Maximum Rule		
		Median Rule		

(*continued*)

Table 2. (*continued*)

Characteristics	Methods	Descriptions	
		Product Rule	Classifiers output which represents the support multiplied to yield the final output
		Decision Templates	The decision templates of each class are likening to the test instance v, then the class label which has DT is closed, using appropriate similarity measure, is selected as the ensemble final decision
		Dempster-Shafer Based Combination	The Dempster-Shafer (DS) hypothesis is based on evidence, and it checks the proof available from each classifier using belief functions (rather than probability), which are then combined using Dempster's combination method

2.3 Related Works

Over time, the Intrusion Detection System (IDS) has piqued the interest of researchers. This prompted them to suggest a wide range of strategies for improving the performance of their proposed IDSs using machine learning and data mining techniques. A survey of anomaly detection created utilizing machine learning and statistical methods is presented by Hodge et al. [26]. Markou et al. [27, 10] provide a comprehensive evaluation of neural network and statistical methods for detection. Table 3 below will highlight those important studies that mainly concentrate on ensemble techniques when promote intrusion detection systems for the period between (2009–2020) considering the entries (Author(s)/Year, ensemble structure, ensemble component, combination method, pre-processing, the dataset used, and metrics for evaluation).

Table 3. Summary Table of the Interesting Works in the Last 10 Years That Employ Ensemble Techniques for IDSs (Homogenous **H**, Heterogenous **G**).

Author(s)	Ensemble structure	Ensemble base learners	Fusion method	Pre-processing	Dataset	Evaluation metric(s)
Roberto Perdisci et al. [25]	H	SVMs	average of probabilities	Clustering features	DARPA'99, GATECH	ROC, AUC, FP
Song et al. [28]	H	SVMs	Maximum rule	Clustering, feature selection	Real traffic	ROC Curve
Te-Shun Chou et al. [29]	G	NN, Fussy KNN, Naive Bayes classifier	majority voting, average rule, Dempster-Shafer technique, and Bayesian combination method	Remove redundant records	KDD99	Detection rate (DR), false positive rate (FPR), and classification rate (CR)
GangLiu et al. [30]	G	BP neural network, probabilistic neural network and SVM	Dempster-Shafer evidence theory	None	2358 normal programs and 65 1 virus programs	ROC
M. Govindarajan et al. [31]	G	MMP, RBF	Vote	None	UNM Send-Mail Data	Accuracy
P. Arun Raj Kumar et al. [32]	H	Resilient Back Propagation (RBP)	WMV, Weighted Product Rule(WPR), and Neyman Pearson cost minimization strategy	Normalization	KDD'99, DARPA'99, and generated DDoS attack in author lap	Accuracy, TP, FP, Cost per sample, ROC
Sivatha et al. [33]	G	NN,C4.5	Vote	Genetic algorithm	KDD'99	TP, FP, Precision, Recall and F-measure
Debojit Boro et al. [34]	G	C4.5, Naive Bayes, and Decision Table	Meta ensemble, weighted majority vote	Information Gain	KDD'99, TUIDS Information	Accuracy
Eduardo de la Hoz et al. [35]	H	SVCs	Selection	PCA, Kernel PCA, Isometric Mapping Isomap	NSL-KDD	Accuracy, TP, FP
Alexandre Balon-Perin et al. [36]	H	DT	Majority vote	SVM, linear genetic programming (LGP), and multivariate adaptive regression splines (MARS) for features selection	KDD'99	Accuracy, FP, FN

(*continued*)

Table 3. (*continued*)

Author(s)	Ensemble structure	Ensemble base learners	Fusion method	Pre-processing	Dataset	Evaluation metric(s)
Saman Masarat et al. [37]	H	J48 tree	Fuzzy combination based on tree cost and detection rate	gain ratio feature selection	KDD'99	Accuracy, Cost
Shalinee Chaurasia et al. [38]	G	NN, KNN	Majority vote	None	KDD'99	Accuracy, TP, FP
Bayu Adhi Tama et al. [39]	G	C4.5, Random Forest, and CART	Majority vote, Average of Probabilities Rule	particle swarm optimization (PSO) for attribute selection	NSL-KDD	Accuracy, FPR
D.P.Gaikwad et al. [40]	H	Partial Decision Tree	Vote	Genetic algorithm	NSL-KDD	Accuracy, TP, FP, and model building time
Aburomman et al. [41]	G	SVM, k-NN	Weighted Majority Vote (WMV)	None	KDD'99	Classification accuracy
Kailas Shivshankar Elekar [42]	G	(J48 and Random Tree), (RandomForest and Random Tree),(J48 and Random Forest Correct)	Vote	None	KDD'99	Attack detection rate and false attack detection rate
M A Jabbar Et al. [43]	G	Random Forest(RF), Average One-Dependence Estimator (AODE)	Vote	Pre-processing Numeric to binary	Kyoto	Accuracy, DR, FAR, Hubert Index (HI)
Valentina Timenko et al. [44]	H	C4.5	Bagged tree, AdaBoost, LogitBoost, GentleBoost, RUSBoost(Vote)	None	UNSW-NB15	Accuracy, ROC, AUC, TP, FP
Ngoc Tu Pham et al. [45]	H	J48	Bagging and Boosting (Vote)	leave-one-out" techniques and Naive Bayes classifier for feature selection	NSL-KDD	Accuracy, FAR
H. P. Vinutha et al. [46]	H	J48	AdaBoost, Bagging, and Stacking	Cfs, Chi-square, SU, Gain Ratio, Info Gain, and OneR used for feature selcetion	NSL-KDD	TP rate, FP rate, Precision, Recall, ROC, Accuracy

(*continued*)

Table 3. (*continued*)

Author(s)	Ensemble structure	Ensemble base learners	Fusion method	Pre-processing	Dataset	Evaluation metric(s)
Fadi Salo et al. [47]	G	SVM, Instance-based learning algorithms (IBK), and multilayer perceptron (MLP)	Vote	Information gain (IG) and principal component analysis (PCA) for dimensionality reduction	ISCX 2012, NSL-KDD, and Kyoto 2006 +	Accuracy DR, FAR, Precision, F-Measure, Building time (s) Testing time(s)
Santosh Kumar Sahu et al. [48]	G	SVM, k_means	Majority vote	Feature selection and normalize data	NSL-KDD, GureKDDCup, and KDDCorrected	Confusion Matrix, ROC, F1 Score, FDR, False Omission Rate (FOR), True Positive Rate (TPR), True Negative Rate (TNR), Accuracy ACC, Positive Predictive Value PPV, Negative Predictive Value NPV, False Negative Rate FNR, False Positive Rate FPR, Positive Likelihood Ratio LR +, Negative Likelihood Ratio LR
Kunal and Mohit Dua [49]	G	IBk, Random Tree, REP Tree, j48m,and Random Forest	Vote	ranker-based attribute evaluation	NSL-KDD	Accuracy, FPR, Recall, and ROC
Amir Andalib and Vahid Tabataba [50]	G	gated recurrent unit (GRU), convolutional neural network,and Random forest	Majority vote, OR logic	numericalization and normalization	NSL-KDD	Accuracy, FPR, DR

3   Rule Extraction

Decompositional and Pedagogical are two important strategies for rule extraction from neural networks, according to Andrews et al. [51]. These strategies could be applied to other models as well. The key distinctions between these strategies are the methods used to extract the rules. The first method focuses on extracting rules from the underlying machine learning method. The second, on the other hand, treats the original model as a black box, necessitating collaboration with additional machine learning techniques with latent ability to explain the basic principles of the original ML method. This necessitates using the original model (black-box) to develop patterns that will be employed in the second model, which will be in charge of generating rules as output.

3.1 Naïve Bayes Rule Extraction

The proposed rule extraction (Hint: in this paper, the terms Extraction and Construction can be used interchangeably) method from Naïve Bayes could be viewed as a decompositional [52]. Hence, a set of classification rules from the NB model could be derived. The construction process is conducted by constructing a rule to every attribute of instances and it takes the following forms.

$$\text{Rule (R)} : T_i \Rightarrow Z_k : P$$

The pattern with its attributes is represented by Ti(T1, T2, T3....Tt) and the target class is represented by Zk (Z1, Z2...Zk). The letter (P) denotes the rule's potency or strength. If the dataset is vast, this extraction procedure technique will generate a lot of rules. As a result, a parameter that regulates this process (i.e. Rule construction) is required to address this issue, and the (P) parameter will serve this role. Rules with low-P will be deleted and removed from the rule-set depending on the parameter (P), boosting the correctness of the system (RBC). Algorithm 1 shows the rule extraction process that was inspired by [53] and is based on previous assumptions.

Algorithm (1): NB Rule Extraction

Input: NB conditional probability P(Xi /C);
            T, threshold;
Output: Rule-set(R)
```
1 begin
2     for i=1 to No.pf instances do
3         for k=1 to No.of classes do
4             L:= P(Xi /C)
5             IF(L ≥ T) OR(L ≤ 1-T)Then
6                 R=R ∪ (Xi➔C,f(L))
7         endfor
8     endfor
9 end
```

Equal Width (EW) and Equal Frequency (EF) are two unsupervised binning algorithms that have been used as pre-processing to make rule extraction easier. These two approaches rely on important variables known as Bin (which indicates the interval of data and represents the subdivision of identical size in the case of EW or divides the data into N groups in the case of EF; each of them includes the same number of values).

3.2 Extracting J48 Rules

The extraction of rules from DT is done in a unique way. The decision rule has been produced by acquiring the path from the root to the leaf of a tree (path will represent rule antecedent, while leave will represent the class label), such that the decision rule will be retrieved for each path from root to leave. Algorithm 2 shows the pseudo-code for the rule building from DT, which is based on [21]:

Algorithm (2): DT Rule Extraction

Input: T, a training dataset;
           DT, a decision tree classifier;
Output: Rule-set(R)
```
1 begin
2    Build DT by training DT classifier on T
3    Apply pruning procedure on generated tree
4        for i=1 to (No.of paths to leafs) do
5            Extract rules from each path to the corresponding
             leaves as R=R ∪ (Path_i →Leaf_i)
6        endfor
7 end
```

---

4 Rule Evaluation Metrics REMs

Through considerable analysis between these two components, a contingency table, also known as a two-way frequency table, has been developed to represent important information between class C and the rule R. The contingency table is a vital numerical that is widely used in ML tasks [15] for presenting categorical data in frequency counts and can be represented by a 2×2 matrix [54]. The contingency table is shown in Table 4:

Table 4. Absolute Frequency of Contingency Table

	Class C	Not class C	
Covered by rule R	n_{rc}	$n_{r\bar{c}}$	n_r
Not covered by rule R	$n_{\bar{r}c}$	$n_{\bar{r}\bar{c}}$	$n_{\bar{r}}$
	n_c	$n_{\bar{c}}$	N

where: n_{rc}: represents the counts of instances within training data which are covered by rule R and related to class C; $n_{r\bar{c}}$: represents the counts of instances within training data that are covered by R but not related to class C; and so forth to the rest. n_r, $n_{\bar{r}}$, n_c, $n_{\bar{c}}$: represent marginal totals, that is: $n_r = n_{rc} + n_{r\bar{c}}$ represents the count of instances covered by R. N: total number of training instances. Table 5 depicted the contingency table as a relative frequency table rather than an absolute frequency table.

where $f_{rc} = \frac{n_{rc}}{N}$, $f_{r\bar{c}} = \frac{n_{r\bar{c}}}{N}$ and so forth.

Table 5. Relative Frequency of Contingency Table

	Class C	Not class C	
Covered by rule R	f_{rc}	$f_{r\bar{c}}$	f_r
Not covered by rule R	$f_{\bar{r}c}$	$f_{\bar{r}\bar{c}}$	$f_{\bar{r}}$
	f_c	$f_{\bar{c}}$	1

4.1 Empirical Evaluation Metrics

According to Bruha et al. [55], several REMs exhibit complex behavior for analyzing rules. These measures are known as empirical metrics since they are based on guesswork rather than statistical or other information theories. The study will give two rule formulae that were utilized to derive the Empirical REMs in order to present the most appealing empirical REMs. The first is known as accuracy (also known as consistency), and the second is known as coverage (also known as completeness) of rule R.; the consistency is defined as follows in Eq. 1:

$$Cons(R) = \frac{n_{rc}}{n_r} \tag{1}$$

The coverage of rule R Eq. 2 below is derived as follow:

$$Cover(R) = \frac{n_{rc}}{n_c} \tag{2}$$

These two measures are critical indicators of the rule's consistency. When utilizing these two metrics as a measure of rule quality, there are two considerations to keep in mind. We can state for the first metric that the rule that applies to positive elements may also apply to negative elements. When it comes to the second parameter, "Accuracy," using this scale alone can result in rules that only cover a small number of elements, which can lead to poor forecasting because rules may overfit the dataset. It is beneficial to combine the two metrics in order to create a more robust and efficient rule assessment metric. The empirical evaluation indicators are summarized in Table 6.

4.2 Metrics for Statistical Evaluation

Despite the fact that empirical REMs have been distinguished by their simplicity, comprehensibility, and comparative output. They do not, however, rely on any theoretical concept. Empirical REMs, on the other hand, could be regarded reasonable measures. Authors continue to search for new REM to improve rule quality; Bruha, Ivan, and Kockova, S [55], Aijun An and Nick Cercone [59] provide three sets of REM based on statistics. These metrics are entirely dependent on the contingency table's statistical relationship. The statistical evaluation indicators will be summarized in Table 7.

Table 6. Empirical Evaluation Metrics

Rule metric	Author(s)	Equation	notes
Weighted sum of consistency and coverage	Michalski and Ryszard [56]	$Qws(R) = W1 \times \text{cons}(R) + W2 \times cove(R)$ (3) where W_1, W_2 represent weights realized by a user, values of these weights in ranges (0, 1) and summed to 1. $Qws(R)$ has been utilized in YAILS learning system [57] $W1 = 0.5 + \frac{1}{4}\text{cons}(R)$ and $W2 = 0.5 - \frac{1}{4} \times \text{cons}(R)$	The weights influenced by the consistency that is the larger consistency, the more influence rule by consistency. One can exchange between consistency and the coverage metric
Product of consistency and coverage	Torgo, L y[58]	$Q_{prod}(R) = \text{cons}(R) \times f(cover(R))$ (4) where f is a function	After conducting several extensive experiments, the researchers concluded that the best value for f is the exponential function as $= e^{x-1}$. Furthermore, they discovered that f reduces the influence of rule metric coverage discrepancies

Table 7. Statistical Evaluation Metrics

Type of Metric	Rule metric	Author(s)	Equation		Notes
Measures of Association	Pearson x^2 Statistic	Yvonne M et al. [54]	$x^2 \sum \dfrac{\left(n_{rc} - \frac{n_r\, n_c}{N}\right)^2}{\frac{n_r\, n_c}{N}}$	(5)	Whenever class C and rule R are highly connected, the x^2 value is modest.
	G2 Likelihood Ratio Statistic	Clark, P et al. [60]	$G2 = 2\left(\frac{n_{rc}}{n_r} log \frac{n_{rc}N}{n_r n_c} + \frac{n_{r\bar{c}}}{n_r} log \frac{n_{r\bar{c}}N}{n_r n_{\bar{c}}}\right)$ where the logarithm is of base e	(6)	If the correlation between the two distributions is just coincidental, G2 has a low value

(continued)

Table 7. (*continued*)

Type of Metric	Rule metric	Author(s)	Equation	Notes
Measures of Agreement (Evaluation metrics obtained under this category used contingency table with relative frequencies and focus only to diagonal elements)	Cohen's Formula	Cohen, J [61]	$$Q_{Cohen} = \frac{f_{rc} + f_{\overline{rc}} - (f_r f_c + f_{\overline{r}} f_{\overline{c}})}{1 - (f_r f_c + f_{\overline{r}} f_{\overline{c}})} \quad (7)$$ $f_{rc} + f_{\overline{rc}}$ will calculate actual agreement, while the chance agreements obtained as: $f_r f_c + f_{\overline{r}} f_{\overline{c}}$	Cohen suggests a new rule evaluation metric that compares the actual and chance agreements
	Colman's Formula	Yvonne M et al. [54]	$$Q_{coleman} = \frac{f_{rc} - f_r f_c}{f_r - f_r f_c} \quad (8)$$	calculates the relationship between the first column and any row in the contingency table
	C1 and C2 Formulas	Bruha et al. [55]	$$Q_{C1} = Q_{coleman} \times \frac{2 + Q_{Cohen}}{3} \quad (9)$$ $$Q_{C2} = Q_{coleman} \times \frac{1 + cover(R)}{2} \quad (10)$$ where the coefficients 2, 3 and 1, 2 are used for the normalization purpose	Coleman's metric is dissected in detail by Bruha, who discovers that it does not compromise coverage. Also, come to the conclusion that Cohen's metric is more reliant on Cover (R). As a result, Coleman's metric has been altered
Measure of Information	information score	Kononenko et al. [62]	$$Q_{IS} = -log \frac{n_c}{N} + log \frac{n_{rc}}{n_r} \quad (11)$$	The information required to classify an instance into class C with a prior probability of P(C) can be obtained as (-log P(C))
Measure of logical sufficiency	Quality logical sufficiency	Y.Y. Yao et al. [63]	$$Q_{LS} = \frac{P(R|C)}{P(R|\overline{C})} \quad (12)$$ P represents the probability. The Q_{LS} could be written using contingency table as follow: $$Q_{LS} = \frac{\frac{n_{rc}}{n_c}}{\frac{n_{r\overline{c}}}{n_{\overline{c}}}} \quad (13)$$	A rule with a big Q_{LS} indicates that R's observation is encouraging for class C, and vice versa

(*continued*)

Table 7. (*continued*)

Type of Metric	Rule metric	Author(s)	Equation	Notes
Measure of Discrimination	Quality Measure of Discrimination	Aijun et al. [64]	The following formula can be used as a measure of how well rule R is able to recognize between positive and negative patterns of class C $$Q_{MD} = log \frac{P(R|C)(1-P(R|\overline{C}))}{P(R|\overline{C})(1-P(R|C))} \quad (14)$$ P represent probability. The above formula can be recalculated via contingency table as follow $$Q_{MD} = \frac{\frac{n_{rc}}{n_{\overline{r}c}}}{\frac{n_{r\overline{c}}}{n_{\overline{r}\overline{c}}}} \quad (15)$$	This metric used in ELEM2 [65]
Measure Depend on Coverage	Laplace	Peter Clark et al. [66]	$Laplace = \frac{f_+ + 1}{n+k} \quad (16)$	Used in CN2 rule induction system
	M-estimate	Savso Dvzeroski, et al. [67]	$M - estimate = \frac{f_+ + kp_+}{n+k} \quad (17)$	Used in CN2 rule induction system as alternative of Laplace metric

5 Proposed Ensemble System

Figure 1 shows the suggested system which relays on two heterogeneous classifiers and two ensemble methods. We'll break down this diagram into five steps to make it easier to understand. To begin with (step 1), A training dataset is chosen. The CICIDS2017 dataset was used as the most recent intrusion detection dataset for this research. The second stage (step 2) is a preprocessor, which comprises dimensionality reduction and feature selection procedures that are required because the selected dataset is large and has many attributes. The authors use a filtering strategy to choose the most essential features that improve classification performance. The orientation in (step 3) will be for the purpose of training two heterogeneous classification models (i.e. NB & J48).

Models will be trained on the same training dataset, resulting in two learnt models, each with its own classification capabilities. The fourth stage (step 4) governs the construction process. Using proposed rule extraction algorithms from the NB&J48 models mentioned in Sects. 3.1 and 3.2, a set of rules (i.e., Rule-set) from each classifier will be extracted. Following Step 4, a pool will have two unique rule sets. Step 5 consists of two threads that make up the core of our suggested systems. The first, EBREMs, begins with rule evaluation, which comprises calculating a collection of REMs from extracted Rule-sets to be utilized in integrating ensemble base classifiers and resolving conflicts as stated in the next subsection (Sect. 5.1). The second SBRC will leverage the cover property of rules to create metadatasets from extracted Rule-sets, which will then be used to train a meta classifier, which will then be used to combine the base classifiers, as shown in detail in (Sect. 5.2). The proposed ensemble methods will be evaluated in the last stage.

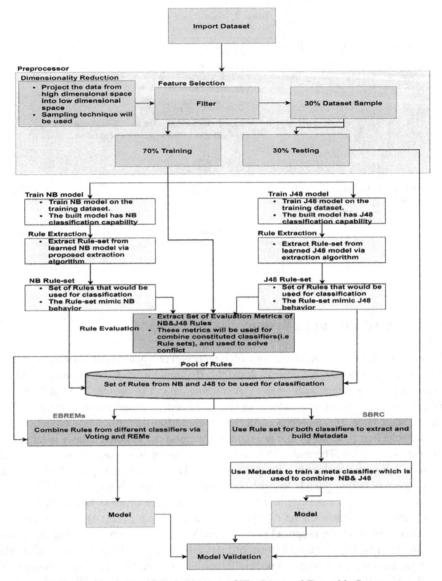

Fig. 1. The General Block Diagram of The Proposed Ensemble System

5.1 Ensemble-Based Rule Evaluation Metrics (EBREMs)

The authors created the ensemble system utilizing two heterogeneous classifiers (NB and J48) as base classifiers in the EBREMs approach. Diversity is a "Cornerstone of Ensemble Systems," according to Robi Polikar [19]. If a classification model has perfect generalization and performance, there is no need to apply ensemble techniques. There are no ideal classifiers because of noise, outliers, and overlapping data distributions. Researchers are looking for classifiers that can reliably identify data fields in the vast majority of cases. As a result, ensemble approaches aim to find a group of classifiers and combine their results to increase the system's performance. This implies that each model makes errors at various times. The idea behind this inference is that if each classifier makes its own mistake, merging them could reduce the overall error. To be more specific, an ensemble system's success necessitates classifiers with sufficiently different judgment boundaries from one another. Diverse is a term used to describe an ensemble with a variety of unique characteristics.

Ensemble diversity can be enforced by altering classifier inputs, outputs, or models, according to [23, 68]. The piece's diversity is achieved by the use of two separate models. After training the base classifiers on the training set, we have two learned models. Each one has its own set of classifying abilities. We then extract Rule-set from each learned model, as discussed in Sects. 3.1 and 3.2. As a result, there are currently two different Rule-sets, each of which can emulate the categorization behavior of the model from which it was formed. The authors apply the REMs stated in Sect. 4 to all Rule-sets prepared by both classifiers once the Rule-sets have been extracted. As a result, each rule in the Rule-sets will be linked to a set of evaluation metrics that will be used to settle any conflict that emerges during categorization activities. Algorithm 3 shows the pseudo-code for evaluating Rule-sets on REMs. To merge the classifier's results, the voting schema will be changed.

When there is a conflict between Rule-sets while voting on classifier output, authors employ two proposed conflict resolution strategies based on REMs that are associated to each rule in the Rule-sets. The following is the first strategy (A):

1) REMs values should be accumulated for each triggered rule in both Rule-sets and classes.
2) As the final class, choose the one with the greatest value from the previous stage.

Algorithm (3): Rule-set Evaluation

Input: R, a Rule-set;
          K, No.of Rules;
          EM, the Evaluation metrics;
Output: ER(R), the evaluated Rule-set;
```
1 begin
2    ER(R) = Ø;
3    for i=1 to K do
4       for j=1 to (No. EM) do
5          Calculate F by evaluate R_i on EM_j utilizing evalua-
           tion metrics equations
6          ER(R) = ER(R) ∪ F
7       endfor
8    endfor
9 end
```

The above two steps could be explained statistically as follow: assume that $(REV)_{i,j}$ represents the evaluation value of Trigger rule i and class j where $i = 1,...P$, P is number of rules in Pool;

$j = 1,...C$, C number of classes;

Then ensemble decision (ED) will choose class J according to Eq. 18

$$(ED)_J = \underset{j=1}{\overset{C}{Max}} \sum_{i=1}^{P} (REV)_{i,j} \tag{18}$$

The second strategy (B) is identical to the first, but instead of using the accumulation, the winning class is determined by the class with the highest rule assessment metrics for activated rules.

The aforementioned two procedures might be applied to each of the metrics listed in Sect. 4, providing insight into the impact of REMs when employed as a combiner and dispute resolution technique in accordance with the two recommended procedures above. The EBREMs pseudo-code is shown in Algorithm 4.

5.2 Stacking-Based Rule Cover (SBRC)

Our second proposed ensemble method has been relayed on stacking concept. Stacking ensemble is usually used to combine heterogeneous classifiers. Stacking consist of two level of classifiers. The first level (level-0) contained base learners which uses different base models to learn from training dataset. The output of each model is collected to form new dataset (sometimes called metadataset) to be used in the second level. The second level (level-1) includes meta learner. Each pattern (i.e. instance) in the metadataset is assigned to real value that it supposed to predict. Meta learner (level-1) is responsible for training on the constructed metadataset and provide the final output [22].

The key idea of the SBRC method is to utilize the information of a cover property of Rule-sets to re-encode the original dataset and construct new metadataset to be used by meta learner which is responsible for final decision. So, the main differences of original stacking method and our proposed stacking method is the constructing of metadataset. The next sub-section illustrates in details how constructing metastases.

Algorithm (4): EBREMs

Input: T1, a training dataset;
   T2, a testing dataset;
   NB, the Naïve base classier;
   J48, the decision tree classifier;
Output: Classification of (T2);

1	begin
2	Read training dataset T1
3	H_{NB} =NB(T1)//Training base learner NB on T1
4	H_{J48} =J48(T1)//Training base learner J48 on T1
5	Extract Rule-set from H_{NB} and H_{J48} utilizing Rule-set Extraction Algorithms
6	Calculate REMs for every Rule-set using Rule-set Evaluation Algorithm
7	Attach to each rule in the Rule-sets a set of REMs obtained in step 6
8	Read testing dataset T2
9	Test each instance in T2 by finding rule(s)in both Rule-set that satisfy the incoming instance
10	Combine results obtained from each Rule-set using Voting and REMs values utilizing either strategy (A) or (B)according to Eq 19
11	Obtain classification Result of T2
12	end

Constructing Metadataset

Meta dataset consisting of a set of attributes as long as the correct class. In the original stacking method, the meta dataset includes the original attributes of the dataset and the base learner's predictions as well as the correct class. Some Stacking methods include just the predictions of base learners as attributes along with a correct class. In the proposed SBRC method, meta dataset is constructing differently and attractively. Instead of utilizing the predictions of base learners, the orientation is to focus on the rules itself. Rules with its antecedents provide more information than the rule's predictions. The intention is to use a cover property of the rule which is more informative than predictions itself. So the attributes of our proposed meta dataset are not the predictions of the base classifiers rather, we replace it with information that reflects which is the first rule of a given base classifier that covers the patterns (i.e. information about if a specific rule covers the patterns). The information obtained from the cover property could be encoded in two different ways:

1. Combination of Nominal and Numerical Attributes

For each base learner (i.e. NB & J48), a combination of nominal and numerical have been created to construct an attribute whose domain consisting of the identifier of the rule followed with rule number and the nominal name of the base learner. A meta instance is represented via the first covering rule of each classifier and its original class value. The constructed piece of feature could be viewed as follow:

Attribute *F*1 (*R0*, *NB*)

Attribute *F*2 (*R3*, *J*48)

The first piece of attribute F1 means that R0 is the first rule in Naïve Bayes Rule-set that cover a given instance and the second piece of attribute F2 indicates that R3 is the first rule in J48 Rule-set that cover a given instance. The pseudo-code for constructing meta dataset utilizing combination of numerical-nominal attribute is illustrated in Algorithm 5.

Algorithm(5): Nominal-Numerical Meta dataset Construction

Input: T, a training dataset;
          K, No. of instance in T;
          R, the Rule-set;
          M, No. of Rules;
Output: Meta-dataset;

```
1   begin
2   Meta-dataset= Ø
3   for i=1 to k do
4      Flag=1,j=1
5      while (Flag=1) and (j≠M) do
6         IF Rⱼ Cover Instᵢ(T) Then
7            begin
8            Append instance with an order pair F ((Rⱼ,Model
             name ),actual class)
9            Meta-dataset= Meta-dataset ∪ F
10           Flag=0,j++;
11           end
12        Else
13        IF (j=M)Then //no rule cover instance
14           begin
15           append instance with a default attribute ordered
             pair F ((default, Model name), actual class)
16           Meta-dataset= Meta-dataset ∪ F
17           end
18      end while
19   end for
20   end
```

The full instance with above features could be viewed in Fig. 2.

2. Combination of Nominal, Numerical, and Binary Attributes

For each rule in the Rule-sets of classifier ensemble, we create a combination of nominal, numerical, and binary attributes. The binary attribute will take Boolean values.

```
@attribute F1
{'(R0,NB)','(R1,NB)','(R10,NB)','(R11,NB)','(R12,NB)','(R2,NB)','(R3
,NB)','(R4,NB)','(R5,NB)','(R6,NB)','(R7,NB)','(R8,NB)','(R9,NB)',BE
NIGN}
```
(a)Constructed feature of NB

```
@attribute F2
{'(R0,J48)','(R1,J48)','(R10,J48)','(R11,J48)','(R12,J48)','(R13,J48)','(R
14,J48)','(R15,J48)','(R16,J48)','(R2,J48)','(R3,J48)','(R4,J48)','(R5,J48
)','(R6,J48)','(R7,J48)','(R8,J48)','(R9,J48)', ATTACK}
```
(b)Constructed feature of J48

Fig. 2. Example of instance with new extracted features of meta dataset using combination of nominal and numerical characteristics

More specifically, the binary value is true if the corresponding rule covers the given patterns, otherwise false. The constructed piece of feature could be viewed as follow:

Attribute F3 (R5, NB, true)

Attribute F4 (R7, J48, false)

The first piece of attribute F3 means that R5 is a Naïve Bayes rule (i.e. the index of the rule in NB Rule-set) that cover a given instance, and the second piece of attribute F4 indicate that R7 is a J48 rule (i.e. the index of the rule in J48 Rule-set) not cover a given instance. Constructing meta dataset utilizing combination of numerical-nominal-binary characteristics is illustrated as pseudo-code in Algorithm 6. The general pseudo-code of SBRC is illustrated in Algorithm 7.

6   Dataset, Experiments, and Findings

This section highlights the dataset that has been used to evaluate this work, the procedures of experiments, and shows the important results of the evaluation processes.

6.1   Dataset and Data Pre-processing

This work has adapted CICIDS-2017's most recent dataset developed by the Canadian Institute for Cybersecurity [69] to evaluate proposed works. The CICIDS-2017 dataset meets all eleven requirements for a legitimate intrusion detection dataset: anonymity, attack diversity, complete capture, complete interaction, complete network configuration, available protocols, complete traffic, feature set, metadata, heterogeneity, and labeling [70, 71]. This dataset includes data acquired via real-world data captured in a form of (PCAPs). While normal records in this dataset tagged as benign, the malicious records tagged as 14 different types of attacks.

Algorithm(6): Nominal-Numerical-Binary Meta dataset Construction

Input: T, a training dataset;
        K, No. of instance in T;
        R, the Rule-set;
        M, No. of Rules;
Output: Meta-dataset;

```
1   begin
2   Meta-dataset= Ø
3   for i=1 to k do
4     for j=1 to M do
5       IF R_j Cover Inst_i(T) Then
6         begin
7           Append instance with an order pair F ((R_j,Model
            name,true),actual class)
8           Meta-dataset= Meta-dataset ∪ F
9         end
10      Else
11        begin
12          Append instance with an order pair F ((R_j,Model
            name, false ),actual class)
13          Meta-dataset= Meta-dataset ∪ F
14        end
15    end for
16  end for
17  end
```

CICIDS-2017 has 2,830,743 records divided into eight files, each with 79 attributes in addition to the class label. The distribution of different attack types and benign data is summarized in Table 8.

Table 8. CICIDS2017 Dataset Summarization

Label	Total
BENIGN	2273097
DDoS	128027
DoS slowloris	5796
DoS Slowhttptest	5499
DoS Hulk	231073
GoldenEye	10293
Heartbleed	11
PortScan	158930

(continued)

Table 8. (*continued*)

Label	Total
Bot	1966
FTP-Patator	7938
SSH-Patator	5897
Web Attack-Brute Force	1507
Web Attack-XSS	652
Web Attack-Sql Injection	21
Infiltration	36
Total	2830743

Algorithm (7):SBRC

Input: T1, a training dataset;
      T2, a testing dataset;
      NB, the Naïve base classier;
      J48, the decision tree classifier;
      L, a meta learner (Stacker);
Output: Classification of (T2);

```
1   begin
2   Read training dataset T1
3   H_NB =NB(T1)//Training base learner NB on T1
4   H_J48 =J48(T1)//Training base learner J48 on T1
5   Extract Rule-set from H_NB and H_J48 utilizing Rule-set
    Extraction Algorithms
6   Construct training meta-dataset_(T1) utilizing Algorithms
    5&6
7   H=L(meta-dataset_(T1))//train meta learner L on
    meta-dataset_(T1)
8   Read testing dataset T2
9   Construct testing meta-dataset_(T2) utilizing Algorithms
    5&6
10  Classify each instance in meta-dataset_(T2) utilizing H
    Model
11  Obtain classification result of meta-dataset_(T2)
12  end
```

According to Table 9, the total number of our sample are (849222) instances. To make our sample is representative according to the dataset class distributions, authors extract training and testing instances depend on the distributions of classes as follows: For begin class, the overall instances are (681929) we take (477350) instances for training and (204578) instances for testing. The selection is done using random selection without replacement. Since there are fractions in the number of instances for both training and testing sets, we make algebra of fractions. This led that some classes have included a bit more instances that the originally proposed distributions. Due to the previous consideration, our training and testing samples will include (594473) and (254792) instances respectively.

Table 9. Demonstration of class distribution research sample

Label	Percentage of Class in Dataset	Sample we try to get (%)	#No of Instances per class	#No of Training 70%	#No of Testing 30%
BENIGN	80.3004%	30% (849222.9)instances	681929.1	477350.37	204578.73
DDoS	4.5227%		38408.1	26885.67	11522.43
DoS slowloris	0.2048%		1738.8	1217.16	521.64
DoS Slowhttptest	0.1943%		1649.7	1154.79	494.91
DoS Hulk	8.1630%		69321.9	48525.33	20796.57
GoldenEye	0.3636%		3087.9	2161.53	926.37
Heartbleed	0.0004%		3.3	2.31	0.99
PortScan	5.6144%		47679	33375.3	14303.7
Bot	0.0695%		589.8	412.86	176.94
FTP-Patator	0.2804%		2381.4	1666.98	714.42
SSH-Patator	0.2083%		1769.1	1238.37	530.73
Web Attack-Brute Force	0.0532%		452.1	316.47	135.63
Web Attack-XSS	0.0230%		195.6	136.92	58.68
Web Attack-Sql Injection	0.0007%		6.3	4.41	1.89
Infiltration	0.0013%		10.8	7.56	3.24
Total	100.0000%		849222.9	594456.03	254766.87

After the preparation of our experiment sample which is considered as a representative, we get a sample that contains begin class and different fourteen attack classes. Since the proposed work concentrations on anomaly detection, we need that our sample has just two classes that are benign and attack classes. This required that we should change all malicious instances class into just one class called (ATTACK). The resultant dataset sample will have (BENIGN & ATTACK) classes.

The next important step is cleaning our sample. It is important to mention that not all features in the CICIDS2017 dataset are important in the classification task, some features must be eliminated since they do not affect the overall performance. These features contain values equal to "Zeros" or "NaN". At the end of these preprocessing steps, we get a sample with 68 features. Table 10 below shows a part of the features and instances in the CICIDS2017 dataset.

Table 10. A sample of features and instances in CICIDS2017 dataset

Destination port	Flow duration	Total Fwd Packets	Total Backward Pakects	Total length of Fwd packets	Total length of Bwd packets	Fwd packet Length Max	Fwd packet Length Min
443	5300564	7	4	617	164	517	0
80	111330	3	3	485	834	479	0

6.2 Experiments Design

This subsection highlights the procedure for implementing our proposed ensemble methods as well as the most important performance metric for evaluating our anomaly IDS systems.

Implementing EBREMs

For the first ensemble method described in Subsect. 5.1, the two heterogeneous classifiers have been built (i.e. NB & J48). Thereafter for each model, Rule-sets from NB&J48 have been extracted according to rule extraction algorithms described in Subsects. 3.1 & 3.2 respectively. The following step is to calculate a REMs for each rule in the Rule-sets and attach these metrics to the rules. Table 10 shows a sample of evaluation metrics for both Rule-sets. Then we supply our prepared test set and obtained the results via combining Rule-sets (i.e. NB&J48 models) using voting schema and REMs. In Table 11, one can recognize the powerful for each rule in both Rule-sets and for the same class. For example, the REMs of CONS for the first rule of J48 which is tagged as (J48 R0) is considered as more powerful rule for J48 Rule-set than rule tagged as (NB R0) as first rule of Naïve Bayes Rule-set. On the other hand, there is a diverse value for (NB R0) in CONS and COVER which means that each evaluation metric gives the importance of rule in the Rule-set according to a different point of view. For example, CONS gives more important for (NB R0) which is (0.840) than COVER which is (0.684) for the same class. It's important to mention that some REMs values is between [0, 1] like (CONS, COVER, QWS, Qprod) while other evaluation metrics values exceed 1 like (X2, Qcohen, Qcoleman).

Implementing SBRC

In the second proposed ensemble method we also train two base classifiers NB, J48 on the training dataset, thereafter Rule-sets form both learned models are extracted. After that, a meta dataset from Rule-sets is extracted utilizing the cover property of rules as described in Subsect. 5.2. The second level (meta-learner) which is responsible for combining the base learners is trained on the constructed meta dataset. In the test mode,

Table 11. Sample of REMs for NB&J48 for Benign Class

NO	CONS	COVER	QWS	Qprod	QC2	QIS	QLS	Laclace	M-estimate
NB R0	0.840758	0.684527	0.795481	0.613286	2136685	0.066327	1.295446	0.840756	0.840758
NB R1	0.850831	0.758502	0.824305	0.668285	2257238	0.083508	1.399487	0.850829	0.85083
NB R2	0.866465	0.677059	0.81279	0.627335	2192253	0.109777	1.592065	0.866463	0.866465
NB R3	0.850202	0.754807	0.82278	0.665328	2250830	0.082441	1.392581	0.8502	0.850202
NB R4	0.795859	0.945248	0.84083	0.753456	2335622	-0.01285	0.956559	0.795858	0.795859
NB R5	0.81727	0.981686	0.865885	0.802439	2443385	0.025449	1.097391	0.817269	0.81727
NB R6	0.795859	0.945248	0.84083	0.753456	2335622	-0.01285	0.956559	0.795858	0.795859
NB R7	0.802935	0.999713	0.861824	0.802704	2422363	-8.2E-05	0.999713	0.802934	0.802935
NB R8	0.848878	0.741546	0.81799	0.655541	2230343	0.080193	1.378233	0.848876	0.848878
NB R9	0.836719	0.712565	0.800613	0.627694	2161813	0.059379	1.25733	0.836717	0.836719
NB R10	0.784235	0.883984	0.814553	0.698331	2229024	-0.03408	0.891804	0.784234	0.784235
J48 R0	0.999628	0.005625	0.751034	0.369817	1516582	0.316027	658.7939	0.999256	0.999481
J48 R1	1	6.28E-06	0.750002	0.367882	1508670	0.316564	0	0.8	0.921192
J48 R2	0.992049	0.002353	0.742658	0.365814	1500187	0.305048	30.61558	0.991182	0.991716
J48 R3	1	0.000287	0.750072	0.367985	1509093	0.316564	0	0.992806	0.997165
J48 R4	0.974771	0.00089	0.725158	0.358917	1471907	0.279699	9.479851	0.972603	0.973986
J48 R5	1	1.89E-05	0.750005	0.367886	1508689	0.316564	0	0.909091	0.964178
J48 R6	1	0.001309	0.750327	0.368361	1510636	0.316564	0	0.998405	0.999372
J48 R7	1	0.051116	0.762779	0.387173	1585776	0.316564	0	0.999959	0.999984
J48 R8	1	3.35E-05	0.750008	0.367892	1508711	0.316564	0	0.944444	0.978109
J48 R9	1	5.45E-05	0.750014	0.367899	1508743	0.316564	0	0.964286	0.985927
J48 R10	1	0.000385	0.750096	0.368021	1509242	0.316564	0	0.994624	0.997882

the testing dataset is supplied and each instance on it is transformed into the form using the same approach of constructing meta dataset. The trained model test each coming instance and decided if it an Attack or Benign.

6.3   Results and Discussions

This sub-section will show the performance metrics that have been used to evaluation our proposed systems and the experimental results when applying our two proposed ensemble methods on the CICIDS2017 dataset. First, the most important results of the first method in both strategies (i.e. strategy A&B) are presented followed by the results acquired for the second proposed stacking method.

Performance Metrics
The evaluation of any IDS is derived via its capability of discriminate the network traffic (in the case of network-based IDS) into a correct type. This evaluation is obtained based on the number of quality measures which in turn are extracted from the well-known matrix called Confusion Matrix. This matrix shows all possible classification cases. Table 12 shows the confusion matrix.

The components of a confusion matrix can be explained as follow:

- TN: is the number of benign instances correctly classified.
- FP: is the number of benign instances incorrectly classified.
- FN: is the number of attack instances incorrectly classified.
- TP: is the number of attack instances correctly classified.

Table 12. Confusion Matrix

		Predicted class	
		Negative class	Positive class
Actual class	Negative class	True negative (TN)	False positive (FP)
	Positive class	False negative (FN)	True positive (TP)

To evaluate our proposed work, several evaluation metrics are adapted namely Accuracy (AC), Recall (R), Precision (P), F-measure (F), True positive rate (TPR) sometime called sensitivity, False Positive Rate (FPR), True Negative Rate (TNR) also called specificity, and False Negative Rate (FNR). All previous metrics are calculated based on information presented by the confusion matrix as follows:

$$Accuracy(AC) = \frac{(TP + TN)}{(TP + TN + FP + FN)} \tag{19}$$

$$RecallR = (TP)(TP + FN) \tag{20}$$

$$Precision(P) = \frac{(TP)}{(TP + FP)} \tag{21}$$

$$F - measure(F) = \frac{2.R.P}{(R + P)} \tag{22}$$

$$Sensitivity(TPR) = \frac{(TP)}{(TP + FN)} \tag{23}$$

$$FPR = \frac{(FP)}{(FP + TN)} \tag{24}$$

$$Specificity(TNR) = \frac{(TN)}{(FP + TN)} \tag{25}$$

$$FNR = \frac{(FN)}{(FN + TP)} \tag{26}$$

Results of EBREMs

- *Empirical Evaluation Metrics*

The complete results of our first proposed ensemble method utilizing empirical evaluation metrics and strategy A are shown in Table 13.

Table 13. Evaluation results of EBREMs method (strategy A & Empirical Metrics)

Evaluation metrics	Accuracy	TP Rate	FP Rate	Precision	Recall	F-Measure	TN Rate	FN Rate
consistency R	99.8626%	0.9959	0.0007	0.9972	0.9959	0.9965	0.9993	0.0041
coverage R	47.2499%	0.2720	0.0002	0.9998	0.2720	0.4276	0.9998	0.7280
QWS	99.7139%	0.9958	0.0025	0.9896	0.9958	0.9927	0.9975	0.0042
QProd	99.7139%	0.9958	0.0025	0.9896	0.9958	0.9927	0.9975	0.0042

Form the above result it's clear that consistency topping the highest percentage of accuracy followed with (QWS & QProd) where coverage metric got lest and worst accuracy. The degradation in coverage accuracy is as we said previously that is rules which cover positive patterns may also cover negative ones. But this consideration not applicable for all datasets which means that coverage metric depends on dataset behavior and strategy that utilize this metric as we see next. The following table (Table 14) shows complete evaluation results for EBREMs method also utilizing empirical metrics but implement strategy B.

Table 14. Evaluation results of EBREMs method (strategy B & Empirical Metrics)

Evaluation metrics	Accuracy	TP Rate	FP Rate	Precision	Recall	F-Measure	TN Rate	FN Rate
consistency R	99.7162%	0.9958	0.0025	0.9897	0.9958	0.9928	0.9975	0.0042
coverage R	87.3929%	0.6111	0.0027	0.9908	0.6111	0.7560	0.9973	0.3889
QWS	99.5490%	0.9875	0.0025	0.9896	0.9875	0.9886	0.9975	0.0125
QProd	99.7139%	0.9958	0.0025	0.9896	0.9958	0.9927	0.9975	0.0042

Table14 also shows that a consistency metric outperformed to all other empirical metrics followed by (QWS & QProd). But regarding coverage metric, it is shown excellent results compared with strategy A. From tables (13 and 14), it seems that overall accuracy for empirical evaluation metrics for both strategies is high except for coverage metric which is relatively low in both strategies compared with other metrics. However, strategy B has enhanced the accuracy of the coverage metric compared with strategy A.

- *Statistical Evaluation Metrics*

Results of EBREMs method utilizing statistical evaluation metrics and strategy A is shown in Table 15 below.

Table 15 shows the highest accuracy for all statistical metrics except for (X2&QIS) that show lower accuracy compared with other statistical metrics. Qcohen metric the winning statistical metric for strategy A with the highest accuracy that reaches (99.8630%). Table 16 illustrates the results of statistical metrics in strategy B.

Table 15. Evaluation results of EBREMs method (strategy A& Statistical Metrics)

Evaluation metrics	Accuracy	TP Rate	FP Rate	Precision	Recall	F-Measure	TN Rate	FN Rate
X^2	77.7356%	0.4695	0.0003	0.9992	0.4695	0.6388	0.9997	0.5305
G2	99.8560%	0.9954	0.0007	0.9973	0.9954	0.9963	0.9993	0.0046
Qcohen	99.8630%	0.9959	0.0007	0.9972	0.9959	0.9965	0.9993	0.0041
Qcoleman	99.7139%	0.9958	0.0025	0.9896	0.9958	0.9927	0.9975	0.0042
QC1	99.7139%	0.9958	0.0025	0.9896	0.9958	0.9927	0.9975	0.0042
QC2	99.7139%	0.9958	0.0025	0.9896	0.9958	0.9927	0.9975	0.0042
QIS	60.9474%	0.3353	0.0002	0.9996	0.3353	0.5022	0.9998	0.6647
QLS	99.8556%	0.9954	0.0007	0.9973	0.9954	0.9963	0.9993	0.0046
QMD	99.0004%	0.9537	0.0006	0.9977	0.9537	0.9752	0.9994	0.0463
Laplace	99.8626%	0.9959	0.0007	0.9972	0.9959	0.9965	0.9993	0.0041
M-estimate	99.7170%	0.9958	0.0025	0.9898	0.9958	0.9928	0.9975	0.0042

- *Execution Time Results of EBREMs*

Table 17 shows the results obtained by comparing the run time[1] and accuracy of EBREMs for strategy (A) and original voting method. Note that each experiment is repeated 10 times and take the average of execution time with (± standard deviation).

From Table 17, it clear that the accuracy of EBREMs is better that original vote method except for (Coverage, X2, and QIS). In addition, the execution time of the proposed method showed superiority speed that not reach 6 s while the original vote method exceeds eighteen seconds in execution time. This superiority also applies to Strategy B as shown in Fig. 3.

---

[1] The proposed IDSs have been implemented using java with JDK.13 run on pc machine with intel processor Core™ i5 2410M,2.30 GZ, 4 GB RAM, and under Window7.

Table 16. Evaluation results of EBREMs method (strategy B& Statistical Metrics)

Evaluation metrics	Accuracy	TP Rate	FP Rate	Precision	Recall	F-Measure	TN Rate	FN Rate
consistency ST(B)	99.7162%	0.9958	0.0025	0.9897	0.9958	0.9928	0.9975	0.0042
coverage ST(B)	87.3929%	0.6111	0.0027	0.9908	0.6111	0.7560	0.9973	0.3889
QWS ST(B)	99.5490%	0.9875	0.0025	0.9896	0.9875	0.9886	0.9975	0.0125
Qprod ST(B)	99.7139%	0.9958	0.0025	0.9896	0.9958	0.9927	0.9975	0.0042
X2 ST(B)	77.7320%	0.4695	0.0003	0.9992	0.4695	0.6388	0.9997	0.5305
G2 ST(B)	99.8513%	0.9952	0.0007	0.9973	0.9952	0.9962	0.9993	0.0048
Qcohen ST(B)	99.6899%	0.9946	0.0025	0.9896	0.9946	0.9921	0.9975	0.0054
Qcoleman ST(B)	99.7139%	0.9958	0.0025	0.9896	0.9958	0.9927	0.9975	0.0042
QC1 ST(B)	99.7139%	0.9958	0.0025	0.9896	0.9958	0.9927	0.9975	0.0042
QC2 ST(B)	99.7139%	0.9958	0.0025	0.9896	0.9958	0.9927	0.9975	0.0042
QIS ST(B)	62.0549%	0.3418	0.0002	0.9996	0.3418	0.5094	0.9998	0.6582
QLS ST(B)	99.8532%	0.9953	0.0007	0.9973	0.9953	0.9963	0.9993	0.0047
QMD ST(B)	98.8520%	0.9468	0.0005	0.9978	0.9468	0.9716	0.9995	0.0532
Laplace ST(B)	99.7162%	0.9958	0.0025	0.9897	0.9958	0.9928	0.9975	0.0042
M-estimate ST(B)	99.7162%	0.9958	0.0025	0.9897	0.9958	0.9928	0.9975	0.0042

Results of SBRC

In the second proposed stacking method, authors suggest to carry out the experiments using four different classifiers families to perform the combination (i.e. stacker model level-1). These families include (Bayes, Rules, Function, and Tree). The arbitrarily in the selection of the meta learner will provide insight about which is the best model to be selected as a stacker model. The selected classifiers are Naïve Bayes, Decision Table, Support Vector Machine, and Random Forest. Moreover, our evaluation will be done on two different manners: split test set and 3-cross-validation test on a training dataset. Table 18 shows the total evaluation results for the SBRC method on our test set.

The first round of experiments on our proposed stacking method for anomaly IDS shows spurious results for all selected meta-learner that exceeded (99.85%) and (99.7%) for accuracy and sensitivity metrics respectively.

Table 17. Execution Time Comparisons of Original Vote and EBREMs

Method	Accuracy	Average Execution Time (Sec)	STDEV(±)
Original Vote	86.91%	18.58	
consistency	99.8626%	4.8238	0.201
coverage	47.2499%	5.5635	0.457
QWS	99.7139%	5.6382	0.351
Qprod	99.7139%	5.6105	0.501
X2	77.7356%	5.64	0.433
G2	99.8560%	5.6732	0.424
Qcohen	99.8630%	5.5578	0.327
Qcoleman	99.7139%	5.5475	0.386
QC1	99.7139%	5.4662	0.432
QC2	99.7139%	5.741	0.113
QIS	60.9474%	5.7063	0.203
QLS	99.8556%	5.548	0.421
QMD	99.0004%	5.7105	0.225
Laplace	99.8626%	5.7091	0.159
M-estimate	99.7170%	5.6494	0.333

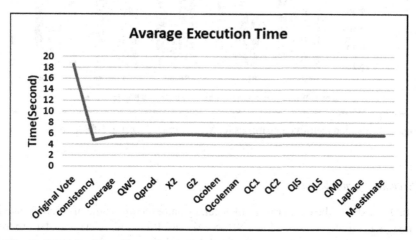

Fig. 3. Execution Time Comparison of original vote method and EBREMs Strategy-B

The following chart (Fig. 4) illustrates comparisons of evaluation metrics for meta-learners when implemented according to a cross-validation evaluation approach using 3 folds as seed. The chart shows high accuracy for all models with a very slight height accuracy for the Decision Table model. If we compare the accuracy of the EBREMs

Table 18. Evaluation results of SBRC implemented on test set

Meta-learner	Accuracy	TP Rate	FP Rate	Precision	Recall	F-Measure	TN Rate	FN Rate
Naiv Bayes	99.8552%	0.9974	0.0012	0.9953	0.9974	0.9963	0.9988	0.0026
Decision Table	99.8642%	0.9974	0.0011	0.9957	0.9974	0.9966	0.9989	0.0026
SVM	99.8591%	0.9971	0.0010	0.9958	0.9971	0.9964	0.9990	0.0029
Randon Forest	99.8642%	0.9974	0.0011	0.9957	0.9974	0.9966	0.9989	0.0026

and SBRC, obviously, both methods have shown high accuracy in classifying the CICIDS2017 dataset.

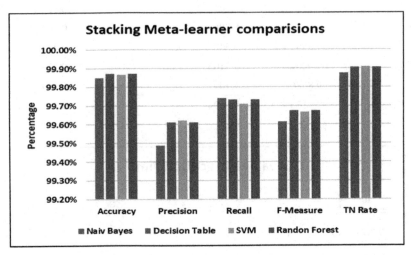

Fig. 4. Evaluation metrics comparisons for Meta learners by using 3-folds cross-validation

• *Execution Time Results of SBRC*

Table 19 shows the comparisons of accuracy and execution time of original stacking method[2] with three combiner (i.e. NB, SVM, and RandomForset) and the proposed SBRC using the same combiner in the level-1 and (NB&J48) as base learners ensemble components.

---

[2] Weka [72] tool has been used to conduct the experiments of original Voting and Stacking methods.

Table 19. Execution Time Comparisons of Original Stacking and SBRC

Combiner	Original Stacking		SBRC		
	Accuracy	Execution Time (Sec)	Accuracy	Execution Time (Sec)	± STDEV
NB	99.8932%	13.710	99.8552%	0.250	0.091802832
SVM	99.8932%	46.020	99.8591%	81.405	0.142334957
Random Forest	99.8634%	19.240	99.8642%	2.480	0.076926523

From the above table, it is clear that the proposed SBRC method showed supremacy in terms of execution time except for SVM. In addition, the accuracy of both methods are comparable. The superiority in the speed of implementation with the high accuracy of the proposed model opens new orientation to implement it as on-line IDS.

7 Conclusion

This paper presents two novel ensemble methods for anomaly detection in network traffic. Two heterogeneous classification model named (NB & J48) are employed as base learners for building the proposed ensemble methods. In both methods, Rule-sets is extracted from the base learners and utilized to build the proposed systems. CICIDS2017 is used to evaluate our methods.

The conclusion of this paper could be summarized as follow:

1. REMs could be utilized in ensemble methods for combining and solve rules conflict with high performance.
2. A cover property is a very important metric that holds information more than rule prediction itself. This is clear from the meta dataset of the SBRC method which constructed with the help of this vital metric and produces high accuracy with exactly just four features.
3. It's clear that (QIS, X2, and Coverage) metrics got less efficiency compared with other metrics.
4. In SBRC method, SVM shows high performance compared with other meta learners (i.e. Decision Table, NB, and Random Forest).
5. The execution time for both proposed methods shows superiority compared with original voting and stacking methods where the lowest execution time was obtained via SBRC with NB combiner which is (.25 s)

Shortly, the authors indent to expand the proposed methods to discover all fourteen attack types in the CICIDS2017 dataset. Also, the intention is to implement the proposed methods onto different IDS datasets, moreover, we plan to apply our proposed methods on different problem domains (like medical) and try to discover the relationships between dataset and REMs. In addition, the supremacy in the execution time and accuracy, especially for the SBRC with NB combiner, opened new horizons for the purpose of implementing the system on-line in the near future.

References

1. Lin, W.C., Ke, S.W., Tsai, C.F.: CANN: an intrusion detection system based on combining cluster centers and nearest neighbors. Knowl. Based. Syst. **78**(1), 13–21 (2015). https://doi.org/10.1016/j.knosys.2015.01.009
2. Elbasiony, R.M., Sallam, E.A., Eltobely, T.E., Fahmy, M.M.: A hybrid network intrusion detection framework based on random forests and weighted k-means. Ain Shams Eng. J. **4**(4), 753–762 (2013). https://doi.org/10.1016/j.asej.2013.01.003
3. Chen, Y., Abraham, A., Yang, B.: Hybrid flexible neural-tree-based intrusion detection systems. Int. J. Intell. Syst. **22**(4), 337–352 (2007). https://doi.org/10.1002/int.20203
4. Folino, G., Pizzuti, C., Spezzano, G.: An ensemble-based evolutionary framework for coping with distributed intrusion detection. Genet. Program Evolvable Mach. **11**(2), 131–146 (2010). https://doi.org/10.1007/s10710-010-9101-6
5. Garg, S., Batra, S.: A novel ensembled technique for anomaly detection. Int. J. Commun. Syst. **30**(11), e3248 (2017). https://doi.org/10.1002/dac.3248
6. Zhou, Z.H.: Ensemble Methods: Foundations and Algorithms. Chapman and Hall/CRC (2012). https://doi.org/10.1201/b12207
7. Kittler, J., Hatef, M., Duin, R.P.W., Matas, J.: On combining classifiers. IEEE Trans. Pattern Anal. Mach. Intell. **20**(3), 226–239 (1998). https://doi.org/10.1109/34.667881
8. Mohammad, M.N., Sulaiman, N., Muhsin, O.A.: A novel intrusion detection system by using intelligent data mining in WEKA environment. Procedia Comput. Sci. **3**, 1237–1242 (2011). https://doi.org/10.1016/j.procs.2010.12.198
9. Ni, X., He, D., Ahmad, F.: Practical network anomaly detection using data mining techniques. VFAST Trans. Softw. Eng. **9**(2), 1 (2016). https://doi.org/10.21015/vtse.v9i2.403
10. Patcha, A., Park, J.M.: An overview of anomaly detection techniques: existing solutions and latest technological trends. Comput. Netw. **51**(12), 3448–3470 (2007). https://doi.org/10.1016/j.comnet.2007.02.001
11. Mannila, H., Smyth, P., Hand, D.J.: Principles of data mining MIT press. In: A Comprehensive, Highlytechnical Look at the Math and Science Behind Extracting Useful Information from Large Databases, vol. 546 (2000)
12. Bhuyan, M.H., Bhattacharyya, D.K., Kalita, J.K.: Network traffic anomaly detection techniques and systems. In: Network Traffic Anomaly Detection and Prevention. CCN, pp. 115–169. Springer, Cham (2017). https://doi.org/10.1007/978-3-319-65188-0_4
13. Roesch, M.: Snort – lightweight intrusion detection for networks. Lisa **99**(1), 229–238 (2015)
14. Folino, G., Sabatino, P.: Ensemble based collaborative and distributed intrusion detection systems: a survey. J. Netw. Comput. Appl. **66**, 1–16 (2016). https://doi.org/10.1016/j.jnca.2016.03.011
15. Han, J., Kamber, M., Pei, J.: Data Mining: Concepts and Techniques, 3rd ed. Elsevier (2012). https://doi.org/10.1016/C2009-0-61819-5
16. Dasarathy, B.V., Sheela, B.V.: A composite classifier system design: concepts and methodology. Proc. IEEE **67**(5), 708–713 (1979). https://doi.org/10.1109/PROC.1979.11321
17. Hansen, P., Salamon, L.K.: Neural network ensembles. IEEE Trans. Pattern Anal. Mach. Intell. **12**(10), 993–1001 (1990)
18. Schapire, R.E.: The strength of weak learnability. Mach. Learn. **5**(2), 197–227 (1990). https://doi.org/10.1023/A:1022648800760
19. Polikar, R.: Ensemble based systems in decision making. IEEE Circuits Syst. Mag. **6**(3), 21–44 (2006). https://doi.org/10.1109/MCAS.2006.1688199
20. Bhuyan, M.H., Bhattacharyya, D.K., Kalita, J.K.: Network Traffic Anomaly Detection and Prevention: Concepts, Techniques, and Tools. Springer, Cham (2017). https://doi.org/10.1007/978-3-319-65188-0

21. Tan, P.-N., Steinbach, M., Kumar, V.: Pang-Ning Tan - Introduction to Data Mining (2006). https://doi.org/10.1152/ajpgi.1999.276.5.G1279

22. Syarif, I., Zaluska, E., Prugel-Bennett, A., Wills, G.: Application of bagging, boosting and stacking to intrusion detection. In: Perner, P. (ed.) MLDM 2012. LNCS (LNAI), vol. 7376, pp. 593–602. Springer, Heidelberg (2012). https://doi.org/10.1007/978-3-642-31537-4_46

23. Woźniak Michałand Graña, M., Corchado, E.: A survey of multiple classifier systems as hybrid systems. Inf. Fusion 16(1), 3–17 (2014). https://doi.org/10.1016/j.inffus.2013.04.006

24. Giacinto, G., Roli, F., Didaci, L.: Fusion of multiple classifiers for intrusion detection in computer networks. Pattern Recogn. Lett. 24(12), 1795–1803 (2003). https://doi.org/10.1016/S0167-8655(03)00004-7

25. Perdisci, R., Ariu, D., Fogla, P., Giacinto, G., Lee, W.: McPAD: a multiple classifier system for accurate payload-based anomaly detection. Comput. Netw. 53(6), 864–881 (2009). https://doi.org/10.1016/j.comnet.2008.11.011

26. Hodge, V.J., Austin, J.: A survey of outlier detection methodologies. Artif. Intell. Rev. 22(2), 85–126 (2004). https://doi.org/10.1023/B:AIRE.0000045502.10941.a9

27. Markou, M., Singh, S.: Novelty detection: a review_part 1: statistical approaches. Signal Process. 83(12), 2481–2497 (2003)

28. Song, J., Takakura, H., Okabe, Y., Kwon, Y.: Unsupervised anomaly detection based on clustering and multiple one-class SVM. IEICE Trans. Commun. E92-B(6), 1981–1990 (2009). https://doi.org/10.1587/transcom.E92.B.1981

29. Chou, T.-S.S., Fan, J., Fan, S., Makki, K.: Ensemble of machine learning algorithms for intrusion detection. In: IEEE International Conference on Systems, Man and Cybernetics, pp. 3976–3980 (2009). https://doi.org/10.1109/ICSMC.2009.5346669

30. Liu, G., Chen, W., Hu, F.: A neural network ensemble based method for detecting computer virus. In: 2010 International Conference on Computer, Mechatronics, Control and Electronic Engineering, CMCE 2010, vol. 1, pp. 391–393 (2010). https://doi.org/10.1109/CMCE.2010.5610520

31. Govindarajan, M., Chandrasekaran, R.: Intrusion detection using neural based hybrid classification methods. Comput. Netw. 55(8), 1662–1671 (2011). https://doi.org/10.1016/j.comnet.2010.12.008

32. Raj Kumar, P.A., Selvakumar, S.: Distributed denial of service attack detection using an ensemble of neural classifier. Comput. Commun. 34(11), 1328–1341 (2011). https://doi.org/10.1016/j.comcom.2011.01.012

33. Sindhu, S.S.S., Geetha, S., Kannan, A.: Decision tree based light weight intrusion detection using a wrapper approach. Expert Syst. Appl. 39(1), 129–141 (2012)

34. Boro, D., Nongpoh, B., Bhattacharyya, D.K.: Anomaly based intrusion detection using meta ensemble classifier. In: Proceedings of the 5th International Conference on Security of Information and Networks, SIN 2012, pp. 143–147 (2012). https://doi.org/10.1145/2388576.2388596

35. de la Hoz, E., Ortiz, A., Ortega, J., de la Hoz, E.: Network anomaly classification by support vector classifiers ensemble and non-linear projection techniques. In: Pan, J.-S., Polycarpou, M.M., Woźniak, M., de Carvalho, A.C.P.L.F., Quintián, H., Corchado, E. (eds.) HAIS 2013. LNCS (LNAI), vol. 8073, pp. 103–111. Springer, Heidelberg (2013). https://doi.org/10.1007/978-3-642-40846-5_11

36. Balon-Perin, A., Gambäck, B.: Ensembles of decision trees for network intrusion detection systems. Int. J. Adv. Secur. 6(1 & 2) (2013)

37. Masarat, S., Taheri, H., Sharifian, S.: A novel framework, based on fuzzy ensemble of classifiers for intrusion detection systems. In: Proceedings of the 4th International Conference on Computer and Knowledge Engineering, ICCKE 2014, pp. 165–170 (2014). https://doi.org/10.1109/ICCKE.2014.6993345

38. Chaurasia, S., Jain, A.: Ensemble neural network and k-NN classifiers for intrusion detection. Int. J. Comput. Sci. Inf. Technol. **5**(2), 2481–2485 (2014)

39. Tama, B.A., Rhee, K.H.: A combination of PSO-based feature selection and tree-based classifiers ensemble for intrusion detection systems. In: Advances in Computer Science and Ubiquitous Computing, vol. 373, pp. 489–495. Springer, Heidelberg (2015). https://doi.org/ 10.1007/978-981-10-0281-6_71

40. Gaikwad, D.P., Thool, R.C.: Intrusion detection system using bagging with partial decision tree base classifier. Procedia Comput. Sci. **49**(1), 92–98 (2015). https://doi.org/10.1016/j. procs.2015.04.231

41. Aburomman, A.A., Bin Ibne Reaz, M.: A novel SVM-kNN-PSO ensemble method for intrusion detection system. Appl. Soft Comput. J. **38**, pp. 360–372 (2016). https://doi.org/10.1016/ j.asoc.2015.10.011

42. Elekar, K.S.: Combination of data mining techniques for intrusion detection system. In: IEEE International Conference on Computer Communication and Control, IC4 2015, pp. 1–5 (2016). https://doi.org/10.1109/IC4.2015.7375727

43. Jabbar, M.A., Aluvalu, R., Reddy, S.S.: RFAODE: a novel ensemble intrusion detection system. Procedia Comput. Sci. **115**, 226–234 (2017). https://doi.org/10.1016/j.procs.2017. 09.129

44. Timčenko, V., Gajin, S.: Ensemble classifiers for supervised anomaly based network intrusion detection. In: Proceedings - 2017 IEEE 13th International Conference on Intelligent Computer Communication and Processing, ICCP 2017, pp. 13–19 (2017). https://doi.org/10.1109/ICCP. 2017.8116977

45. Pham, N.T., Foo, E., Suriadi, S., Jeffrey, H., Lahza, H.F.M.: Improving performance of intrusion detection system using ensemble methods and feature selection. In: ACM International Conference Proceeding Series, p. 2 (2018). https://doi.org/10.1145/3167918.3167951

46. Vinutha, H.P., Poornima, B.: An ensemble classifier approach on different feature selection methods for intrusion detection. In: Bhateja, V., Nguyen, B.L., Nguyen, N.G., Satapathy, S.C., Le, D.-N. (eds.) Information Systems Design and Intelligent Applications. AISC, vol. 672, pp. 442–451. Springer, Singapore (2018). https://doi.org/10.1007/978-981-10-7512-4_44

47. Salo, F., Nassif, A.B., Essex, A.: Dimensionality reduction with IG-PCA and ensemble classifier for network intrusion detection. Comput. Netw. **148**, 164–175 (2019). https://doi.org/ 10.1016/j.comnet.2018.11.010

48. Sahu, S.K., Katiyar, A., Kumari, K.M., Kumar, G., Mohapatra, D.P.: An SVM-based ensemble approach for intrusion detection. Int. J. Inf. Technol. Web. Eng. **14**(1), 66–84 (2019). https:// doi.org/10.4018/IJITWE.2019010104

49. Kunal, Dua, M.: Attribute selection and ensemble classifier based novel approach to intrusion detection system. Procedia Comput. Sci. **167**, 2191–2199 (2020). https://doi.org/10.1016/j. procs.2020.03.271

50. Andalib, A., Vakili, V.T.: An autonomous intrusion detection system using an ensemble of advanced learners. In: 2020 28th Iranian Conference on Electrical Engineering (ICEE), pp. 1– 5 (2020). https://doi.org/10.1109/ICEE50131.2020.9260808

51. Andrews, R., Diederich, J., Tickle, A.B.: Survey and critique of techniques for extracting rules from trained artificial neural networks. Knowl. Based Syst. **8**(6), 373–389 (1995). https://doi. org/10.1016/0950-7051(96)81920-4

52. Al-Aaraji, N., Al-Mamory, S., Al-Shakarchi, A.: Constructing decision rules from naive Bayes model for robust and low complexity classification. Int. J. Adv. Intell. Inf. **7**(1), 76–88 (2021). https://doi.org/10.26555/ijain.v7i1.578

53. Śnieżyński, B.: Converting a naive Bayes model into a set of rules. In: Kłopotek, M.A., Wierzchoń, S.T., Trojanowski, K. (eds.) Intelligent Information Processing and Web Mining, pp. 221–229. Springer, Heidelberg (2006). https://doi.org/10.1007/3-540-33521-8_22

54. Holland, P.W., Bishop, Y.M., Fienberg, S.E.: Discrete Multivariate Analysis: Theory and Practice. The MIT Press (1977)
55. Bruha, I., Kockova, S.: Quality of decision rules: empirical and statistical approaches. Informatica **17**, 233–243 (1993)
56. Michalski, R.S.: Pattern recognition as rule-guided inductive inference. IEEE Trans. Pattern Anal. Mach. Intell. **4**, 349–361 (1980)
57. Torgo, L.: Controlled redundancy in incremental rule learning. In: European Conference on Machine Learning, pp. 185–195 (1993)
58. Torgo, L.: Knowledge integration. In: Current Trends in Knowledge Acquisition, vol. 8, p. 90 (1990)
59. An, A., Cercone, N.: Rule quality measures for rule induction systems: description and evaluation. Comput. Intell. **17**(3), 409–424 (2001). https://doi.org/10.1111/0824-7935.00154
60. Clark, P., Niblett, T.: The CN2 induction algorithm. Mach. Learn. **3**(4), 261–283 (1989)
61. Cohen, J.: A coefficient of agreement for nominal scales. Educ. Psychol. Measur. **20**(1), 37–46 (1960)
62. Kononenko, I., Bratko, I.: Information-based evaluation criterion for classifier's performance. Mach. Learn. **6**(1), 67–80 (1991)
63. Yao, Y.Y., Zhong, N.: An analysis of quantitative measures associated with rules. In: Zhong, N., Zhou, L. (eds.) PAKDD 1999. LNCS (LNAI), vol. 1574, pp. 479–488. Springer, Heidelberg (1999). https://doi.org/10.1007/3-540-48912-6_64
64. An, A., Cercone, N.: Rule quality measures improve the accuracy of rule induction: an experimental approach. In: Raś, Z.W., Ohsuga, S. (eds.) ISMIS 2000. LNCS (LNAI), vol. 1932, pp. 119–129. Springer, Heidelberg (2000). https://doi.org/10.1007/3-540-39963-1_13
65. An, A., Cercone, N.: ELEM2: a learning system for more accurate classifications. In: Conference of the Canadian Society for Computational Studies of Intelligence, pp. 426–441 (1998)
66. Clark, P., Boswell, R.: Rule induction with CN2: some recent improvements. In: Lecture Notes in Computer Science (including subseries Lecture Notes in Artificial Intelligence and Lecture Notes in Bioinformatics), vol. 482. LNAI, pp. 151–163 (1991). https://doi.org/10.1007/BFb0017011
67. Džeroski, S., Cestnik, B., Petrovski, I.: Using the m-estimate in rule induction. J. Comput. Inf. Technol. **1**(1), 37–46 (1993)
68. Bagui, S.C.: Combining Pattern Classifiers: Methods and Algorithms, vol. 47, no. 4 (2005). https://doi.org/10.1198/tech.2005.s320
69. Ghorbani, A.A., Sharafaldin, I., Lashkari, A.H.: Toward generating a new intrusion detection dataset and intrusion traffic characterization. In: ICISSP, pp. 108–116 (2018)
70. Gharib, A., Sharafaldin, I., Lashkari, A.H., Ghorbani, A.A.: An evaluation framework for intrusion detection dataset. In: ICISS 2016 - 2016 International Conference on Information Science and Security, pp. 1–6 (2017). https://doi.org/10.1109/ICISSEC.2016.7885840
71. Ahmim, A., Maglaras, L., Ferrag, M.A., Derdour, M., Janicke, H.: A novel hierarchical intrusion detection system based on decision tree and rules-based models. 2019 15th International Conference on Distributed Computing in Sensor Systems (DCOSS), pp. 228–233 (2018). http://arxiv.org/abs/1812.09059
72. Frank, E., Hall, M.A., Witten, I.H.: The WEKA Workbench. Online Appendix for "Data Mining: Practical Machine Learning Tools and Techniques", Morgan Kaufmann, Fourth Edition (2016)

New Security Mechanism of Health Data Based on Blockchain–NFV

Hayder A. Jawdhari$^{(\boxtimes)}$ and Alharith A. Abdullah

Al Qasim Green University, Babil, Iraq
haider.satar@uoqasim.edu.iq, alharith@itnet.uobabylon.edu.iq

Abstract. Health data security has permanently been essential trouble for humanity. In spite of its significant social position, modern approaches for handling health data are uneventful, complex, occasionally costly, and risky to human mistakes and misconceptions. On the health aspect, the Healthchain approach appears to own the possibility to evolve a unique measure for addressing health records utilizing virtual functions that are stable within blockchain technology. In this study, we provide a one-of-a-kind example that uses a licensed blockchain-NFV (Network Function Virtualization) to manage and store patient electronic health records (EHR). This method ensures transparency and, more precisely, immutability, which are required for secure administration and storage, ensuring a well-organized system that involves both doctors and patients, and, hopefully, restoring confidence in the overall health situation. Our profession may also present to obtain a speed of the blockchain system to EHR and promote different dialogues with health organizations to fully employ the potential of the stated technology, according to the requested purpose.

Keyword: blockchain · NFV · health-data security · electronic health record

1 Introduction

A distributed ledger, or blockchain, records and preserves all transactions. Particularly, it is known by utilizing peer-to-peer records for transactions constructed from associated blocks of transactions things are unchangeable and are sent across a network [1]. A distribution ledger is a database that is transmitted, duplicated, and synced among nodes in a network. The ledger keeps track of all transactions, such as data transfers, that take place between the parties in the network [2]. The ledgers have two kind: public in addition to private ledgers. The first one is unspecified in the understanding that every node contains a duplicate of the ledger in addition to the participates in verifying data independently, in contrast, the second one is not anonymous. Also, there are two types of blockchain permissioned, and permissionless blockchain, The first requires people to be given a replica of the ledger as well as permission from the ledger's manager to participate in verifying or confirming data, trades, and transactions. Because most data should be kept private and require authorization, blockchain allows organizations to deal with reservations regarding privacy and the Health Insurance Portability and Accountability Act (HIPAA).

A. M. Al-Bakry et al. (Eds.): NTICT 2022, CCIS 1764, pp. 230–247, 2023.
https://doi.org/10.1007/978-3-031-35442-7_12

Blockchain disapplies any structure of centralized control [28]. The logs of transactions are general and readily checkable. In the health care system, all blocks are partially general or public, whereas only those who are offered approval will be awarded access to confirm if the details are valid before it evolves to be a component of the blockchain. For confirmation purposes, an audit log logs each transaction, and each transaction includes a timestamp as well as a unique digital signature, which permits a servant to sign with a private key to follow the production of the details of transaction. Through two keys, a public key and a private key, the blockchain system based on encryption for ensure security, management, and verification [31]. A public key refers to the user's address in the environment, while a private key is equivalent to an access code that primates access the content of the blockchain e.g. data. The blend of mentioned keys guarantees the contents of the blockchain are impossible to damage and traceable to the source of the data while maintaining that root unidentified.

Public health consider as science and art of controlling whole illness [29], extending life and elevating health via the managed efforts of community. The important field in this area, we may discover health security via the secure of people via the practical cooperation of specialists in determining, averting and mitigating the effects of infections and of ecological, chemical and X-rays and other high-energy radiation threats.

Health care is a complicated endeavor with different significant stakeholders [30]. Possibility whole technologies that based on blockchain has the ability to throw into disorder the logistics of the industry of health care via creative explanations to the difficulties encountered in the industry, as contain whereas are not restricted to the challenges, for example, the processing of the outpour of transactions and services between the basic industrialization and utilizing via the client (supply chain management), problems that faced technical in data administration, and smart contracts.

As regards healthcare is worried, the insistence of growth gains too great rates. Now the demand is for good health skills backed by developed and more further technologies. Now, Blockchain would recreate an essential part in converting the healthcare area. Moreover, the view of the health strategy is locomoting to a patient-case-centered procedure concentrating on many major characteristics such as available services in addition to the suitable healthcare resources continuous. Healthcare enhanced based on Blockchain by improving communities to supply sufficient patient care and excellent health skills. Utilizing Blockchain systems, whole people may participate to learn more and more about the health investigation programs. Many centralized databases are used to handle the whole healthcare system and communities [3–5].

Yet, the considerable important concerns encountered are data security, sharing, in addition to the interoperability in people health administration. This distinct issue is dedicated by utilizing Blockchain. This technology improves safety, data sharing, interoperability, confintionalty, and access when accurately executed. Furthermore important problems regarding data security, particularly in the areas of personalized treatment and wearables. All components of health care system such as patients and medical stuff demand secure and explicit standards of enrollment, sending, and conferring data through networks unaccompanied by security matters therefore, Blockchain system is executed to fix these problems [6, 7]. That may be achieving also through using Network Function Virtualization (NFV).

Network Function virtualization can be run on a regular public server managed by Hypervisor using NFV. Because the network runs on virtual computers that are readily provisioned and managed for wired and wireless connections, network design and management is much easier with a virtual network, and the best part is that network functionalities may be altered or added on demand. [17].

In this work, we have worked hard using modern and powerful methods to protect the components of the health system, and this was done using the blockchain in addition to NFV, so we used the blockchain to save and protect patient reports with its results (Positive or negative) and be known to all the nodes. In addition, we applied the NFV tool to the functions that exist in all the nodes to get the virtual ledger in addition to all the functions inside the nodes.

1.1 BlockChain Challenges

Whereas blockchain has the ability to maintain powerful promises, furthermore there are many difficulties to overpower. Some researchers state many troubles in utilizing the blockchain such as elasticity of data dealing, expenditure, scalability, adequacy, or qualification [25]. Also look out that the costs of transaction in addition to the threats of centralization, too possibility to occur quantum attack. The common blockchains (e.g. Bitcoin's) are ineffective as well as suffer from scalability issues in which its ability is to do below six transactions per second [25]. Others note that blockchain is inappropriate for dealing with medical data (e.g. storing) also calculated scans of X-rays or ultrasound that will increase the size of the blockchain data and cause many problems in its management [26]. Likewise states that displaying a person's private key to an investigator basically converts it to the public key, thus strategies should permit for the abolition of a key whether authorization to display data is inverted. Eventually, Giordanengo displays that abstracting any data from the blockchain system, like running out the duration of the legal reservation, that puts institutions at stake due to the immutability of blockchain maintaining data is considered from its a liability [26]. Ultimately, investigators are confronted with problems generated via governance blockages and technological problems regarding data sharing [24]. An additional problem that faced researchers is the segment out exclusively the important data whole health data, whose may put unnecessary load on them to guard unnecessary data [27].

2 Related Work

The blockchain is attracting a lot of attention from the scientific community and the media, in addition to people's eagerness regarding its possible services and function in pushing decentralization of community [8] and independence from central controls. Greatly concentration has been earmarked to the favorable or unruly alteration that the wide assumption of using blockchain ought to get to the communities. In spite of mentioned above consideration, some literature has been devoted to the difficulties it might review. Beck and Muller-Bloch [9] noted that the root of the blockchain system can be analogized to Internet innovation, displaying the possibility for revolutionary changes inside many industries. Nevertheless, as stated to [10], a foremost analogical instance of this technology has been offered via the outcome of [11], which suggested a distributed ledger broadcasted in general newspaper and other media for timestamping the invention of each outcome of the human mind that the law saves from unauthorized usage via others, there is researcher positioned the foundation of current cryptocurrency that depend on blockchain invention, Also, the first action was to supply an authorized non-territorial digital coin [12], with leaving relying on centralized and economic organizations, while confirmed via [13]. Actually, Many studies have been conducted in the Bitcoin area, considering that Bitcoin is presently the most widely used and significant environment leveraging blockchain technology, supported by the biggest user foundation. Some years ago, the blockchain system, progressed further to cryptocurrencies, whereas yet small is comprehended around its pledged disruptive prospect that moves past IT [9]. The important thing is that the security side considers one of the main investigation issues in blockchain-concerning to diffecltieites and limitations like directions and consequences of security happenings, 51% attack, data moldability issues, in addition to cryptography problems. In spite of the fact that many explanations to handle mentioned problems have been introduced, Some of them are merely a simple viewpoint provides with no objective evaluation of their efficacy. Additionally, blockchain applications are expected in almost each humanistic sector, and the blockchain utilizes have a high level of expectations that are appealing. The results of the literature review revealed that much emphasis should be placed on those aspects that have been identified as the most ambiguous or complex in regard to blockchain and its components, such as smart contracts and distributed ledgers, as well as the consensus process. As known the blockchain promises to profoundly change to the applications of its components and the correlated organizations due to its possible implementations are vastly more comprehensive from currency [14] and exceeding economic services [15]. Finally, we applied the same architecture to files with common paths such as pdf and PNG without file status reporting [17]. Some study's objective was to develop and test a mHealth system that makes use of blockchain - based to provide interoperability, confidentiality, and scalability of health data [32]. Legacy systems typically solely communicate medical resources locally in the area of healthcare industry [33]. And cannot be used with other systems [34]. However, data in [35, 36] identifies a variety of advantages of linking such systems for more effective and integrated healthcare, urging health informatics experts to find a way to connect various companies. However, data in [35, 36] identifies a variety of advantages of linking such systems for more effective and integrated healthcare, urging health informatics experts to find a way to connect various companies.

3 Curent Work

We describe a Blockchain-based strategy for exchanging patient data in this paper. By predicating consensus on the demonstration of structural and virtual functions, this moves toward sacrificing a single, central source of confidence in favor of network consensus.

3.1 Blockchain Execution

A blockchain appears to be a series of blocks that are encrypted [17, 18]. Immutability is the significant characteristic and most attractive about this to numerous industries.

Various data that are added to the database of the blockchain never be modified; thus, depending on the consensus, a checkable, and rectified ledger of kinds of data can be constructed. That gives the blockchain specifically power and is appropriate to duties wheresoever the confidentiality of the blockchain data is of greatest significance, a functional instance of the immutability is ProvChain [19] as architecture to gather and confirm the source of cloud data, that operates through entrenching the provenance data at transactions of the blockchain.

As known there are different implementations of the blockchain, the main field contains Bitcoin [12], that based on Blockchain to execute the cryptocurrency coin execute on it. Ethereum [20] is a ledger that is built on the blockchain and contains a Turing-complete virtualization feature that allows code to be implemented using consensus protocol within the blockchain; in addition to numerous different blockchain applications. There are differences between Ethereum, Bitcoin and our private blockchain in the approach of smart contracts implementation. Smart contracts are executable code implemented on all nodes in the blockchain environment. Smart contracts are automatic contracts [17] in which the deal is executed on whole partners within the blockchain. They determine the advantages, responsibilities, and punishments that are related to conducting associated with the contract similar to the manner a standard contract approaches. As they simulate common contracts that are implemented on paper and regulations, they may be utilized, For example, to create a healthcare model depend on the Health Insurance Portability and Accountability Act (HIPAA). A modern type of blockchain confidence model is gaining traction: consortium confidence (a group of health care providers (HCPs)). Microsoft recently developed a framework called Coco that enables the creation of blockchain-agnostic consortiums [21]. These consortiums rely on a pre-defined group of permitted organizations. Via implementing smart contracts exclusively on these authorized members' devices, the consensus is created without the necessity of the miners. That given perfect outcomes in extremely more incredible performance with many modifications to the Coco blockchain make it has the capability to do approximately 1550–1600 transactions per second [22].

3.2 Shared Data

It is possible to improve data exchange by using BlockChain technology [16], in addition, to achieving optimization of the health provides chain through obtaining characteristics like immutability transparency, traceability to the software. Nevertheless, impossible for the blockchain system to ensure its content confidentiality and security. Therefore, this system is never offered as an ability to operate independently technology, whereas as an integrated with cryptographic strategies. Disregarding the different samples presented that rely on blockchain in healthcare systems, on account of the limitations of the assumption e.g., lawful, social, and technical. Desiring to overpower the above limitations, we suggest forthcoming research approaches that contain the design of holding privacy mixture data warehouse, interoperable hardware and software architecture, that obedient with the global laws and rules. Data sharing denotes one of the most significant possibilities for modifications toward the better in the healthcare system whereas furthermore one of the most considerable privacy challenges. Absolutely, some researchers like [23] handle the necessity to supply transparency on the possibility of the data of patients being communicated or shared with other parties utilizing DeepMind cooperation with Royal Free London NHS Foundation Trust.

4 Proposed Framework

This section includes the method used in this work, the method used in the use of virtualization in the blockchain and the health system data. We started from building the blockchain and transferring its functions to virtualization and using the cloud as a virtual incubator for the system, in addition to the method of sharing the health files of the system.

4.1 Virtual Blockchain Environment

With this, we show that the proposed environment that was built consists of a complete network of Blockchain with its components (nodes, smart contract, peer network, ledger). Furthermore, the NFV was created as a generic notion that encompasses a range of functions and services, with no precise standard to characterize it. After constructing the network, customizing it to perform within the blockchain ecosystem, we introduced this tool to the node functions hash, ledger, and key distribution to get a virtual blockchain environment.

The framework of proposed system is briefed in many include the below steps Fig. 1.

Step 1: Covers constructing a private blockchain network based on a given setting. [17].

Step 2: This depicts the process of connecting the blockchain to the cloud in order to use NFV services. [17].

Step 3: This features a revolutionary effort based on cloud services that virtualizes hashing blocks and leger (blockchain database). [17].

Step 4: The last phase includes applying the proposed system novel to healthcare.

4.2 Virtual Blockchain in Healthcare

The health care system consists of various organizations, Individuals and procedures whose major responsibility is to manage, enhance, and maintain people's health, who should provide specific services, such like medical centres, pharmacy, hospitals, and insurance companies. Properly complete systems provide a high-quality service level and safety of the e-community while also improving illness treatment and budgeting. And this is achieved by taking into account several aspects:

Figure 2 illustrates the structure of the suggested healthcare system. We clarify the structure of the sub-system that performs as stated in the next steps.

Step 1: In suggested system, we give permission to the user to enter into the system via an interface of our private blockchain, then ask for the wished health record.

Step 2: The condition of the smart contract is initiated for privacy in addition to transparency. It will examine security and entrance control. When the user tries to access has permitted user records, at that point they are supplied with access to an exact health record.

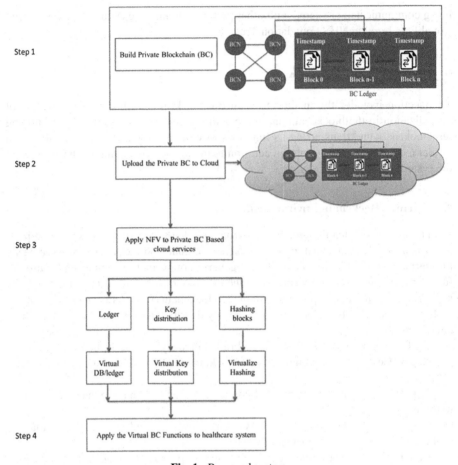

Fig. 1. Proposed system.

Step 3: The smart contract verifies that the nodes have suitable privacy.

Step 4: The permission status is based on the access control policy for every user.

The complete process is illustrated in Fig. 2, and it performs based on the subsequent steps.

Step 1: The user should log into the private blockchain- healthcare then looks for their wished health record.

Step 2: For examinations privacy, the smart contract is started.

Step 3: The privacy is guaranteed by the suggested smart contract. Next, monitoring the access control permission, users are reported that they have the ability to see the report with the result.

Figure 3 illustrates the architecture of the blockchain- healthcare; the main component of that system is a user interface, blockchain in two approaches (local and global). The topology of this system consists of many components (nodes, local blockchain, and root blockchain).

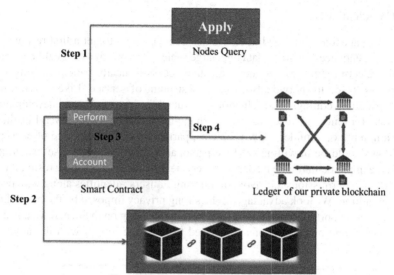

Fig. 2. Healthcare subsystem.

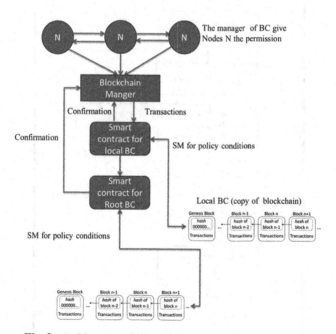

Fig. 3. Architecture of virtual blockchain- healthcare system.

4.3 Confidentiality

Health care agencies will need to distribute necessary data to get a first response plan to diseases, enhance statistical data on a large scale, and optimize the healthcare quality in which electronic health systems use actual access to health patient records to give prompt assistance to individuals at the closest point of service. Like a result, health data distribution, editing, and evaluation are crucial for identifying and developing new treatments for emerging diseases. But, exchanging health data over several institutions poses a number of confidentiality problems, particularly in the absence of encryption. Individuals could be unwilling to share personal data with anyone else, which might stymie the implementation that connects every health practitioners. As a result, it is vital to ensure safe permissions and avoid monitoring of users' identities along with original data recognition. We took advantage of the strong privacy imposed by the blockchain in saving patient reports and preventing others from intruding on them, and we considered each node as one of the sections authorized to view the report, with the addition of

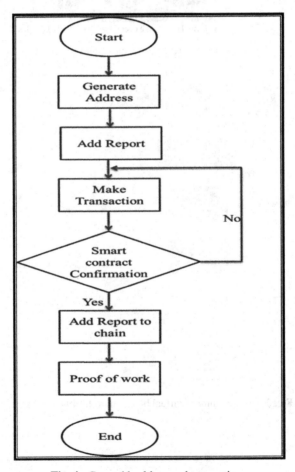

Fig. 4. General health record transactions.

another field showing the content of the report without opening it through the use of the two terms (negative and positive) Fig. 4.

5 Implementation and Results

In this section, the implementation and results of the proposed system are shown, starting from creating the keys and how to encrypt the files that are preserved inside the ledger, in addition to implementing the smart contract and obtaining optimal speeds, and finally, the comparison between the traditional and virtual ledger based on a transaction per second and number of nodes.

5.1 Key Generation

A public key is used to encrypt all blockchain transactions. As well as the transactions decrypting through the private key, and the process generation of key with time of encryption and decryption Tables 1 and 2. We observed below the Table 1 the file size is increased in the encryption process because the RSA is asymmetric encryption gets bigger the data size by 1/3 through the encryption process. The number of bits in the key of an encryption scheme is comparable to the length of the key. Poor security results from a small key length. But excellent security does not always entail a lengthy key length. The utmost number of combinations needed to defeat an encryption technique depends on the key length.

Table 1. Key generation and time (ms) of encryption and decryption for RSA algorithm

Size of file (KB)	Size of key	Time of generation key	Time of encrypted	Time of decrypted	Encrypted file size
711	512	90	310	911	905
711	1024	108	372	1105	810
711	2048	205	512	1812	780

From the above table, we can see that the time increases with the length of the key, also the encryption time increases with decryption time. However, the file size is decreased when the length of the key is increased when using RSA.

From the above table, we can see that the time increases with the length of the key, but the encryption time varies with its increase and decrease. However, decryption depends on the length of the key, meaning that the decryption time increases with the increase in the length of the key with the stability of the file encrypted using ECC.

Even though the key length is the same in both systems, key creation times vary, and it can sometimes take a very long time to generate the keys. Figure 5 illustrates that the key creation time is about identical in both situations for smaller key sizes, though as the key size increases, RSA consumes more time to produce the keys, but this time rises linearly with the key size.

Table 2. Key generation and time (ms) of encryption and decryption for ECC algorithm

Size of file (KB)	Size of key	Time of generation key	Time of encrypted	Time of decrypted	Encrypted file size
711	160	25	101	45	711
711	224	30	80	95	711
711	256	41	98	112	711

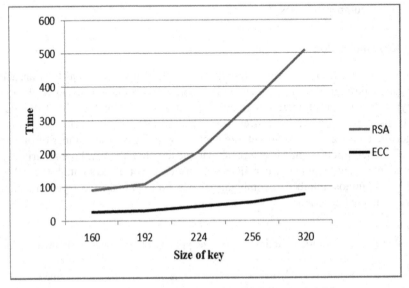

Fig. 5. Key Generation Time Comparison RSA & ECC

Encryption timings for the ECC and RSA methods are shown in Fig. 6.

Figure 7 show that the bigger the number of hash bits, the much more secure the system is. As a result, the output bits of SHA-1, SHA-512, and SHA-256 are equivalent. While choosing a secure hash algorithm, the file type for execution is a significant consideration.

The time it takes to execute a file of type character and number, image file, or text file is shown in Fig. 8. As a result, SHA-1 takes much less time to process huge files than SHA-256 and SHA-512.

With these two loops, the configuration is executed on localhost, and the results of many samples are compiled and analyzed. There are three main samples, which are listed in Table 3, 4 and 5.

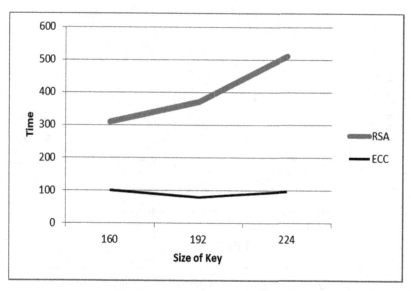

Fig. 6. Encryption Time RSA & ECC

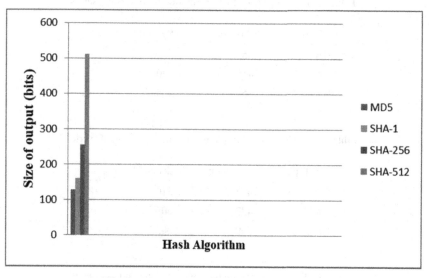

Fig. 7. Comparing Hash Algorithm Evaluation

5.2 Smart Contracts

The smart contract that was implemented was very fast and also has sufficient protection for all the nodes and this speed decreases very slowly with the increase of the nodes as shown in the Table 6 below.

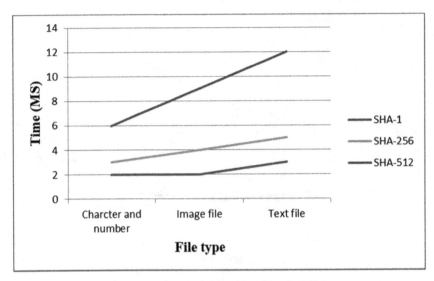

Fig. 8. Comparing Hash Algorithms based on file type.

Table 3. Two loops (ms) Implementation time to small series

Hash Type	First loop	Second loop
SHA-1	355	372
SHA-256	415	390
SHA-512	366	455

Table 4. Two loops (ms) Implementation time to middle series

Hash Type	First loop	Second loop
SHA-1	417	510
SHA-256	433	605
SHA-512	399	602

Table 5. Two loops (ms) Implementation time to large series

Hash Type	First loop	Second loop
SHA-1	715	810
SHA-256	680	805
SHA-512	680	802

Table 6. Speed of smart contract in our system

Number of Nodes	Time (ms)
2	1
5	1.2
10	1.5
20	1.8
40	2
60	2.2

5.3 Virtual Distributed Ledger Technology

In comparison to DLT, vDLT boosts transaction speeds to roughly 120 transactions per second Fig. 9. We build a network with sixty nodes. We create a variety of block levels ranging from 0 to 10. The block size has been fixed at 65 transactions per block. The pace of arrival of transactions is 77 transactions per second.

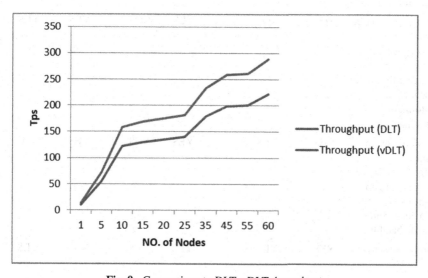

Fig. 9. Comparison to DLT, vDLT throughput

5.4 Comparison Metrics

In concluding, Table 7 compare the suggested work with some other options. The outcome demonstrates the various benefits of the suggested approach.

Table 7. Comparison among our proposed system and related works.

Paper title	Metrics					
	Tamper resistance	Nonrepudiation	Search in blocks	Attack Resistance	Offering key security	Ledger structure
A Blockchain-Based Solution for Electronic Medical Records System in Healthcare[37]	NO	YES	YES	NO	NO	YES
A blockchain-based medical data preservation scheme for telecare medical information systems[38]	YES	NO	NO	YES	YES	YES
Blockchain-based multi-level privacy-preserving location sharing scheme for telecare medical information systems[39]	NO	NO	YES	NO	YES	YES
Towards secure and privacy-preserving data sharing in e-health systems via consortium blockchain[40]	YES	YES	YES	YES	YES	NO
Proposed scheme	YES	YES	YES	YES	YES	YES

6 Conclusion and Future Work

This research solves the shortcomings of earlier methods and created a blockchain-NFV-based system for the protection of medical data. We highlighted the advantages of adopting a blockchain system for healthcare data protection in this work, through used a virtual blockchain to safeguard and distribute patient data. The blockchain's tamper-resistance and decentralized attributes in the developed framework ensure the confidentiality of virtual medical and health records and safeguard patients' privacy. We started with the construction private blockchain and the turn functions of it into a virtual function by using NFV. Adopting the virtual Blockchain to deploy the healthcare data fixes the important problems of availability of access and authority. The virtual Blockchain permits the comfort of access to the data of healthcare. Due to it being deployed and distributed over different networks, also may it available from anywhere. Additionally, a smart contract between the nodes has been developed with a fast execution time to ensure time acquisition and address privacy, legal, and performance problems. In future work, we will apply the framework to IoT environment and its influences will be investigated well and in more virtually.

References

1. Transaction, Cost Per, and Master Patient Index MPI. Blockchain: Opportunities for health care. CP transaction (2016)
2. Attili, S., Ladwa, S.K., Sharma, U., Trenkle, A.F.: Blockchain: the chain of trust and its potential to transform healthcare–our point of view. In: ONC/NIST Use of Blockchain for Healthcare and Research Workshop. Gaithersburg, MD: ONC/NIST (2016)
3. Marko, H., Kompara, M., Kamišalić, A., Zlatolas, L.N.: A systematic review of the use of blockchain in healthcare. Symmetry 10(10), 470 (2018)
4. Farouk, A., Alahmadi, A., Ghose, S., Mashatan, A.: Blockchain platform for industrial healthcare: vision and future opportunities. Comput. Commun. 154, 223–235 (2020)
5. Ariel, E., Azaria, A., Halamka, J.D., Lippman, A.: A case study for blockchain in healthcare:"MedRec" prototype for electronic health records and medical research data. In: Proceedings of IEEE Open & Big Data Conference. vol. 13, p. 13 (2016)
6. Dhillon, V., Metcalf, D., Hooper, M.: Blockchain enabled applications. Apress, Berkeley, CA (2017)
7. Dimitrov, D.V.: Blockchain applications for healthcare data management. Healthc. Inform. Res. 25(1), 51–56 (2019)
8. Rousseau, D.M., Sitkin, S.B., Burt, R.S., Camerer, C.: Not so different after all: a cross-discipline view of trust. Acad. Manag. Rev. 23(3), 393–404 (1998)
9. Gupta, V.: The promise of blockchain is a world without middlemen. Harv. Bus. Rev. 6(3), 2017 (2017)
10. Roman, B., Bloch, C.M.: Blockchain as radical innovation: a framework for engaging with distributed ledgers as incumbent organization (2017)
11. Yermack, D.: Corporate governance and blockchains. Rev. Finance 21(1), 7–31 (2017)
12. Nakamoto, Satoshi. "Bitcoin: A peer-to-peer electronic cash system." *Decentralized Business Review* (2008): 21260
13. Haber, S., Stornetta, W.S.: How to time-stamp a digital document. J. Cryptology 3(2), 99–111 (1991). https://doi.org/10.1007/BF00196791
14. Catalini, C., Gans, J.S.: Some simple economics of the blockchain. Commun. ACM 63(7), 80–90 (2020)
15. Darcy WE, A.: Discovering and developing the blockchain cryptoeconomy. SSRN 2815255 (2017)
16. Hayder A.J., Abdullah, A.A.: A new environment of blockchain based multi encryption data transferring. Webology 18(2), 1379–1391 (2021)
17. Jawdhari, H.A., Abdullah, A.A.: A novel blockchain architecture based on network functions virtualization (NFV) with auto smart contracts. Periodicals Eng. Nat. Sci. 9(4), 834–844 (2021)

18. Hayder A.J, Abdullah, A.A.: The application of network functions virtualization on different networks, and its new applications in blockchain: a survey. Comput. Technol. Inf. Manage. **18**, 1007–1044 (2021)

19. Liang, X., Shetty, S., Tosh, D., Kamhoua, C., Kwiat, K., Njilla, L.: ProvChain: a blockchain-based data provenance architecture in cloud environment with enhanced privacy and availability. In: 2017 17th IEEE/ACM International Symposium on Cluster, Cloud and Grid Computing (CCGRID), pp. 468–477. IEEE (2017)

20. Wood, G.: Ethereum: A secure decentralised generalised transaction ledger. Ethereum Proj. Yellow Pap. **151**(2014), 1–32 (2014)

21. Microsoft. The Coco Framework (2017)

22. Microsoft. Microsoft announces the Coco Framework to improve performance, confidentiality and governance characteristics of enterprise blockchain networks (2017)

23. Powles, J., Hodson, H.: Google DeepMind and healthcare in an age of algorithms. Heal. Technol. **7**(4), 351–367 (2017). https://doi.org/10.1007/s12553-017-0179-1

24. Shabani, M.: Blockchain-based platforms for genomic data sharing: a de-centralized approach in response to the governance problems? J. Am. Med. Inform. Assoc. **26**(1), 76–80 (2019)

25. Zheng, X., Sun, S., Mukkamala, R.R., Vatrapu, R., Ordieres-Meré, J.: Accelerating health data sharing: a solution based on the internet of things and distributed ledger technologies. J. Med. Internet Res. **21**(6), e13583 (2019)

26. Alain, G.: Possible usages of smart contracts (blockchain) in healthcare and why no one is using them. In: MEDINFO 2019: Health and Wellbeing e-Networks for All, pp. 596–600. IOS Press (2019)

27. Johnson, M., Jones, M., Shervey, M., Dudley, J.T., Zimmerman, N.: Building a secure biomedical data sharing decentralized app (DApp): tutorial. J. Med. Internet Res. **21**(10), e13601 (2019)

28. Marcella, A.: Blockchain technology and decentralized governance: Is the state still necessary?. SSRN 2709713 (2015)

29. Kenneth, C.C.: The potential for health (1998)

30. Chandwani, R.: Stakeholders in the Indian Healthcare Sector. Vikalpa **46**(2), 65–70 (2021)

31. Bin, L., et al.: A blockchain-based security framework for secure and resilient smart grid. J. Phys. Conf. Ser. **2218**(1), 012033 (2022). IOP Publishing

32. Tomomitsu, M., et al.: Secure and scalable mHealth data management using blockchain combined with client hashchain (2019)

33. Miller, A.R., Tucker, C.: Health information exchange, system size and information silos. J. Health Econ. **33**, 28–42 (2014)

34. Anil, S.A., Laleci Erturkmen, G.B.: A federated semantic metadata registry framework for enabling interoperability across clinical research and care domains. J. Biomed. Inform. **46**(5), 784–794 (2013)

35. Featherstone, I., Keen, J.: Do integrated record systems lead to integrated services? an observational study of a multi-professional system in a diabetes service. Int. J. Med. Informatics **81**(1), 45–52 (2012)

36. Christoph, R., et al.: Improving the informational continuity of care in diabetes mellitus treatment with a nationwide Shared EHR system: Estimates from Austrian claims data. Int. J. Med. Inform. **92**, 44–53 (2016)

37. Sharma, S., Kaushal, S., Gupta, S., Kumar, H.: A Blockchain-based solution for electronic medical records system in healthcare. In: Luhach, A.K., Jat, D.S., Hawari, K.B.G., Gao, X.-Z., Lingras, P. (eds.) Advanced Informatics for Computing Research: 5th International Conference, ICAICR 2021, Gurugram, India, December 18–19, 2021, Revised Selected Papers, pp. 232–243. Springer International Publishing, Cham (2022). https://doi.org/10.1007/978-3-031-09469-9_20

38. Lee, T.-F., Li, H.-Z., Hsieh, Y.-P.: A blockchain-based medical data preservation scheme for telecare medical information systems. Int. J. Inf. Secur. **20**(4), 589–601 (2020). https://doi.org/10.1007/s10207-020-00521-8
39. Yaxian, J., et al.: BMPLS: Blockchain-based multi-level privacy-preserving location sharing scheme for telecare medical information systems. J. Med. Syst. **42**(8), 1–13 (2018)
40. Zhang, A., Lin, X.: Towards secure and privacy-preserving data sharing in e-health systems via consortium blockchain. J. Med. Syst. **42**(8), 1–18 (2018)

Use Multichannel EEG-Based Biometrics Authentication Signal in Real Time Using Neural Network

Nadhim Azeez Sayel[1]($\boxtimes$), Salah Albermany[2], and Bayan Mahdi Sabbar[3]

[1] University of UoITC, Baghdad, Iraq
nazim201369@uoitc.edu.iq
[2] University of Kufa, Kufa, Iraq
salah.albermany@uokufa.edu.iq
[3] Nahrain University, Baghdad, Iraq
bayan.Mahdi@coie-nahrain.edu.iq

Abstract. As EEG brainwave, which represent human brain activities, are more private, sensitive, and hard to steal or copy, the signals show a lot of promise as a biometric method for user authentication that is much safer. The current study shows a biometric security framework that is based on EEG. In particular, the plan is to lower the noise level with ensemble averaging and a band pass filter, pull out frequency features with fast Fourier transform (FFT), and to use an artificial neural network to do classification. The study followed two different scenarios to show how different authentication applications work. The findings demonstrate that, the average accuracy was about 93.13% when it is used with one person from a group of people. But it has also been revealed there is a classification rate of less than 68.88% is achieved when all subjects are picked out of a large group. The study establishes a strong starting point for future investigation into new biometric approaches considering brainwaves.

Keywords: Electroencephalogram (EEG) · Feature Extraction · classification

1 Introduction

For future research into new biometric methods based on brainwaves. The inevitable spread of brain-computer interfaces (BCIs) into society could change the way people interact with each other today. BCI devices are expected to be used by a wide range of people in the future, including children, adults, medical patients, inventors, and government workers. There are four main types of BCI applications, which are: "1) neuromedical applications 2) Logging in as a user 3) Games and entertainment, and 4) base applications for smart phones" [1]. Because brain biometrics are more secure than other biometrics like fingerprints, retina scans, and voice authentication, BCI devices have been added to the user authentication process. Recent technological advances, such as man-in-the-middle attacks, data impersonation, and the straight-up theft of body parts, have shown that these biometrics are easy to hack. These security risks have led to

A. M. Al-Bakry et al. (Eds.): NTICT 2022, CCIS 1764, pp. 248–263, 2023.
https://doi.org/10.1007/978-3-031-35442-7_13

security problems, like when a hacker from the Chaos Computer Club (CCC) stole the thumbprint of German Defense Minister Ursula von der Leyen at a news conference by using standard imaging and software devices [2].

Brain biometrics are collected by BCI devices that record an individual's electroencephalogram (EEG) to collect brainwave data. This information can then be used to find out things about the brainwave patterns of each person, such as an Event-Related Potential (ERP), which is the brain's response to a stimulus that is time-locked [3]. Through these tests, a person's unique brainwave pattern can be found. But brainwave fingerprints data are different from other biometrics in a few ways, they are more complicated and therefore harder to copy, the authenticator must be alive to create an EEG signal, and EEGs and ERPs cannot be controlled by the user [3, 4].

But this is not the case with DNA, fingerprints, a person's face, or the iris, which can be used to identify a person for a few hours after death before slowly changing [7, 8].

The main focus of the research will be on authentication, since there is a strong desire to make BCIs as safe as possible when people use their brain biometrics to claim a certain identity. Finally using this concept to ensure brainwave data from customer well-disposed EEG devices is essentially as protected as could be expected.

2 Background of EEG

With an EEG, you can record the electrical activity of the brain on the scalp. When numerous neurons in the brain fire at the same time, ions flow through the brain. This makes voltage changes that vary from 5 to 100 V and have a frequency of between 0.5 and 40 Hz [9]. By looking at the dominant frequencies and amplitudes of EEG waveforms in distinct parts of the brain, you can learn some things about the person. This can help us to figure out how they feel or how their bodies are doing [10]. Based on how fast they move, there are five different types of brain waves [11]:

- In terms of amplitude, delta waves (0.1–3.5Hz) are the slowest and usually the highest waveforms. Children, adults who are drowsy, and people who want to remember things all have the delta band.
- the theta (4–7.5 Hz) band. The delta band is seen in babies and when people are in deep sleep. There is usually less than 100 V of amplitude in Theta waves.
- Alpha waves (8–13 Hz) are usually the most common frequency band and show up when you are relaxed, or your eyes are closed. Theta waves have a low amplitude. The amplitude of the Alpha band is reduced when you pay attention or relax with your eyes open. Normally, these waves do not have more than 50 V.
- Beta waves (14–30 Hz) are linked to thinking, active concentration, and focused attention. Also, when you move your body or see other people move their bodies, your Beta power increases [12].
- Gamma waves (over more than 30 Hz) are seen when the brain is processing a lot of distinct forms of information. Beta waves usually have less than 30 V of amplitude [13]. Gamma patterns have the lowest amount of energy.

In addition to function-frequency relationships, it is also thought that each part of the brain does a different physical or mental job. It is important to explore not only the dominant frequency but also recordings from the part of the brain that corresponds to each task [9].

In addition to function-frequency relationships, it is also thought that each part of the brain performs a different physical or mental job. It is important to inspect not only the dominant frequency but also recordings from the part of the brain that corresponds to each task. Table 1 shows the functions that are linked to each part of the brain [9].

Table 1. Functions associated to different parts of the brain

Region	Functions
Parietal Lobe	Problem Solving, grammar, attention
Frontal Lobe	Memory, emotions, concentration
Occipital Lobe	Reading, vision
Temporal Lobe	Memory, word recognition, hearing, face recognition

To get the EEG signals, electrodes with low impedance are put on the scalp to pick up the electric potentials that the brain makes. The electrodes can be put on with conductive gel, which is called a wet electrode, or they can touch the skin directly, which is called a dry electrode. Most of the time, dry electrodes are easier to attach, but they are more sensitive to the motion artifacts that happen. There are some rules for where and how to place and label the electrodes on the scalp, like 10–20 standard electrodes [9]. Ten percent and twenty percent points on lines of longitude and latitude, respectively, are where the electrodes are placed. They are marked with the lobe that is attached to them. Odd numbers are given to the electrodes on the left side of the brain, and even numbers are given to the electrodes on the right side.

2.1 Emotiv Capabilities

The Emotiv software can perform countless of different tasks. The Facial Expressions suite can detect a wide range of facial expressions, such as blinking, winking with the left or right eye, and expressions of surprise, frowning, smiling, and clenching one's face, among other things [23].

The experiment used the Emotiv Insight. It records on five channels: AF3, AF4, T7, T8, Pz, and one reference node. Gel made of glycerin was used to connect the leads to each other and it can connect wirelessly to most computers with Bluetooth. Because of its design, it is easy to put on your own head without any help from anyone else. In combination with the BCI software that Emotiv makes available, it is a quite easy EEG device. This could make it possible for even the least-experienced people to use a BCI quickly and easily, even if they do not know how.

The output data from the headset is transferred to the PC using Bluetooth USB receiver model. The captured EEG signal is already filtered with a built-in digital 5th order sinc bandpass filter, whose passband ranging from (0.16 ~ 43) Hz (range of EEG frequencies), with two digital notch filters at 50Hz and 60Hz, to eliminate AC power line harmonics.

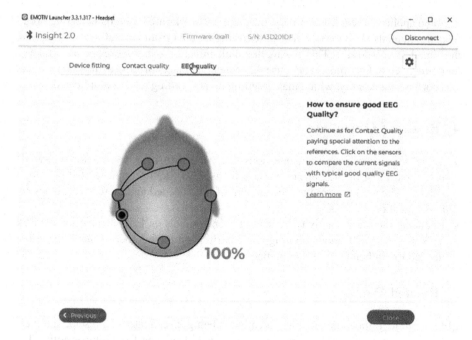

Fig. 1. Emotiv EEG headsets with their electrode positions in 10–20 system

Because of the high resistance between the scalp and the electrodes, EEG data might be contaminated. The conductive media employed, such as saline solutions, can lower impedance and increase contact quality, hence improving signal quality. High impedance can cause EEG signal distortion by allowing extraneous electrical frequencies to be induced on the system, making it harder to distinguish from the original signal. Figure 1 shows "EMOTIV Launcher 3.3.0.311", which is the impedance monitoring program included with the EMOTIV INSIGHT headsets used to measure impedance in real-time. If the impedance raises beyond 5K Ohms, the application will warn you by changing the electrode colors. This will eliminate the distortion in the signal.

3 Problem Statement

There are three types of authentication and identification methods: something the user knows, something the user owns, and something the user does [5]. Traditional methods, like passwords and ATM cards, have been shown to have major flaws when it comes to things that the user knows and remembers. The user knows about or has tokens that it can be lost, stolen, or forgotten, which could cause authentication to fail or data to be leaked. EEG, a type of biometric, can help to solve these problems. Because biometrics are things about a person's body or behavior, they do not need to be learned. This demonstrates that each person's EEG signal may be different, so it could be used as a biometric signal. The EEG is different from other biometrics in a number of important ways [6].

Even though these previous investigations have contributed great strides in EEG-based authentication, there are still some key challenges that need to be resolved before it can be applied in real life. Primary, most current works are based on detecting event-related potentials (ERPs), which require averaging data from several trials to improve the signal-to-noise ratio. This means that authentication using these methods takes a long time. Secondary, most works use 32 or more channels of EEG acquisition devices to record neural activity, which makes setting up and getting ready complicated.

4   Research Objectives

- There were some important questions that needed to be answered for real-world use. First, most of the current work is focused on finding event-related potentials (ERPs). The goal is to reduce the amount of time needed and increase accuracy for authentication.
- Reducing the brain's activity by using fewer channels on EEG acquisition devices. This makes setting up and getting ready easier, and the number of math operations needed for authentication is extremely low.

5   Related Works

EEG-based identification and authentication is being investigated at present, and these early studies have revealed that brainwave signals from the EEG can be utilized to identify and authenticate a person.

Palaniappan [14] proposed a two-stage threshold method based on the features of autoregressive coefficients (AR), channel spectral powers and inter-hemispheric channel spectral power differences (IHPD), inter-hemispheric channel linear complexity (IHLC), and non-linear complexity on six channels to verify five subjects. For this approach, the false reject error (FRE) ranged between 0 and 1.5 percent. (1) Using the naive Bayes model, (2) authenticated four participants based on mAR attributes. The HTER, or half total error rate, was 6.7%. C. He and J. Wang, [15] also employed the naïve Bayes model to verify seven patients, yielding HTERs ranging from 2.2 to 7.3%. This model based on AR and power spectral density (PSD) was also employed by Kathikeyan and Sabarigiri [16], who had an equivalent error rate (EER) of 4.16%.

Ashby et al. [17] used the linear support vector machine (SVM) classifier to authenticate 5 people using the AR, PSD, spectral power (SP), IHPD, and IHLC from the 14 EEG channels. They got a false rejection rate (FRR) of 2.4% to 5.1% and a false acceptance rate (FAR) of 0.7% to 1.1%. Yeom et al. [18] used the signal difference and least square error of time derivative features on 18 channels with the Gaussian kernel SVM on 10 subjects and got an accuracy of about 86%. Dan et al. [19] employed a polynomial kernel SVM based on a single channel wavelet transform (WT) and AR. On average, they were right about 85% of the time on 13 subjects.

Because SVM theory only allows for two classes, when there are three or more, there are two options for classification: one against one (any two classes) and one against all (taking a random class as the first group and all the other classes as the second group). Ferreira et al. [20] classified 13 subjects based on the gamma band using the linear and radial basis function (RBF) SVM. The error rate for the one against one method was between 15.67% and 38.21%, and the error rate for the one against all method was between 17.43% and 30.57%.

Chen et al. [21] suggested a fast visual presentation-based EEG login system. The tests let the people quickly look at the randomly chosen target images. Then, shrinkage discriminant analysis was used to classify the images. The test results showed that the average accuracy of classification could be as high as 77.5.9%. Gui et al. [22] came up with a plan for an experiment in which the subjects had to read out loud the right words, the wrong words, acronyms, and their own names. It used wavelet packet decomposition to get frequency features and neural networks to classify the data. This gave it an average accuracy of 90%.

6   Materials and Methods

Based on Fig. 2, the authentication system composed of a registration subsystem, login and authentication subsystem.

Figure 2 shows that the data flow of each subsystem in the authentication framework is made up of four parts. The first step is to get EEG signals in their raw form. After that, a band pass filter and ensemble averaging are used to cut down on the noise. Then, FFT is used to pull out the features of the EEG signals based on the Theta frequency sub-bands. One of these features is used to train the neural network, and the other features are used to measure how well the system is working.

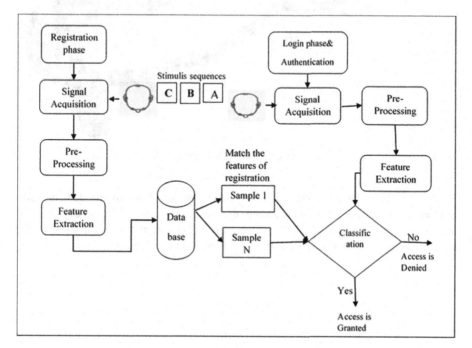

Fig. 2. Authentication Model

A number of important tools are used to help with BCI in this study. The software used was written in a language called MATLAB. We are using a laptop or tablet PC with Windows 10 or a higher version (R2020 b). The brainwave reader used is called an EEG Sensor (Emotiv Insight). This is the fresher adaptation of the old Emotiv Insight. It accompanies additional libraries that assist the researchers with getting raw EEG data from the device.

Emotiv Insight has five EEG channels and two references that make it easy to locate the right position for accurate spatial resolution. Based on the 10–20 electrode system, these are the names of the channels. They are marked with AF3, T7, Pz, T8, and AF4, with CM S/DRL references where P3/P4 would be. With digital signal processing and sorting, it takes a lot of effort to convert raw EEG data into pure EEG signal, which can then be investigated. The current study is based on EEG data in its raw form. Emotiv Insight headset and the five EEG channels shown in Fig. 3 are shown in this picture.

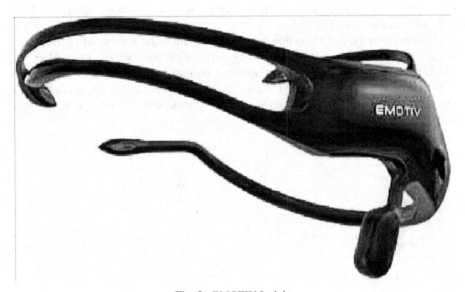

Fig. 3. EMOTIV Insight

The theta brainwave is utilized to carry out this project. Low-amplitude beta waves that have various different frequencies are often linked to thinking that is busy, anxious, or active. Calm activity is linked to the alpha wave. If you want to keep the 4–8 Hz theta wave, you should use a Bandpass Filter to filter the EEG so that they stay in.

The filtered EEG is then put through a "windowing" function, which turns non-periodic EEG signals into periodic ones so that the FFT does not leak the spectrum when it looks at the EEG (Fast Fourier Transform).

- Hardware Requirements

- EEG Sensor (Emotiv Insight)

- Software Requirements

- Matlab (R2020 b)

6.1 Subjects

Ten participants between the age of 19 to 23 participated in the experiment to construct the EEG signal dataset,7 male and 3 female. Before the test, they were all healthy and had not taken any drugs or medicines.

Then, at that point, they were asked to sit quietly in a quiet room and try to remain as quiet as possible. Before the experiment began, all of the participants who participate in experiment to sign a written consent to participate. Then their neural responses were recorded.

6.2 Signal Acquisition

When each individual tried to perform a certain cognitive task, their EEG was recorded. EEG is used with the EMOTIV neuro headset to find out how the brain's electricity is being used. It uses two reference electrodes (CM S/DRL) and five electrodes (AF3, AF4, T7, Pz, and T8) to pick up neural signals that are caused by different actions. The EEG signal is sent to the laptop wirelessly by the Bluetooth dongle, so the laptop can recognize it. A sampling rate of 128 Hz to save the EEG data as an edf file is used. In the MATLAB workspace, the live EEG feed from the Emotiv headset can be seen.

In this study, the researchers examined how the brain is reacted to the acronym's stimuli from the AF3 and AF4 channels, which were regarded to be the best channels for displaying the subject's brain activity. The raw data from Channels AF3 and AF4 are shown in Fig. 4 to give a sense of what they appear. The raw EEG data were noisy because they varied quickly, as it can be seen from the waveform.

Prior to the recording session, the participant is asked to rest for five to ten minutes. This enables a broad relaxation of brain activity and improves the precision of recorded EEG data. The participant is then asked to keep his eyes open while placing his hands on the armrest.

By blinking with both eyes, the user selects between two alternatives in the visual stimulus window that opens, one for recording and the other for logging in, as shown in the Fig. (5) and Fig. (6).

The recording is then first chosen after that when the registration is selected, a window appears asking to register the name to start the registration process and acquire the required signal, as shown in the Fig. (7).

In the authentication stage the same steps as in Fig. 7 are followed, choosing to log in to start the process of classifying subject.

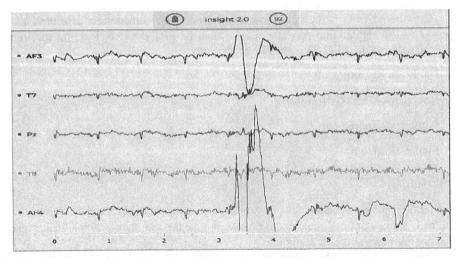

Fig. 4. Raw data from EMOTIV headset

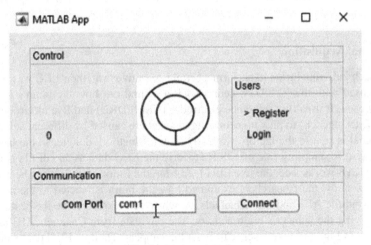

Fig. 5. Register interface

After the registration period ends, it appears on the same window, asking him/her to blink on the right or left eye randomly the registration process is conducted 5 times for each case 10 times randomly with varying times so that 100 samples for each participant could be collected, it is saved in the database in order to be analyzed, all this is done at sample rate of 128 per second to measure the correlation process between both eyes.

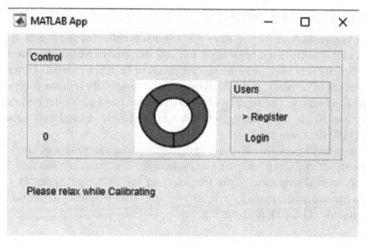

Fig. 6. Registration mode and relax

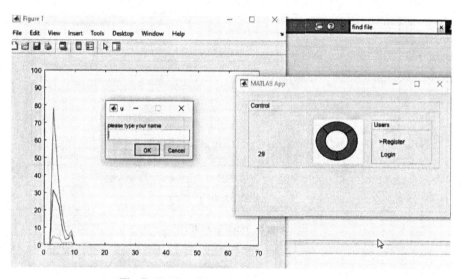

Fig. 7. Registration and storage in the database

6.3 EEG Signal Preprocessing

In the 2020b MATLAB workspace, real-time EEG signals are processed and then investigated. For the proposed method of study, a Core i5 processor with a speed of 2.60 GHz is used. At the beginning, EEG responses are brought into the MATLAB workspace.

During the pre-processing phase, the signal-to-noise ratio was improved, and the quality of the signal was improved without any information being lost. The first step was to find events in the data that were related and get rid of events that were not needed. Then, independent component analysis (ICA) was used to remove the eye and heart artifacts that were in the raw data.

6.4 Filtering, Artifact Removal

During EEG signal acquisition, the raw EEG signal is collected and stored. But the raw signal has a lot of noise that is not related. Because the hand moves and the line frequency changes, the artifacts may make noise that needs to be taken care of. Using different ways to get rid of artifacts in the MATLAB environment, these noises were removed of the raw EEG signal. The signal had to go through a band pass filter because the line frequency was 50 Hz. For filtering between 4 Hz and 8 Hz, a band pass finite impulse response (FIR) filter was used.

Utilizing a band-pass filter function designed for a frequency range of 4 to 8 Hz (theta) the frequency of the input samples is 128 samples and calculate the first frequency of the stop band (Fstop1) = 3, the frequency of the first band (Fpass1) = 4, band frequency Second pass (Fpass2) = 8, second stopband frequency (Fstop2), first stop band attenuation (Dstop1), as in the Fig. 8.

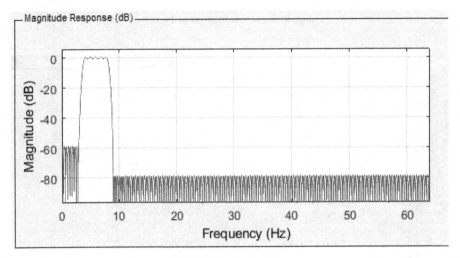

Fig. 8. Band-pass filter

6.5 EEG Feature Extraction

EEG features are normally separated into three fundamental gatherings: time, frequency, and time- frequency.

6.5.1 Frequency-Domain Features

Participants who use EEG to figure out how someone is feeling have found that frequency-domain features are better at this than time-domain features. If someone is in a different kind of mood, the strength of the EEG signal in different frequency bands is a good way to tell. Different frequency bands, like Theta, should be used to get information like the power spectrum, the logarithm of the power spectrum, the maximum, the minimum, and the standard deviation.

6.5.2 Time–Frequency Domain Features

The main problem with frequency-domain features is that individuals do not tell info about time. So, features in time–frequency domain are helpful at catching signals that do not stay still and change over time, which can help us to figure out how people feel at various times. It has numerous innovative and fascinating features, such as the Fast Fourier transform (FTT). The Fast Fourier transformation has several more characteristics that can be used to figure out basic emotions, such as power, root mean square. The Gamma, Beta, Alpha, Delta, and Theta frequency bands were extracted from emotiv insight for AF3 and AF4 channels We note the frequency strength in the theta range of the above channels. We note the frequency strength in the theta range of the above channels., as show in Fig. 9.

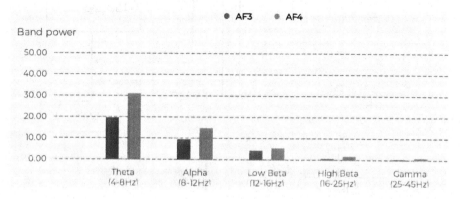

Fig. 9. Frequency bands for AF3 and AF4 channels

6.6 EEG Signal Classification

Classification is the process of comparing the input vectors to the stored feature vectors to see if they are the same. Researchers have used Artificial Neural Networks (ANNs) a lot to sort EEG signals into groups. In this study, the classifier for EEG patterns is a back-propagation, multi-layer perception NN. The extracted features were used to tell the neural network what to do. 70% of the data in each training dataset was utilized to train the model, and the remaining 30% was used to test the model. Each time, the researchers increased the number of neurons in the buried layer by 5, from 5 to 25. As a result, five examples with varying numbers of neurons were examined to evaluate how well they functioned, and which one performed the best.

In Fig. 10 the flowchart diagram of the BCI appears which was created can be seen. It contains the steps of acquisition, processing, as well as classification, as can be seen from the flowchart in the classification stage. If the threshold limit in the AF3 channel is greater than the threshold1 and the second threshold, the direction is to the blink left eye. Here, the threshold1 limit is 25 power and the threshold2 is 30 powers for channels AF3 and AF4, and through the flowchart we see of the conditions in the figure.

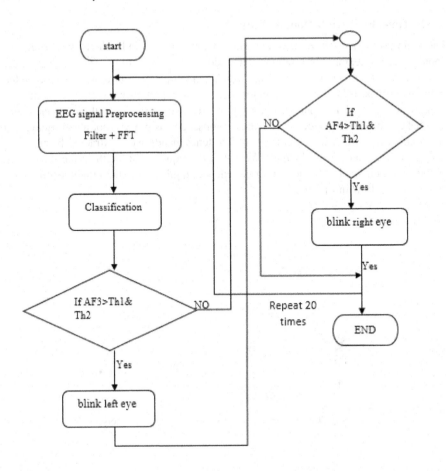

Fig. 10. Flowchart of MATLAB code for applying FFT on the EEG dataset from INSIGHT headset.

7   Results and Discussion

The researchers looked at two distinct application situations that may be used for user authentication in the experiment.

SCENARIO 1: Correctly identify all ten participants: The purpose of this scenario was to correctly identify each of the ten participants. As a result, the training dataset included all 10 participants' attributes, and the outputs included 10 separate classifications. On the basis of the training dataset, a NN model was created to test the inputs.

SCENARIO 2: Choose one individual out of the other 9: The goal of this scenario was to test how well it can differentiate participant from another. All of the data from one participant's training dataset was put into the training dataset, and the same amount of data from all of the other participant' training datasets was collected at random and put in the same place.

Table 2. Showed the rates of classification for each situation

Scenarios	Description	No of Neurons	Correct Classification Rate		
			Minimum	Maximum	Average
1	1 case	5	46.84%	57.68%	52.26%
		10	46.80%	63.45%	55.12%
		15	50.46%	66.53%	58.49%
		20	63.73%	74.04%	68.88%
		25	56.33%	68.31%	62.32%
2	10 cases	5	81.38%	95.84%	88.61%
		10	79.48%	98.90%	89.19%
		15	75.23%	97.56%	86.39%
		20	85.13%	96.66%	90.89%
		25	86.91%	99.36%	93.13%

Utilizing the Correct Classification Rate (CCR) in the following equation to measure how well each scenario worked:

$$CCrate = C_t / T_n * 100\% \tag{1}$$

where Ct is the total number of right answers and Tn is the total number of times the test was done.

SCENARIO 1: in which all 10 participants had to be identified, was the least accurate, with a range of 52.26 to 68.88 percent. The best accuracy was in the hidden layer of 20 neurons, and adding more neurons did not help to improve the performance.

SCENARIO 2: was a case of picking out one person from a group of people. The average accuracy of the hidden layer of 25 neurons was 93.13 percent. The accuracy did not change much when the number of neurons was cut down, since the minimum average accuracy is 90.89 percent. Even though everyone has different brainwaves, there are times when some participants have brainwaves that are very close to each other and times when they are very different. So, it may be difficult to inform some participants separately, but it may be very convenient to inform others away from each other/. The table's minimum and maximum accuracy numbers show this. The worst case for being able to tell one thing from another was 75.23%, and the best case was 99.66%.

The results, show that that SCENARIO 2 had the highest average accuracy for to select the one subject apart from others. However, for some people, the average accuracy was low, at 75.23%. This was mostly because the patterns of some of the EEG signals recorded from some of the subjects were very similar. So, when we tried to select one of these participants apart from the others, the NN classifier couldn't tell all the feature vectors apart correctly. It was more likely to have some wrong classifications, which would lower the accuracy. When we increased the number of participants The researchers were trying to find, the average, minimum, and maximum accuracy all went down.

8   Conclusions

In this research, the focus relies on a pilot study of how to use EEG signals for authentication. To minimize noise, ensemble averaging, and a band pass filter were utilized, and the Fast Fourier transform (FTT) was used to extract features. The neural network was used to classify the data. In two separate approaches, we put the authentication situations to the test. The classification rates for separating one subject from others or a small group of subjects from others were very accurate around 93.13% of the time. Determining which of the participants performed the worst. It was difficult to correctly identify all ten of participants.

References

1. Ienca, M., Haselager, P.: Hacking the brain: brain–computer interfacing technology and the ethics of neurosecurity. Ethics Inf. Technol. **18**(2), 117–129 (2016). https://doi.org/10.1007/s10676-016-9398-9
2. Kleinman, Z.: Politician's fingerprint 'cloned from photos' by hacker, BBC News, vol. 29 (2014)
3. Ruiz-Blondet, M.V., Jin, Z., Laszlo, S.: CEREBRE: A novel method for very high accuracy event-related potential biometric identification. IEEE Trans. Inf. Forensics Secur. **11**(7), 1618–1629 (2016)
4. Pham, T., Ma, W., Tran, D., Nguyen, P., Phung, D.: Multi-factor EEG-based user authentication. In: 2014 International Joint Conference on Neural Networks (IJCNN). IEEE (2014)
5. Pasupathinathan, V.: Hardware-based identification and authentication systems. Macquarie University (2009)
6. van Beijsterveldt, C.E.M., Boomsma, D.I.: Genetics of the human electroencephalogram (EEG) and event-related brain potentials (ERPs): a review. Hum. Genet. **94**(4), 319–330 (1994)
7. Saripalle, S.K., McLaughlin, A., Krishna, R., Ross, A., Derakhshani, R.: Post-mortem iris biometric analysis in Sus scrofa domesticus. In: 2015 IEEE 7th International Conference on Biometrics Theory, Applications and Systems (BTAS) (2015)
8. Trokielewicz, M., Czajka, A., Maciejewicz, P.: Post-mortem human iris recognition, In: 2016 International Conference on Biometrics, ICB 2016 (2016)
9. Bidgolya, A.J., Bidgoly, H.J., Arezoumanda, Z.: A survey on methods and challenges in EEG based authentication (2020)
10. Sanei, S.: Adaptive processing of brain signals. John Wiley \& Sons (2013)
11. Sanei, S., Chambers, J.a.: EEG Signal Processing:ppt, p. 289 (January 2013)
12. Zhang, Y., Chen, Y., Bressler, S.L., Ding, M.: Response preparation and inhibition: the role of the cortical sensorimotor beta rhythm. Neuroscience **156**(1), 238–246 (2008)
13. Read, G.L., Innis, I.J.: Electroencephalography (Eeg). Int. Encycl. Commun. Res. Methods, 1–18 (2017)
14. Palaniappan, R.: Two-stage biometric authentication method using thought activity brain waves. Int. J. Neural Syst. **18**(1), 59–66 (2008)
15. He, C., Wang, J.: An independent component analysis (ICA) based approach for EEG person authentication. In: 2009 3rd International Conference on Bioinformatics and Biomedical Engineering. IEEE (2009)

16. Kathikeyan, T., Sabarigiri, B.: Countermeasures against IRIS spoofing and liveness detection using Electroencephalogram (EEG). In: 2012 International Conference on Computing, Communication and Applications, pp. 1–5 (2012)
17. Ashby, C., Bhatia, A., Tenore, F., Vogelstein, J.: Low-cost electroencephalogram (EEG) based authentication. In: 2011 5th International IEEE/EMBS Conference on Neural Engineering. IEEE (2011)
18. Yeom, S.-K., Suk, H.-I., Lee, S.-W.: Person authentication from neural activity of face-specific visual self-representation. Pattern Recognit. **46**(4), 1159–1169 (2013)
19. Dan, Z., Xifeng, Z., Qiangang, G.: An identification system based on portable EEG acquisition equipment. In: 2013 Third International Conference on Intelligent System Design and Engineering Applications. IEEE (2013)
20. Ferreira, A., Almeida, C., Georgieva, P., Tomé, A., Silva, F.: Advances in EEG-based biometry. In: International conference image analysis and recognition, pp. 287–295 (2010)
21. Chen, Y., et al.: A High-Security EEG-Based Login System with RSVP Stimuli and Dry Electrodes. IEEE Trans. Inf. Forensics Secur. **11**(12), 2635–2647 (2016)
22. Gui, Q., Jin, Z., Xu, W.: Exploring EEG-based biometrics for user identification and authentication. In: 2014 IEEE Signal Processing in Medicine and Biology Symposium (SPMB). IEEE (2014)
23. Turner, M.D., Burnet, D.H., Turner, J.A.: Expanding EEG research into the clinic and classroom with consumer EEG systems (March 2017)

Machine Learning-Based DDoS Attack Detection in Software-Defined Networking

Mohammed Ibrahim Kareem[1] and Mahdi Nsaif Jasim[2]($\boxtimes$)

[1] Department of Information Networks, University of Babylon, Hillah, Iraq
Mohamed.ibrahim@uobabylon.edu.iq
[2] Department of Business Informatics, University of Information Technology and Communications, Baghdad, Iraq

Abstract. Software-defined networking (SDN) has recently become a prominent technique for addressing the inherent difficulties of traditional distributed networks. The main advantage of SDN is the decoupling of the control plane and the data plane, which makes the network more flexible and manageable. SDN is a network architecture of the future; nevertheless, its configuration settings are centralized, leaving it vulnerable to DDoS attacks. Distributed Denial of Service (DDoS) represents a grave threat to computer networks. These attacks are common because they are simple to execute and difficult to detect. Due to this vulnerability, the SDN controller will be flooded by the incoming packets from the switches, resulting in its overload. This project intends to create and deploy an attack detection system based on machine learning (ML) algorithms for detecting DDoS attacks over SDN network traffic. Using the CICIDS2017 dataset, the ML models were trained and tested. The feature sets for classification were determined using a proposed features selection algorithm, evaluation via multiple tests, and the filtered features are the most applicable and relevant in an SDN environment. The performance of each classifier was evaluated using different performance metrics for the four feature sets obtained from the feature selection algorithm. Using either 6 or 11 features, the candidate PART classifier achieves an accuracy of 99.77% and 99.96%, respectively. The proposed classifier shows high accuracy for both UDP and SYN attacks on the CICDDoS2019 dataset.

Keywords: SDN · Machine Learning · Features Selection · DDoS · CICIDS2017 · PART classifier

1 Introduction

SDN is a new networking technology that overcomes the constraints of traditional networks. Traditional networks' bottlenecks were their complicated design, the setup of individual network devices using language programming of the vendors, and a lack of a global perspective of the network [1]. A global view of networks became feasible with the introduction of SDN, allowing for faster network setup and management [2]. SDN is a new architecture comprised of three data, control, and application plane levels, with the data and control layers being independent of one another. The data plane is made up

© The Author(s), under exclusive license to Springer Nature Switzerland AG 2023
A. M. Al-Bakry et al. (Eds.): NTICT 2022, CCIS 1764, pp. 264–281, 2023.
https://doi.org/10.1007/978-3-031-35442-7_14

of switches and routers that are involved in network traffic forwarding; the control plane is made up of network intelligent components [3].

Distributed Denial of Service (DDoS) attacks use malicious ways to reduce the availability of services in computer networks, with the most common method being to send large traffic at the target to deplete either the bandwidth or the target's resources. Attackers typically utilize a large number of machines, known as bots or zombies, to send malicious communications. Bots are frequently infected computers that their genuine controllers are unaware of that [4–6].

In traditional networks, a variety of strategies have been employed to mitigate the impact of DDoS attacks [7]. Packet analysis was resource-intensive in conventional networks; thus, sampling techniques were utilized to validate the packets. For traffic collection and analytics, Cisco's NetFlow flow monitoring technology and S-flow packet sampling technology were employed [8]. When a DDoS attempt is identified, flow rules may be dynamically introduced into the flow table due to the programmable nature of SDN.

According to Mousavi and St-Hilaire [9], a DDoS attack is one of the most crucial challenges in this type of setting. A huge number of packets are sent to a host or group of hosts on a network in this circumstance. The accumulation of authentic and bogus DDoS packets might bind the controller's processing resources to the point where they are completely drained. This may render the SDN controller unreachable to valid incoming packets and may cause the controller to fail, destroying the SDN architecture.

Among the many protection measures recommended for detecting DDoS attacks, ML techniques, which are useful in cybersecurity [10], are being employed to address this issue. There are three classifications for ML-based DDoS detection methods: supervised, unsupervised, and hybrid. The supervised methods utilize a labeled dataset in which the labels of the records are supplied in a column titled "class label." [11].

The flow statistics can be provided through OpenFlow, which is a widely used southbound API for communication between switches and controllers. The relevant features of packets can be derived from the flow statistics supplied by SDN switches and combined with ML techniques for security analytics [12]. Many studies have used OpenFlow's flow capabilities to identify DDoS assaults in SDN [13].

The supervised methods utilize a labeled dataset in which the labels of the records are supplied in a column titled "class label." We used two publicly available labeled {normal, DDoS} datasets to train supervised algorithms, extract significant features, and anticipate packets on the SDN controller. Typically, packets fall into two categories: normal and suspicious. Normal packets are sent directly to their destination, whereas suspicious packets are recognized and categorized further based on the type of attack.

The goal of this research is to use ML algorithms to detect DDoS attacks in early and accurate criteria in an SDN environment. To identify traffic as regular or hostile, the system employs a features selection approaches with a variety of classification methods. A Proposed feature selection algorithm was used to create the feature sets or feature groups for classification. The performance of each of the classifiers was evaluated using various performance metrics for the four feature sets acquired from the feature selection algorithm, and the results were tabulated. The feature set that performs the best in terms of identifying malicious traffic has been discovered.

2 Work's Contributions

The following of the main contributions of this paper: -

1. To recognize DDoS attacks in SDN systems, we created a feature selection algorithm for determining the importance of the features.
2. Training and testing six of the proposed classification algorithms based on the CICIDS2017 dataset offline and reprocessing to build the best model considering accuracy and compatibility with SDN flow statists in real-time. This is achieved by the proposed Overall Process Algorithm.
3. Developed a PART classifier that is efficient because of both quick and accurate, which achieved a high level of accuracy when it was tested on the CICIDS2017 database for DDoS detection.

3 ML Related Work

Recent developments in ML approaches have facilitated improvements in the categorization and forecasting of attack traffic [14]. The detection of DDoS can be accomplished using a variety of different ML strategies. Techniques from the field of ML are utilized in many different industries to solve difficult challenges [15]. These efficient techniques have been used to detect distributed denial of service attacks by a researcher, as detailed in Table 1.

Table 1. DDoS-Detection using Machine Learning

No	Ref	Technique name	Features	Results Discussion
1	[16]	Binary Bat algorithm Random Forest	The dynamic set of features	This project is primarily driven by two processes: Detecting network anomalies can be done by monitoring network traffic. As a classifier, Random Forest is used, while the Bat Algorithm is used to choose features
2	[17]	ASVM	The average number of bytes in a flow, the average number of flow packets, Flow packets and flow bytes come in different sizes. The normal amount of time	The model will take a sample of the traffic and then submit it to the ASVM classifier so that it can identify whether or not an attack has occurred

(continued)

Table 1. (*continued*)

No	Ref	Technique name	Features	Results Discussion
3	[18]	Long Short-Term Memory and Fuzzy Logic	bits/s, packets/s, source IP entropy, destination IP entropy, source Port entropy, destination Port Entropy	In SDN contexts, this paper proposes a solution for detecting and mitigating Distributed Denial of Service (DDoS) and Portscan attacks (LSTM-FUZZY). The three phases of the LSTM-FUZZY system described in this study are characterization, anomaly detection, and mitigation. The dataset used was CICDDoS 2019
4	[19]	The entropy variations	the destination IP address and the threshold	It is observed that early detection is possible, the attack can be detected as early as in the first 250–500 packets of the randomly generated traffic
5	[20]	Naive Bayes, K-Nearest Neighbor, Decision Tree, and Random Forest are also utilized and compared with the SVM	The necessary statistics are used as features	The suggested approach starts by sending regular and attack traffic flow packets across the network. When packets arrive at the controller, the headers are extracted and appropriate flow calculations are performed to get the required characteristics. The characteristics are utilized to construct a dataset for the linear support vector machine classifier. The kernel radial basis function is used to train the model using the classifier. Weaknesses: no list features, use source IP as a feature

(*continued*)

Table 1. (*continued*)

No	Ref	Technique name	Features	Results Discussion
#	Our Proposed	PART Classifier	Subsets features	Use new features in SDN by extracting applicable features in SDN (We applied IP flows collected from the SDN POX controller through emulation on Mininet. On the other hand, in the second scenario, the CICIDS2017 dataset was applied). Source IP is not used features to avoid spoofed IP. Proposed Semi-Supervised. Both Training and Evaluation are offline setups. Realtime is proposed with less testing time aa and a high accuracy rate. Applied two Datasets; CICIDS2017 and CICDDoS2019

4   The ML Algorithms

Using ML techniques, the proposed system creates a classifier that can detect DDoS attacks. According to Das and Behera (2017) [21], ML a method of learning that involves developing a mathematical model to predict outcomes or establish a classification based on historical data. Past data is input into the learning process in the form of a huge dataset with a variety of attributes. This research applies six ML classifiers to complete the binary classification challenge. The classifiers are Random Tree, Random Forest, J48, REP Tree, and Partial Decision Tree [3, 22–24].

5   The Proposed System

The proposed system has main stages shown in Fig. 1. The proposed system model integrated with a POX controller was proposed for detecting DDoS attacks. There are three modules in the system model. The first part of the system is called "Statistics Collection and Monitoring," and it monitors network traffic and is the one who first spots DDoS attacks. The second component, DDoS Detection, ensures that the traffic identified as attack traffic is, in fact, attack traffic, while the third component, Mitigation, creates and enforces rules to block attack flows. Figure 1 depicts the real-time DDoS detection system. This stage is heavy and deep traffic analysis by ML techniques, which is of DDoS detection, the ML algorithms able to determine their normal/abnormal traffic.

5.1   Description of Dataset

This study will make use of the dataset that was collected during CICIDS2017 [25]. It was decided to download the CICIDS2017 dataset with all of its eighty-four features. It

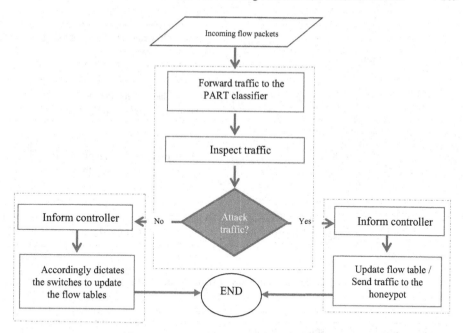

Fig. 1. The block diagram of proposed system

is a well-known and relatively recent benchmark dataset that has been put to use for the purpose of both training and testing ML models.

5.2 Preprocessing and Feature Selections

In this study, the preprocessing resolve that test Dataset issues with NaN values and duplicate columns were eliminated during the initial round of data cleaning. Two features in this file have the name Fwd Header Length, making it redundant; therefore, one of them is eliminated. The normal method of scaling was utilized.

The proposed building mechanism's feature selection is depicted in Fig. 2. Preprocessing of the training data will be done initially by the proposed system.

The feature selection set-up algorithm is used to pick an optimal attribute that distinguishes abnormal traffic from regular traffic. The attack classes in the CICIDS2017 dataset are somewhat unbalanced. The datasets include attributes that aren't relevant for detecting attacks.

The variance-based feature selection approach is proposed to identify useless features among 84 features as the initial phase in ML process. When an applied variance features selection technique, eliminated 20 useless features. So, remain 64 features in CICIDS2017 dataset. After then, study flow features in SDN, there are found that most features in CICIDS2017 data are not applicable with SDN packet features. Algorithm (1) is demonstrated the features selection process. The proposed features selection up algorithm is filtration 14 applicable and useful features.

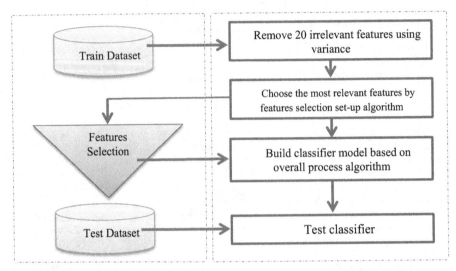

Fig. 2. The system Flow of build of the classifier

Algorithm 1 Features selection set-up

---

1. **Procedure** Selection_Features ()
2. **Split** the dataset train/test 50:50 ratios
3. **Perform** Features Filtering
   - (i)   Calculate variance and info-gain scores of features
   - (ii) Removed 20 features with the lowest variance
   - (iii) Select 64 features with the highest variance from D
   - (iv) Filtration 58 Features using information gain
4. **Input F** = Training dataset, processing 14 features f1, f2, f3... f58
5. **For every feature F**
6. **Select** important features after applying the following criteria
   - (i)   **Multiple** training and testing to deleting less frequent or no redundant features
   - (ii) **Selection** of features based on previous works // help to avoid unimportant features
   - (iii) **Focus** on the features that give higher accuracy and test time decreases. // this help to build fast and accurate model
   - (iv) **Discard** features that cannot be implemented in **real-time**. // this help to avoid complexity in the proposed model.
   - (v)   **Discard** features that incompatibility with SDN flow features. // this help to apply just applicable features.
7. **Create** a classifier model based on the training CICIDS2017 dataset, D
8. **Test** the classifier by using testing dataset, T
9. **Evaluate** performance and accuracy of classifier
10. **Rank** feature with their weight
11. **Store** List of features

In this work, according to the features selection through set-up algorithm (1), Filtration 14 features among 84 features. Table 2 shows 14 selected features.

Table 2. Applicable features with SDN flow

No	Feature name	Description of features
1	SourceIP	Source IP address
2	DestinationIP	Destination IP address
3	SourcePort	Source port number
4	DestinationPort	Destination port number
5	Protocol	Types of protocols (e.g.: tcp or udp)
6	FlowDuration	Duration flow in MS
7	TotalFwdPackets	Total packet in the forward direction
8	FlowPackets/s	Number of packets bytes per second
9	FlowIATMean	Mean of the time between two packets sent in the flow
10	FlowIATStd	Standard deviation of the time between two packets sent in the flow
11	FwdIATTotal	Total of the time between two packets sent in the forward direction
12	FwdIATMean	Mean of the time between two packets sent in forward direction
13	FwdIATStd	Std of the time between two packets sent in forward direction
14	FwdPackets/s	Number of forward packets per second

The next subsection is to develop classifier models using various ML techniques.

5.3 Selection of Classifiers

A utilized the CICIDS2017 dataset to develop classification models using various ML approaches after identifying optimum feature subsets. According to algorithm 2, exploiting the performance of several types of learning models, uses J48, Random Forest (RF), REP Tree (REPT), Partial Decision tree (PART), Random Tree (RT), and Decision Stump (DS), which are all standard supervised learning approaches. The best classifier will be applied real-time as SDN app to detect DDoS attack in SDN environment.

Algorithm 2 Overall Process

1: **Procedure** Process ()

2: **Input**: **FL** = Features_List

3: **Output**: Features Subsets, Accuracy, and Testing time with **Fast and Accurate Model**

4: **Reduce** 8 features to n features based on performance

5: **For** every feature Fr in Feature_Ranked data

6: **Start** to Select from Feature SETS

7:　　　SET1 = 11 features

8:　　　SET2 = 9 features

9:　　　SET3 = 6 features

10:　　　SET4 = 5 features

11: **For each** Feature groups

12: **Feed** Selected Features to RF, REPT, RT, DS, J48, PART using CICIDS-2017

13: **Apply Classifier**

14:　　　C1 = Random Forest model accuracy

15:　　　C2 = Random Tree model accuracy

16:　　　C3 = REP Tree model accuracy

17:　　　C4 = Decision Stump model accuracy

18:　　　C5 = J48 model accuracy

19　　　C6 = PART model accuracy

20: **Calculate** Test time, Tree size, and Accuracy

21: **Compare** the accuracy and testing time of C1, C2, C3, C4, C5 and C6

Based on algorithm 2, the features were chosen, as subsets (see Table 3). Finally, the six classifiers are tested using the test dataset to determine the performance of the proposed method, which relies on both fast and accurate parameters.

Table 3. Features Set

No	Set no	Number Features in sets	No. Features
1	Feature set 1	4,5,6,7,8,9,10,11,12,13,14	11
2	Feature set 1	4,7,8,9,10,11,12,13,14	9
3	Feature set 1	4,7,11,12,13,14	6
4	Feature set 1	7,11,12,13,14	5

6　Discussion of the ML Classifiers Results

Using the three performance measures, the performance of classifiers and feature selection was evaluated. There are three performance measures: Testing time, Tree size, and Accuracy. Accuracy reflects the accuracy of the algorithm in detecting attacks over both normal and attack packets. The accuracy is computing defined using Eq. 1.

$$Accuracy = \frac{TP + TN}{TP + TN + FP + FN} \qquad (1)$$

This work used test mode by split 50% train, remainder test. It is used to help of choosing the suited of ML classifiers. This mode can aid in the development of a lightweight classifier model as well as the selection of important features, because make balancing between accuracy and testing time.

Test time, which indicates the model rules' testing time during the testing step, is also calculated together with the other three evaluation criteria. The Tables 4, 5, 6 and 7 indicate the performance of classifiers in terms of concern in sets. Table 4 presents the performance obtained from several classifiers (feature sets). Within the context of this experiment, the 50:50 ratio split mode of split data was utilized.

When the data are analyzed, it is found that there are five classifiers that have an accuracy that is more than 99% in feature set (1, 2, 3). These classifiers include the REP Tree, Partial decision tree, Random Tree, Random Forest, and the J48 classifier. The Random Forest classifier has a high level of accuracy, reaching 99.8%. However, in order to get an accuracy score of 99.8%, the Random Forest classifier takes more testing time than the other classifiers.

Table 4. Accuracy of Classifiers on Feature Sets with 8 Selected Features

ALGORITHM	SET1	SET2	SET3	SET4
REPTree	99.85%	99.84%	99.76%	98.25%
DecisionStump	82.58%	82.58%	82.58%	82.58%
RandomTree	99.86%	99.89%	99.78%	98.30%
RandomForest	99.93%	99.92%	99.84%	98.54%
J48	99.87%	99.87%	99.77%	98.30%
PART	99.87%	99.82%	99.77%	97.87%

Table 4 shows the classifier's spent time in testing rules with feature four sets. The random forest classifier achieves the highest test time when using feature four sets. While, the decision stump that lowest testing time lowest accuracy score for all feature sets.

A decrease in testing time is observed when the number of features is reduced from eleven to five. It should also be noted that feature set3 contains six features, the test time of the PART, and REP tree classifiers lowest value than another four classifiers.

For features sets, Figs. 3, 4 and 5 provide a comparison of classifier accuracy, testing time, tree size.

Figure 3 illustrates the evaluation of classifiers for each of the four feature sets. The Random Forest and Partial decision tree classifiers achieve the best accuracy of 99.93% and 99.87 for feature set 1 with all 11 features. With 11 features, the PART, REP Tree, J48, and Random Tree classifiers get the highest accuracy.

Table 5. Classifier testing time on Feature sets

ALGORITHM	SET1	SET2	SET3	SET4
REPTree	0.23	0.11	0.08	0.12
DecisionStump	0.27	0.08	0.12	0.14
RandomTree	0.19	0.15	0.17	0.11
RandomForest	2.82	2.74	3.21	12.59
J48	1.34	0.23	0.17	0.15
PART	0.23	0.18	0.1	0.29

Table 6. Classifier Tree size on Feature set 3 with 6 Selected Features

Algorithm	Tree size
REPTree	289
DecisionStump	22
RandomTree	1179
RandomForest	1599
J48	325
PART	65

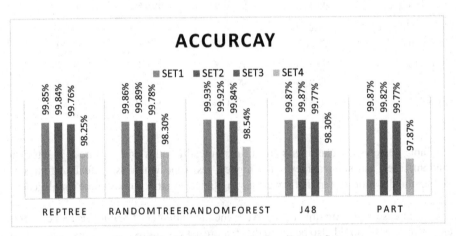

Fig. 3. Classifier's accuracy for four Feature Sets

Figure 4 depicts classifier testing time for the four feature sets. The testing time has huge impact of performance in real-time constant, when it is increase lead to decrease the

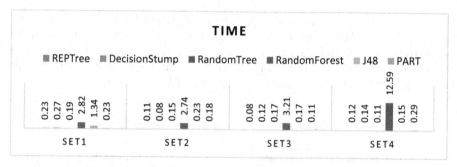

Fig. 4. The classifier testing time period for four feature sets

performance and verse versa. With feature set4, the testing time of classifiers J48, Decision Stump, REP Tree, and PART remains the same but Random Forest was registered highest testing time.

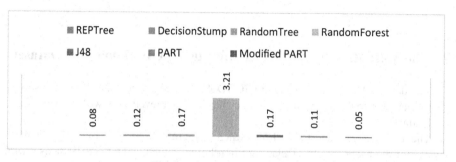

Fig. 5. The classifiers' tree size

Figure 5 represents the tree size, which is the number of rules that will be approved for each classifier. With a dimension that explains to us what is the best classifier in terms of accuracy according to the form, it has become necessary to identify the best classifier in terms of test time and the fewest number of rules according to the result of performance in the Figs. 4 and 5, also shows that the classifiers have different accuracy and different tree sizes. So, in this case, must create a balance to find an efficient classifier with high accuracy and small tree size, so it becomes a high performance when applied in real-time detection of DDoS attacks.

Analyzing the results of the six classifiers on the three performance measures for each of the four feature sets, we find that feature set 1 with all features gets the best overall classifier performance. In this study, we use features selected from the CICIDS2017 dataset using an algorithm 1 that, according to our experiments, DDoS attacks can be identified with 99.87% reliability.

The best accuracy score for each feature set is summarized in Table 7. When all 11 features were used, the Random Forest classifier achieved the highest accuracy of 99.92%.

While conducting the classification with six features, found that PART is lightweight and high accuracy. According to tests of set3, as shown in Figs. 3, 4 and 5, this result has been proved that the PART classifier is the best depending on achieved 99.77% accuracy by using 65 rules and testing time 0.1 MS, while random forest achieved 99.53% with set 4 by using 1599 of rules set and testing time 3.21 MS.

Table 7. Accuracy Score is determined by the best feature.

No	N. of features set	Features	High accuracy
1	Feature set 1	4,5,6,7,8,9,10,11,12,13,14	RandomForest; 99.92%
2	Feature set 2	4,7,8,9,10,11,12,13,14	RandomForest; 99.92%
3	c	4,7,11,12,13,14	**PART**; 99.77% and RandomForest; 99.83%
4	Feature set 4	7,11,12,13,14	RandomForest; 98.53%

7   The Validation of PART Classifier using CICDDoS2019 Dataset

The validated PART classifier using CICDDoS2019, to ensure that the response was appropriate. Up to this point, high accuracy has been achieved 99% with both SYN and UDP attacks.

The test time was reported as 1.59 s when 11 features were used to verify the effectiveness of the proposed PART classifier in relation to the CICDDoS2019 dataset with SYN attach; however, the test time that was taken to test model was 0.87 s.

8   The SDN Environment

This section describes the experimental setup and technologies used to test the performance of proposed PART model and the framework's viability in an SDN environment. To get the best security mechanism, the method of detection and prevention DDoS attack must be executed. To achieve this method, POX controller [26] with the open virtual switch (OVS) will be used. To generate flow packets, the "scapy" tool [27] has used besides the proposed algorithm.

8.1   The Implementation Environment and Tools

Multiple platforms were used for the simulations and analyses. Our detection technique is primarily tested in a Windows 10 environment with a 2.60 GHz Intel Core i7-6600U processor and 16 GB of RAM. Currently, there are two virtual machines active in this setting (Mininet and POX controller). Normal traffic can be initiated using the Scapy tool prior to an attack being launched.

8.2 The SDN Network Configuration

Our experiment begins with the selection of Mininet as the network emulator and POX as the controller platform. The detecting APP will function independently within the L3 Learning module. This allows the controller to perform additional activities, such as installing flows and validating DDoS attacks. A victim node in the Mininet network is the target of both normal and attack traffic generated by a client in the SDN network. Analyze the outcomes of an assault on a virtual host using Mininet and our detection approach. The client IP addresses range from 10.0.0.1 to 10.0.0.8.

As shown in Fig. 6, eight hosts, 3 OVS, and a single POX controller are implemented for this research. The average network contains 12 network devices; nevertheless, because of a lack of resources, the test in the previous section was designed to simulate the same kinds of situations that occur in large networks. We developed and validated the efficacy of our approach in a real time context by first creating a virtual network.

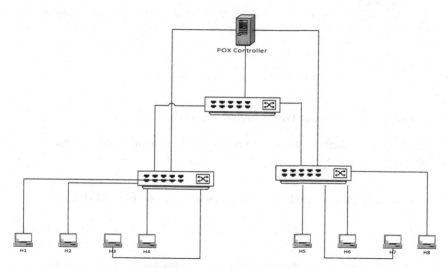

Fig. 6. Mininet topology of 3 switches and 8 hosts with single POX Controller

Scapy imports functions such as sendp, IP, UDP, Ethernet, and TCP. It is used in this study to generate UDP packets with different payloads and traffic intervals (inter = 0.025) for DDoS traffic whereas normal traffic, the interval will be 0.1 s (inter = 0.1). Figure 7 depicts the attacks traffic generated by the Scapy script in a virtual host (h1).

The topology and parameters for simulating attack traffic with multiple victims is the same as those for simulating normal traffic. In this attack scenario with multiple victims, the four packets per second are being used for legitimate traffic. As expected, the attack is found by the algorithm in first a second.

The time it takes to find out about a DDoS attack is first second. It is safe to say that the PART algorithm does a good job of telling the difference between normal traffic and DDoS traffic that is being used to attack.

```
root@mininet-vm:~/mininet/custom# python launchAttack.py 10.0.0.8 ['10.0.0.8']
125.122.177.248
<Ether  type=0x800 |<IP  frag=0 proto=udp src=125.122.177.248 dst=['10.0.0.8']
|<UDP  sport=http dport=1 |>>>
Sent 1 packets.
252.247.14.220 <Ether  type=0x800 |<IP  frag=0 proto=udp src=252.247.14.220
dst=['10.0.0.8'] |<UDP  sport=http dport=1 |>>>
Sent 1 packets.
190.59.1.84  <Ether   type=0x800  |<IP   frag=0  proto=udp  src=190.59.1.84
dst=['10.0.0.8'] |<UDP  sport=http dport=1 |>>>
Sent 1 packets.
217.227.47.14  <Ether  type=0x800  |<IP  frag=0 proto=udp  src=217.227.47.14
dst=['10.0.0.8'] |<UDP  sport=http dport=1 |>>>
Sent 1 packets.
221.225.119.212 <Ether  type=0x800 |<IP  frag=0 proto=udp src=221.225.119.212
dst=['10.0.0.8'] |<UDP  sport=http dport=1 |>>>
Sent 1 packets.
101.101.142.97  <Ether   type=0x800  |<IP   frag=0  proto=udp  src=101.101.142.97
dst=['10.0.0.8'] |<UDP  sport=http dport=1 |>>>
```

Fig. 7. Traffic Generation using Scapy

8.3 Comparison of Recent Works in SDN Network

The accuracy of evaluation obtained in recent works is highlighted in Table 8, which can be found below.

Table 8. Previous Works are Compared with Our proposed PART classifier

No	Authors	Network	Dataset	Accuracy of the classifier %
1	M. Khairi et al. [28], 2021	Mininet simulated	Simulated generation	99.49%
2	C. Fan et al. [29], 2021	Mininet simulated	Simulated generation	91.25%
3	A. Maheshwari et al. [30], 2022	Mininet simulated	CICDDoS2019	99.41%
4	Y. Liu et al. [31], 2022	Mininet simulated	CICIDS2017	98.98%
#	**Our study**	Mininet simulated	CICIDS2017	99.77%
				99.96%

The proposed PART can detect DDoS attacks in a short time and with the fewest number of rules (65 rules). These criteria were applied to the creation of lightweight models. Our proposed is used in SDN network to detection of DDoS attack in real-time coordinate. The classifier by integrated with L3 module of POX controller to monitor and collect flow statistics and then identify the traffic.

9   The Conclusion

In this study, two CIC datasets are used to examine the performance of six supervised ML methods. Performance indicators were used, including testing time, tree size (number of rules), and accuracy.

The proposed PART model with the features set3 is able to detect DDoS attacks with a high degree of accuracy when compared to earlier related works.

The experience of the set3 with six features revealed that PART performed, with an accuracy of 99.77%. It a noteworthy that the high accuracy remains in both the datasets. The proposed PART classifier achieves high efficiency with lower time consumption when used in real-time in an SDN environment for DDoS attack detection. The average detection rate of a DDoS attack is determined within the first second. It is safe to say that the PART algorithm outperforms the other techniques in distinguishing the normal/abnormal traffics. The early detection using PART classifier is suited to save the network resources and a have a higher accurate prediction.

References

1. Kreutz, D., Ramos, F.M.V., Verissimo, P.E., et al.: Software-defined networking: a comprehensive survey. Proc IEEE **103**, 14–76 (2014)
2. Kim, H., Feamster, N.: Improving network management with software defined networking. IEEE Commun. Mag. **51**, 114–119 (2013)
3. Banitalebi Dehkordi, A., Soltanaghaei, M., Boroujeni, F.Z.: The DDoS attacks detection through machine learning and statistical methods in SDN. J. Supercomput. **77**, 2383–2415 (2021)
4. Abubakar, R., Aldegheishem, A., Majeed, M.F., et al.: An effective mechanism to mitigate real-time DDoS attack. IEEE Access **8**, 126215–126227 (2020)
5. Musumeci, F., Fidanci, A.C., Paolucci, F., et al.: Machine-Learning-enabled DDoS attacks detection in P4 programmable networks. J. Netw. Syst. Manag. **30**, 1–27 (2022)
6. Bhushan, K., Gupta, B.B.: Distributed denial of service (DDoS) attack mitigation in software defined network (SDN)-based cloud computing environment. J. Ambient. Intell. Humaniz. Comput. **10**(5), 1985–1997 (2018). https://doi.org/10.1007/s12652-018-0800-9
7. Jarraya, Y., Madi, T., Debbabi, M.: A survey and a layered taxonomy of software-defined networking. IEEE Commun. Surv. Tutor. **16**, 1955–1980 (2014)
8. Jose, A.S., Nair, L.R., Paul, V.: Towards detecting flooding DDOS attacks over software defined networks using machine learning techniques. Rev GEINTEC-GESTAO Innov. E Tecnol. **11**, 3837–3865 (2021)
9. Mousavi, S.M., St-Hilaire, M.: Early detection of DDoS attacks against SDN controllers. In: 2015 International Conference on Computing, Networking and Communications (ICNC), pp 77–81. IEEE (2015)
10. Wang, M., Lu, Y., Qin, J.: A dynamic MLP-based DDoS attack detection method using feature selection and feedback. Comput Secur **88**, 101645 (2020)

11. Kalkan, K., Altay, L., Gür, G., Alagöz, F.: JESS: Joint entropy-based DDoS defense scheme in SDN. IEEE J Sel. Areas Commun. **36**, 2358–2372 (2018)
12. Kokila, R.T., Selvi, S.T., Govindarajan, K.: DDoS detection and analysis in SDN-based environment using support vector machine classifier. In: 2014 Sixth International Conference on Advanced Computing (ICoAC) , pp 205–210. IEEE (2014)
13. Park, Y., Kengalahalli, N.V., Chang, S.-Y.: Distributed security network functions against botnet attacks in software-defined networks. In: 2018 IEEE Conference on Network Function Virtualization and Software Defined Networks (NFV-SDN), pp. 1–7. IEEE (2018)
14. Rangaraju, N.K., Sriramoju, S.B., Sarma, S.: A study on machine learning techniques towards the detection of distributed denial of service attacks. Int. J. Pure Appl. Math. **120**, 7407–7423 (2018)
15. Pitropakis, N., Panaousis, E., Giannetsos, T., et al.: A taxonomy and survey of attacks against machine learning. Comput. Sci. Rev. **34**, 100199 (2019)
16. Li, J., Zhao, Z., Li, R., Zhang, H.: Ai-based two-stage intrusion detection for software defined iot networks. IEEE Internet Things J. **6**, 2093–2102 (2018)
17. Myint, O.M., Kamolphiwong, S., Kamolphiwong, T., Vasupongayya, S.: Advanced support vector machine-(ASVM-) based detection for distributed denial of service (DDoS) attack on software defined networking (SDN). J Comput. Netw. Commun. **2019** (2019)
18. Novaes, M.P., Carvalho, L.F., Lloret, J., Proenca, M.L.: Long short-term memory and fuzzy logic for anomaly detection and mitigation in software-defined network environment. IEEE Access **8**, 83765–83781 (2020)
19. Anil, A., Rufzal, T.A., Vasudevan, V.A.: DDoS detection in software-defined network using entropy method. In: Proceedings of the Seventh International Conference on Mathematics and Computing, pp 129–139. Springer, Heidelberg (2022). https://doi.org/10.1007/978-981-16-6890-6_10
20. Gadallah, W.G., Omar, N.M., Ibrahim, H.M.: Machine learning-based distributed denial of service attacks detection technique using new features in software-defined networks. Int J Comput Netw Inf Secur **13**, 15–27 (2021)
21. Buczak, A.L., Guven, E.: A survey of data mining and machine learning methods for cyber security intrusion detection. IEEE Commun. Surv. Tutor. **18**, 1153–1176 (2015)
22. Awan, M.J., Farooq, U., Babar, H.M.A., et al.: Real-time DDoS attack detection system using big data approach. Sustainability **13**, 10743 (2021)
23. Niranjan, A., Nutan, D.H., Nitish, A., et al.: ERCR TV: ensemble of random committee and random tree for efficient anomaly classification using voting. In: 2018 3rd International Conference for Convergence in Technology (I2CT) , pp 1–5. IEEE (2018)
24. Rahman, O., Quraishi, M.A.G., Lung, C.-H.: DDoS attacks detection and mitigation in SDN using machine learning. In: 2019 IEEE World Congress on Services (SERVICES), pp 184–189. IEEE (2019)
25. Stiawan, D., Bin, I.M.Y., Bamhdi, A.M., Budiarto, R.: CICIDS-2017 dataset feature analysis with information gain for anomaly detection. IEEE Access **8**, 132911–132921 (2020)
26. Installing POX—POX Manual Current documentation. https://noxrepo.github.io/pox-doc/html/. Accessed 7 June 2022
27. Scapy. https://scapy.net/. Accessed 7 June 2022
28. Khairi, M.H.H., Ariffin, S.H.S., Latiff, N.M.A., et al.: Detection and classification of conflict flows in SDN using machine learning algorithms. IEEE Access **9**, 76024–76037 (2021)
29. Fan, C., Kaliyamurthy, N.M., Chen, S., et al.: Detection of DDoS attacks in software defined networking using entropy. Appl. Sci. **12**, 370 (2021)

30. Maheshwari, A., Mehraj, B., Khan, M.S., Idrisi, M.S.: An optimized weighted voting based ensemble model for DDoS attack detection and mitigation in SDN environment. Microprocess. Microsyst. **89**, 104412 (2022)
31. Liu, Y., Zhi, T., Shen, M., et al.: Software-defined DDoS detection with information entropy analysis and optimized deep learning. Futur. Gener. Comput. Syst. **129**, 99–114 (2022)

Author Index

A

Abbas, Hawraa 77
Abdulkhaleq, Ali Hussein 3
Abdullah, Alharith A. 173, 230
Agyeman, Michael Opoku 25
Ahmed, Shaimaa K. 125
Al Hassani, Safaa Alwan 3
Al-A'araji, Nabeel H. 191
Albermany, Salah 248
Al-Chalabi, Hayder Hussein 139
Ali, Israa H. 38
Al-mamory, Safaa O. 191
Alshaibi, Maather 125
Al-Shakarchi, Ali H. 191
Al-Sherbaz, Ali 25

E

El Abbadi, Nidhal K. 3

F

Fadel, Noor 50

G

George, Loay E. 162

H

Hadi, Hend A. 162
Hasson, Saad Talib 25

J

Jaleel, Hanan Q. 107
Jaleel, Qasim 38
Jasim, Mahdi Nsaif 139, 264
Jawdhari, Hayder A. 230

K

Kanakis, Triantafyllos 25
Kareem, Emad I. Abdul 50
Kareem, Mohammed Ibrahim 264

M

Mahdi, Suadad S. 173
Mohammedali, Noor Abdalkarem 25

N

Naji, Sinan A. 107
Naji, Zobeda H. 125

R

Reda, Noor H. 77

S

Sabbar, Bayan Mahdi 248
Sayel, Nadhim Azeez 248
Stephan, Jane J. 107

A. M. Al-Bakry et al. (Eds.): NTICT 2022, CCIS 1764, p. 283, 2023.
https://doi.org/10.1007/978-3-031-35442-7

Printed in the United States
by Baker & Taylor Publisher Services